SO SUE ME!

How to Protect
Your Assets from
the Lawsuit Explosion

ARNOLD S. GOLDSTEIN, J.D., PH.D.

GARRETT PUBLISHING, INC.

By Arnold S. Goldstein, JD, Ph.D.
Copyright 2005 by Arnold S. Goldstein, JD, Ph.D.

Published by
Garrett Publishing, Inc.
2500 North Military Trail
Suite 260
Boca Raton, Florida 33431
Telephone: 561-953-1322
Fax: 561-953-1940
E-mail: info@garrettpub.com
Website: www.garrettpub.com

This book is designed to provide accurate and authoritative information on the subject of asset protection. While all of the cases and examples described in the book are based on true experiences, most of the names and some situations have been changed slightly to protect privacy. It is sold with the understanding that neither the author nor the publisher is engaged in rendering legal, accounting, or other professional advice. As each individual situation is unique, questions specific to your circumstances should be addressed to an appropriate professional to ensure that your situation has been evaluated carefully and appropriately. The author and the publisher specifically disclaim any liability or loss incurred as a consequence, directly or indirectly, of using and applying any of the concepts in this book.

Wealthsaver® is a registered trademark of Arnold S. Goldstein & Associates LLC.

Goldstein, Arnold S.
    So Sue Me!! Arnold S. Goldstein, JD, Ph.D.
        p.   cm.
    Includes bibliographical references
    ISBN 1-880539-60-8
          1. Execution (law)-United States-Popular works.
          2. Property-United States-Popular works.
          3. D creditor-United States-Popular works.
          4. Liability (law)-United States-Popular works. I. Title

                              2005921662
                              PCN

Printed in the United States of America
10 9 8 7 6 5 4 3 2 1

ACKNOWLEDGMENTS

So Sue Me is the culmination of my life's work as an asset protection attorney. My knowledge has been greatly aided by my association with other professionals who each in their own way, added immeasurably to my skills. I thank them all.

Special thanks to David Mandel, Chris Jarvis, Ben Knaupp and Jonathan Curshen who contributed much to the specialty of asset protection and to some of the ideas and concepts presented in this book.

Thanks also to my wife Marlene and my office administrator Barbara Schwartz for their tireless efforts in preparing the manuscript; Sheila Alexander for her expert editorial assistance and Vivian Jorquera and Christina Saenz for their graphic skills. They make a great team!

Finally, I am forever grateful to my many clients who entrusted to me their wealth and financial security. I hope that I have served them well.

CONTENTS

Introduction

The Book A Million Lawyers Don't Want You To Read

Part 1:
Asset Protection Planning

Part 2:
Strategies and Tools

The book a Million Lawyers don't want you to Read

For four decades I have helped America's affluent protect their wealth from lawsuits, creditors, tax collectors, ex-spouses, and other predatory threats. My experience is that while many people know how to make money, far fewer know how to keep their wealth safe and secure.

I truly believe in the concept that each of us must think and act defensively if we are to protect our wealth in what has become a dangerously predatory society - a world that has turned lawsuit crazy - a world where your wealth is no longer safe.

So Sue Me! is essential reading because America has become the world's litigation capital. We have bad laws, too many laws, too many greedy lawyers, too many sue-crazy litigants, and too many juries who spawn outrageous litigation awards. It is also about a nation of 'victims' who believe it is their right to use the courts to redistribute wealth. It is about the destruction of our basic liberties and property rights and a government that grabs whatever it wants from you - and takes much of it arbitrarily. It is also about honest, hard-working people who, through their own talents and efforts, managed to accumulate some wealth for themselves and are now targets for every potential sue-happy litigant. Finally, it is about a country where true financial security has become an illusory goal. These realities are the philosophical underpinnings for this book.

More importantly, *So Sue Me!* is about what you can do - must do - to keep your assets safe and enjoy lifelong financial security. *So Sue Me!* is designed to be your comprehensive asset protection armchair advisor. It is a guide to show you how to protect everything you own from virtually *any* legal or financial threat.

Within its pages are the same precise, proven, and practical strategies to shelter your assets that I have used as an asset protection attorney to successfully shield the wealth of nearly 20,000 individuals, families, and companies nationwide.

Can these same strategies turn your *vulnerable* wealth into *untouchable* wealth?   Absolutely, if you keep three important points in mind:

- **Protect yourself before you have a problem.** Advance planning is essential. Creditors also have rights, so think of asset protection as insurance and buy it before your house is on fire. Commit to implementing your own financial self-defense program starting today, but don't give up even if you are already in deep trouble. Even then there are strategies that can work for you. Your wealth isn't lost until it is in your creditor's pocket!

- **Creating untouchable wealth takes time, effort, and money**, but you will find asset protection to be the best investment you ever make.

- **Asset protection and wealth preservation can involve a wide range of strategies,** from the simplest to the most complex. You will find there is no single correct formula or 'quick fix.' I present the various wealth protection tools and illustrate which strategies may be best in any given situation. *Your* best plan, will, of course, depend on the many factors that are unique to you. While I give you the broad overview and general concepts, you will not need every detail. Let's leave the technicalities to the lawyers.

Use this book as your primer, but retain an experienced asset protection lawyer to help you design *your* best strategy. This book highlights how to protect what you own, but it also makes you a better informed client so you can more intelligently choose and work with a lawyer.

So Sue Me! goes beyond explaining asset protection strategies. These strategies are presented in action, with examples to illustrate how others - people much like you gain lifetime financial security for themselves and their families - and how you can, too!

The Latest Wealth-Saving Strategies

This isn't just another book on wealth protection.

- You discover scores of *little known* strategies and tactics - tricks of the asset protection trade that can make the difference between bulletproof financial safety and going broke. These are the strategies that you *won't* find in other books, but are nevertheless essential tools in your financial self-defense arsenal.

- You get straight talk, not textbook theory. I tell you what *really* works and what *doesn't*. You get the inside facts as if you were in my office paying me hundreds of dollars an hour for the same sound advice.
- I help you to avoid the common mistakes that you may be making right now - fatal errors that may be undermining your financial security.
- I lead you to vital resources - where to go for more help or simply to learn more.

Essential for Everyone With Vulnerable Wealth

This book is for everyday folks with a few bucks in the bank, some equity in their home, and their future security tucked away in a retirement account. These are the middle-class Americans that I help every day - folks who work hard for what they have and are least likely to recover from the devastation of a major lawsuit.

This book is a must read whether you:

- Are wealthy, or have only few assets that you would hate to lose.
- Are totally unprotected against lawsuits or *think* that you are well protected. I show you how to begin protecting your assets as well as how to improve your protection.
- Have never before been sued, are in the middle of a lawsuit, or have suffered through one or more lawsuits and now want better protection.
- Need to protect your own wealth or a client's wealth. (Yes, if you are a financial advisor, accountant, or lawyer, you share responsibility for your client's financial security.)
- Are starting out in life and want to safeguard your

future wealth or are in your twilight years and want to shelter your nest egg or your children's inheritance.

- Need to shield yourself from lawsuits or seek protection against divorce, the IRS, bankruptcy, or any other financial threat that can impoverish you.

I'm Only a Phone Call Away

Let's make this book only the beginning of a relationship. I strive to learn from my many clients and readers who share their experiences with me. My many asset protection clients are my greatest teachers!

Let me hear from you. What ideas can you suggest for my next book? What experiences can you share with my future readers? Most importantly, how can I help you and your family achieve lifelong financial security?

Arnold S. Goldstein, JD, Ph.D.
Boca Raton, Florida

Part 1

Asset Protection Planning

1

Why You Must Lawsuit-Proof Yourself Today

John Mathews and his wife Millie enjoyed the good life. They owned a nice home, had money in the bank, a solid portfolio of stocks and bonds, a six-figure IRA, and a profitable Chicago plumbing supply business. They had worked hard all their lives and were experiencing the American dream. Within a few years they hoped to retire to Florida with the financial security that they had worked a lifetime to achieve.

Life, however, is unpredictable. One day John was handed a lawsuit. An ex-partner on a minor business deal from years earlier was now suing him. A sinking feeling consumed John as he scanned the lawsuit and read the outrageous allegations of all the terrible misdeeds he supposedly committed during their short partnership.

Then came the real shock: John's ex-business associate was demanding millions in 'damages.' Suddenly John's life soured. The ridiculous claims and insane demands for millions seemed unbelievable. Anger quickly turned to fear as John realized that this was one lawsuit for which he had no liability insurance.

John was confident that once he visited his attorney all would be well. Undoubtedly his lawyer would assure him that he had nothing to worry about. However, John's lawyer gave him little consolation. Yes, the lawyer agreed, the ex-partner's case against John appeared shaky, but it was always possible John *could* lose. His lawyer did not expect that the ex-partner would win much money, even if he did win his case. However, John was also being sued for punitive damages, and the lawyer reminded John that "you just never know what a jury will do." All John's lawyer was certain of was that it would cost John thousands of dollars in legal fees to defend this case and could take several years to resolve – years of aggravation, worry, and uncertainty for John and Millie.

The lawyer's words continued to ricochet in John's mind: *"You just never know what a jury will do."*

John became upset. What if he *did* lose the case? What about his assets? Would he and Millie lose their home? Investments? Savings? Could they lose their business? How safe was John's retirement account? Could John be forced into bankruptcy and lose *everything*?

John also wondered if it was too late to protect himself. How could he secure his assets, no matter how this lawsuit ended? John suddenly faced the reality that he could lose everything he had slaved a lifetime to accumulate in the legal lottery he was about to play.

Asset Protection is Vital

I tell you about John and Millie Mathews not because their story is unusual; quite the opposite. Thousands of such stories arise every day. I know. For forty years I have earned my living advising people who share similar tales. Everyone's fears come down to these same nagging questions: What happens to my financial security if I lose this lawsuit? How could I protect myself before all is lost?

While my clients have included sports icons, movie stars, and industry moguls, most are everyday Americans - people very much like the Mathews. They get up every morning to put in a hard day's work and aspire to build some financial security for themselves and their families.

These clients knew about lawsuits. They had heard stories from others who were wiped out by lawsuits or other financial disasters. As with most tragedies, however, such terrible things only happen to others. They could not foresee it happening to them. *Until it does!*

Some folks came to me too late. The sheriff had already auctioned their home, carted away their furniture, or seized their bank account. I could offer little or no help.

Fortunately, many more came to me in time. I could help these people because they wanted to protect their wealth *before* they were sued or before their legal problems progressed too far. I could give these people the protection they needed to survive financially.

It's a sorry fact that 93 percent of Americans have absolutely no lawsuit protection aside from their liability insurance. Even more amazing is that so many successful people who carefully scrutinize every business deal, demand the best business and investment advice - even micro-plan their vacations - do little or no advance planning to fortify their wealth against lawsuits and the hundreds of other financial pitfalls that we all face in a lifetime. Why is this?

"Procrastination is one answer," claims one leading New York personal injury lawyer, who won over $100 million in judgments. He adds, "Few people place lawsuit protection high on their agenda until they are hit with a lawsuit. That's when they begin to sweat. But once the lawsuit strikes, they'll find it considerably more difficult to protect themselves. The procrastinator is always my most vulnerable target because his or her assets are ripe for the picking. Those are the 'deep pocket' defendants I want to sue!"

He is right. Procrastination is the biggest obstacle to timely defensive planning. Only one out of five adult Americans have even a simple will, and what is more certain than death? It is little wonder so few people think about asset protection until they are sued.

Americans are not necessarily risk-takers; we just don't always put things in perspective. For example, fifty million new lawsuits will be filed this year, yet there will be only five million injuries and deaths from car accidents. You are, then, ten times more likely to get sued than to injure or kill someone in a car accident. However, you wouldn't go without car insurance. You would be ten times as foolish to ignore lawsuit protection.

The number of new civil lawsuits this year will be nearly eighty times the number of residential fires. You probably have insurance to protect your home against fire, but what simple steps have you taken to safeguard your home from lawsuits and creditors?

Our Litigious Society

My passion for my profession of asset protection is because America is in the throes of a lawsuit explosion, and it will only get worse. Each year brings more lawsuits and bigger awards. Litigation is America's fastest growing business, and few of us will get through life without being victimized by at least one lawsuit. Fifty million lawsuits filed this year is only one dismal statistic. Actually, there will be many more lawsuit defendants because lawsuits frequently involve multiple defendants. While nobody has precise numbers, we can reasonably assume that there may be as many as 100 million civil lawsuit defendants at any given moment. Whatever the number, it is indisputable that lawsuits are all too common and billions more are paid out each year on the mere threat of a lawsuit.

Why is America so lawsuit crazy? Sociologists, economists, politicians, and lawyers each have their own theories. Having practiced law for four decades, my perception is that we have too many lawyers, and too many laws, and too few judges with the courage or common sense to summarily throw out blatantly frivolous lawsuits. We also have too many juries that don't rule on the basis of liability, but prefer instead to empty a defendant's 'deep pockets' to redistribute wealth.

We also have too many incentives to sue. For example, a punitive damage claim can enrich a plaintiff who has suffered little or no actual damage with a multi-million-dollar windfall. Nor are there many reasons *not* to sue. It usually won't cost them a dime in legal fees because they can always find some lawyer to work on a contingent fee basis.

While there is much wrong with our legal system, it is not only the system's fault, as perverse as it is. The fault is chiefly that as a society we have transformed ourselves into a nation of victims. When things go wrong, as they invariably do, we instinctively point blame elsewhere. The lawsuit is the natural consequence of our distorted national mindset.

Walter K. Olson's *The Litigation Explosion* explains our litigation dilemma from a different perspective:

"The unleashing of litigation in its full fury has done cruel, grave harm and little lasting good. It has helped sunder some of the most sensitive and profound relationships of human life: Between the parents who have nurtured a child; between the healing professions and those whose life and well-being are entrusted to their care. It clogs and jams the gears of commerce, sowing friction and distrust between the productive enterprises on which material progress depends and on all who buy their products, work at their plants and offices or join in their undertakings. It seizes on former love and intimacy as raw materials to be transmuted into hatred and estrangement. It exploits the bereavement that some day awaits the survivors of us all and turns it to an unending source of poisonous recrimination. It torments the provably innocent and rewards the palpably irresponsible. It devours hard-won savings and worsens every animosity of a diverse society. It is the special American burden, the one feature hardly anyone admires of a society that is otherwise envied the world around."

Amen!

No less outspoken about lawsuits is Judicial Watch, a Capital Hill non-partisan, non-profit foundation that claims: "The American legal system is dangerously corrupt. It picks the pockets of hard working Americans by putting literally billions of dollars into the pockets of greedy lawyers, turning neighbor against neighbor and threatening to derail the rule of law." Judicial Watch bolsters its case with interesting statistics:

- The US tort system is the most expensive in the industrial world. US tort costs are 2.2 percent of the gross domestic product - substantially higher than that of other developed countries.
- The cost of the US legal system is growing at four times the rate of our economy.
- Class action filings increased by more than 1000 percent in state courts over the past ten years. Federal class actions increased by more than 300 percent.

- Asbestos claims alone have more than doubled in the past five years.
- There are one million lawyers in America, the highest per capita average.
- There are one million law students in law schools.
- America, with 70 percent of the world's lawyers, has 90 percent of the world's litigation.

With so many lawyers, it is inevitable that there are so many lawsuits. The thought of a million lawyers running around in search of their next victim endangers anyone with assets. You can't blame every lawyer, though. Not every lawyer is in the lawsuit business, and if you look hard you can still find a plaintiff's lawyer or two who will not accept a frivolous lawsuit. They use their good judgment as far as who and when to sue, and they do not abuse the judicial system. I am proud to be part of the legal profession with *these* lawyers as my colleagues. Yet how many lawyers *do* throw lawsuits around like confetti? How many lawyers view the lawsuit as a way to make a fast buck? How many lawyers *don't* care if their lawsuit is meritless as long as they can extort enough money from some hapless defendant to make the exercise worthwhile?

The tide has turned. The *American Bar Association Journal* (the largest US publication for lawyers) in its article *Protect Your Assets Before Lawsuit Arises* counsels their 300,000 members that asset protection is as critical for *them* as it is to their clients. One trial lawyer interviewed for the article frankly admits, "I don't want people doing to me what I do to other people all day in court."

The *Wall Street Journal*, in response to the ABA article, argued that if the lawyers know the legal system is out of control, then they should change the system, not merely protect themselves against it. The fact is that our legal system has yet to be reformed, and it won't be any time soon. The lawsuit threat will not decrease, it will only get worse. It is far wiser to join the lawyers who are themselves becoming lawsuit-proof.

Losing the Legal Lottery

We should not blame only the lawyers. We should never forget that we would have far fewer lawsuits if fewer people were so intent on suing to achieve wealth. Walter Kelly's cartoon character, Pogo Possum, had it right: "We have met the enemy and they is us."

Ask yourself this: Why shouldn't people sue when it costs them nothing and they lose but a few hours, when they have so much to gain if they win? Why work when you can sue your way to great wealth? Why play the lottery when your chances of winning are so much better when you gamble in court? As one client once philosophized, "Why marry for money when it's so much more pleasant to spend a few hours with a good lawyer rather than a lifetime with a bad spouse?"

Everybody wants a piece of the action and their own chance to win the legal lottery. So kids sue parents, partners sue partners, patients sue doctors, customers sue manufacturers, students sue teachers, and, in a more recent wrinkle, parishioners now sue their clergy in record numbers. From toddlers to executors of the deceased, anyone can sue and no one is immune – not even the President of the United States.

More frightening than the blizzard of lawsuits is the sheer number of ridiculous cases that manage to squeeze their way through the court system and reach a jury. It seems that the more ridiculous the case, the greater the plaintiff's victory. Scan the newspapers or magazines. Watch TV. Laugh to the

Saturday night stand-up comics. Who can most scintillate us with the day's craziest lawsuit? Why is litigation our favorite form of entertainment?

I recently chuckled my way through a fascinating book that featured its own macabre brand of lawsuit humor: *Buy This Book or We'll Sue You* (Citadel Press). Authors Laura and Attila Benko compile scores of true cases, more absurd and supposedly funnier than fiction. Think for a moment, though: Are these cases really humorous when you consider the great waste of time, money, and energy that was expended to defend against them? Are these frivolous and bizarre cases truly funny when you consider the aggravation, worry, and grief that so many defendants were forced to endure before they could shake themself free of these nutty litigants and their stupid lawsuits? Some of these whacky plaintiffs actually *won* their cases, which again bolsters my argument that our legal system is indeed a legal lottery where even the bad case has a good chance.

Consider the classic cases: The 82-year-old lady whose MacDonald's coffee landed on her lap while she was simultaneously driving and juggling the hot coffee between her knees. Our geriatric plaintiff not only successfully sued McDonald's for millions, but also Wal-Mart, who sold her the auto cup holder. What can we say about the New York couple who successfully sued the city for ten million dollars after they were struck by a train while enjoying sex on the tracks? There is the Florida drunk who, while climbing a fence, was zapped by a transformer and sued the six taverns that had served him liquor that day as well as the electric company. Consider the Georgia couple who sued Ford after their three-year-old boy died in a Ford van where they locked him up for several hours in 90-degree heat (the parents claim Ford should feature a safety device to cool parked cars). We could list more, because this is the attitude of today's society.

I predicted it years ago. The fast food industry has finally been sued for turning us into a nation of fatties. Can the chocolate industry be far behind? Who's next? More importantly, who *isn't*?

You might argue that these cases are the legal anomalies and rare curiosities within our legal system, but you would be wrong. Hundreds or thousands of equally ridiculous cases are now pending in your local courthouse at this very moment. I know. I have seen enough ludicrous cases in my own practice. Take a few minutes to read the weekly Bar journals. There are plenty of equally far-fetched cases breaking new legal ground. Usually there is also a picture of the grinning victorious plaintiff's lawyer who bagged another defendant.

The lawsuit mongers are abusing the legal system in record numbers. California, America's lawsuit capital, in order to stem the litigation avalanche, created the Vexatious Litigation Act to identify those who overload their courts with frivolous lawsuits. While chronic plaintiffs cannot be denied their 'constitutional right' to sue, they cannot sue in California without an attorney. Nevertheless, one chronic victim still managed to file two hundred lawsuits in seven years. The court clerk who identifies these lawsuit junkies (and who was himself sued unsuccessfully eleven times in two years) admits: "I don't exaggerate when I say I am extremely frightened by these people."

You do not have to do anything wrong to be sued - and lose. You only have to be in the wrong place at the wrong time or somehow come across some greedy lunatic who thinks he or she has reason to be grieved. Voilá! *Your* wealth could soon be in *their* pocket!

Perhaps it's not for me to call any case ludicrous.

After all, juries decide whether a case has merit. What is the law but what a court determines it to be in any given case. That's another problem with our legal system. We have lost all predictability as to what the law is or what the outcome of a case is likely to be. Few lawyers will speculate where a case will wind up: *You never know what a court will do.* How different is that from saying 'You never know what a roulette wheel will do.' It's random chance.

We have so stretched and convoluted our theories of liability that no lawyer really knows the law anymore. This may help explain why lawyers accept cases that others see as patently bizarre, or why no defense lawyer can assure their client that they *can't* lose their case. Our legal system has transformed into a crapshoot where the plaintiff need not play with his own chips and the defendant - win or lose - inevitably loses some or all of his own.

One Lawsuit Can Wipe You Out

Even when you can endure the odds of being sued and the uncertainty of winning or losing, you must consider the potentially devastating awards. You can seldom predict what you could lose in a lawsuit. A plaintiff who wins a few dollars in actual damages may pocket millions more in punitive damages. Anyone who buys a $20 defective product can turn it into a class action case that can cost the company who sold it millions - or even billions. One lawsuit can start an avalanche of others. Enough piddly lawsuits can topple the most powerful business or the wealthiest family, as we have seen with litigation against tobacco, pharmaceuticals, asbestos, and countless other industries.

It is this uncertainty of outcome that also explains why nine out of ten lawsuits are settled before trial. What defendant can go to trial confident of victory? What defendant can know what they stand to lose if their case goes to trial? How many defendants can afford the exorbitant legal fees to get answers to these questions?

Plaintiffs and their lawyers use lawsuits as weapons to extort whopping settlements because the economics are always with the plaintiffs. The defendant is coerced to pay 'go away money, because the defendant with exposed wealth simply has too much to lose by gambling on litigation.

Of course, some lawsuits involve more than money. A lawsuit can attack your personal character, particularly those that allege fraud, racketeering, or conspiracy. You have good cause to get angry when a lawsuit attacks your professional competency. Ask any doctor how it feels to be characterized in a malpractice lawsuit as 'negligent, incompetent or reckless.'

One leading New York thoracic surgeon who was sued only twice in his thirty-year career will tell you, "You know you did nothing wrong, but still you begin to question your own competence. Inevitably your self-confidence and self-esteem drops a few notches."

Any lawsuit can create stress and uneasiness; however, a major lawsuit can disrupt social relationships, cloud thoughts, dampen enthusiasm for the future, and always creates that nagging sense of insecurity. The essence of the lawsuit was perhaps best voiced by the *Tort Informer:* "The law provides incredible financial incentives to seek out a victim with deep pockets, drag him into court, ruin his reputation, wear him down with endless discovery demands, pay a fortune to defend himself and then extort a settlement from him. This is not justice in any sense of the word."

Develop the Survivor Instinct
Not every lawsuit is frivolous. If you breach a lease, default on a loan, or negligently rear-end another car, these spawn

legitimate cases for which a plaintiff has every right to sue.

Does a claim's legitimacy give you any less reason to protect yourself? I don't think so. The bottom line is not whether a lawsuit is justified, but whether you can afford to lose all of your assets defending it. Lose a bonafide lawsuit and you can still be financially wiped out. I consider financial self-defense a necessity regardless of the legitimacy of the claim. Nor can you anticipate a lawsuit only when you do something wrong - you can just as easily be sued when you do everything right.

Some folks are uncomfortable with the objectives of asset protection. They view asset protection as somehow illegal or immoral - a device to cheat creditors of their rightful due. I disagree. Those who seek protection are neither crooks nor immoral. I see them as savvy and with a strong survival instinct. These people are taking advantage of laws created to protect against life's financial uncertainties and risks.

Asset protection, properly practiced, is certainly not illegal. Of course you cannot commit such illegal acts as perjury, violate bankruptcy laws, or fraudulently conceal your assets from creditors; however, a good asset protection plan neither encourages nor permits these or other illegal acts. You can and must implement your asset protection plan fully complying with all laws. This is basic to sound planning.

Ethically, you may consider it improper to shelter your assets from those who assert a rightful claim. Consider asset protection as financial self-defense in its purest form. It combats frivolous and harassing lawsuits. When you are well protected you are a less inviting lawsuit target. You can live your life confident that your financial security can not be stripped away because you were targeted for a lawsuit. The bottom line: Wealth is good. *Vulnerable* wealth is bad.

You must protect your assets and consider defensive

financial planning. There are many good attorneys ready to assist their clients to achieve this goal by recommending corporations, trusts, limited partnerships, and a variety of other asset protection devices.

If the ethical or moral aspects of protecting your assets from a lawsuit still concern you, try this: Protect your assets. If a legitimate lawsuit is filed against you, negotiate a fair settlement and pay the claim. When your assets are protected, you have that option.

Who Needs Asset Protection?

You may feel for many reasons that your wealth is safe and that you do not need asset protection. I claim this attitude is naïve. You may also delude yourself and fall victim to one or more myths:

Myth #1: "I can't get sued. I'm too careful."

While you need not do anything wrong to find yourself on the wrong end of a lawsuit, there are those who tell me, "I have never been sued before and I can't visualize why I would be sued now."

One woman who attended one of my *Wealthsaver* seminars gave me that argument as she explained her apathy for asset protection: "I'm a schoolteacher. What legal problems can a schoolteacher have?" True, she may never be sued as a schoolteacher, yet this woman was sued for a million plus dollars about a year later for negligently handling her mother's estate.

There are many reasons to get sued today. A lawsuit need not relate to your employment. You may be cautious and careful and still get sued. It is not only doctors, real estate developers, or business owners who incur liability or attract lawsuits; *everyone* is a potential target.

It was at this same California *Wealthsaver* seminar when a young man asked, "Dr. Goldstein, what tips do you have to avoid liability?"

I facetiously replied, "Don't get out of bed in the morning."

The young man retorted, "I tried that and got sued for paternity."

That reply brought laughter from all of us. Nevertheless, it goes to show you that no matter how you live your life or what you do for a living, there is ample opportunity to get into legal trouble. So who is safe?

Nobody! Professionals, of course, are the most probable lawsuit targets. When a surgery fails, a trial is lost, or an investment sours, the patient, client, or investor concludes that the professional is to blame. Unfavorable outcomes translate into 'sue the professional.' These plaintiffs 'walk the Yellow Pages' for a lawyer ready and willing to take the case. Others are also high on the lawsuit hit list: Parents of teenage drivers; commercial real estate owners; small business owners; accountants and other business advisors; architects and engineers; corporate officers and directors; directors of charitable organizations; police officers; celebrities; sports figures, and the conspicuously wealthy. It's not what you do, but how much you own that determines your vulnerability.

Even the proverbial little old lady in tennis shoes can get into big legal trouble. For instance, an 83-year-old great grandmother met with me because she accidentally hit the gas rather than the brake and slammed her Lexus through a K-Mart storefront, seriously injuring several shoppers. She is going to be sued for considerably more than her insurance coverage. On the bright side, this will be her first lawsuit in eighty-three years. Eventually we all run out of luck!

Myth #2: "I don't need asset protection. I don't have enough assets to protect."

How many times have I heard this line?

How would you feel if you lost what few assets you do own? While talking to a young man about asset protection, he assured me he was too poor to worry about lawsuits or asset protection. His entire wealth consisted of a used $15,000 car and $10,000 in savings. True, $25,000 is modest wealth.

I asked, "How long did it take you to earn what you own?"

"About five years," he replied. "I'm only a landscape worker."

"How would you feel if tomorrow someone seized your car and bank account?"

"Devastated," he admitted.

My business as an asset protection lawyer has taught me that wealth is relative. It is not only the rich and affluent who need asset protection; if you have *any* assets, they need protection.

While traveling to give another *Wealthsaver* seminar in New York, I passed through LaGuardia airport and got a shoe shine. The affable bootblack engaged me in conversation and asked what brought me to town. I told him that I was to give an asset protection seminar in Manhattan, and he told me about his own financial problems. He was being sued for $100,000 on a bank loan he guaranteed for his son. He then explained that he owned only his Bronx home with a $100,000 equity. To some people, $100,000 is hardly serious wealth. While they would hate to lose it, such a loss would not hurt their lifestyle. That $100,000 was this man's entire lifetime accumulation. How many more shoes must he shine to replace his $100,000 nest egg?

I receive calls from people from throughout the

country who have creditors or lawsuit problems. Many have only a few dollars in the bank, a small house, or perhaps some modest investments. Whatever their wealth, it is precious to *them*. Protecting their assets is as serious a matter as protecting someone else's millions. Wealth is relative, and you must treat your wealth accordingly. You must protect *any* asset that is important to *you*.

Myth #3: "I don't need protection. I'm insured."
This is another fallacy. You buy a liability policy and figure, "That's it, I'm covered. If I'm sued, my insurance will take care of it."

I can give you many reasons why liability insurance is not a substitute for asset protection. In fact, liability insurance covers only about one in three lawsuits. What do you do about the two out of three lawsuits that will not be covered by insurance? Consider the possibilities: You could get sued for breach of contract, a defaulted loan, or on a family dispute. How many *uninsured* claims can be levied against you? The possibilities are endless.

Take a lesson from one of my physician friends. He argued for years that he did not need any more lawsuit protection than his five million dollar malpractice policy. However, you can bet he wished that he had protected his assets after an employee sued him for two million dollars on a sexual harassment claim. His malpractice insurance was also useless to shelter his wealth when Uncle Sam demanded he repay millions that he allegedly over billed Medicaid.

Even when a claim is insured, you must ask whether the insurance will *fully* cover the claim. A million-dollar liability policy does not mean much when you are sued for two million. With today's unpredictable, ludicrous jury awards, you cannot foresee what damages you may someday be forced to pay. Then, too, you may discover that liability insurance is not your complete answer to financial security.

There are countless policy exclusions, the inevitable loopholes that let your insurance company deny coverage. Nor will your insurance company readily defend a claim that is supposedly insured. The many 'bad faith' claims now pending against insurance companies prove this point.

You cannot even be sure that your insurance company will be in business when you need them. I am now trying to protect the assets of scores of physicians in Ohio, New Jersey, and several other states whose insurance companies filed bankruptcy. These doctors *thought* that they were protected, but they are now exposed with little or no coverage. Many are in the middle of lawsuits!

No, I am not against liability insurance. In fact, I want my clients to have good insurance coverage because insurance is a smart first step in any asset protection program. Buy whatever liability insurance you can reasonably afford, but look upon insurance as a starting point. Liability insurance cannot take the place of a good asset protection plan, which you need to protect yourself from *any* type or size claim. Asset protection planning is the *only* way to achieve *complete* financial safety.

Myth #4: "Asset protection is too costly. I can't afford it."
Protecting your assets is not too costly, and probably will not take more than a few hours of your time. I find the average family can gain strong protection for their assets for under a few thousand dollars. We have sheltered larger fortunes for under $20,000, and there are many protective steps that cost you absolutely nothing.

A doctor complained to me that he did not have the spare cash to set up the few entities that he needed to safeguard his three million net worth and considered my proposed $15,000 legal fee too great a cost. However, he spends $65,000 a year for malpractice insurance. This same $65,000 policy only covers malpractice claims, and only for one million dollars. Next year the good doctor will pay another $65,000 (assuming his premiums do not increase) for the same limited protection. In comparison, I offered this physician *complete* protection against *any* lawsuit, in *any* amount, for the *rest of his life*, for less than one-fourth of what he pays each year for malpractice insurance. So, which is the better deal…insurance or asset protection? You can't think of asset protection as an expense. It's an investment - a *great* investment - if you truly want financial security!

Life's Financial Minefield

The lawsuit is, of course, only one way to lose your wealth. It is certainly not the only path to financial devastation. Life can be a financial minefield and no matter how carefully you tread, there is danger with every step:

Divorce. Isn't this one of life's most devastating lawsuits? Yet few people think of divorce that way. You may be happily married today, but the statistics are against you and you may some day divorce. As unlikely as it may seem, you could struggle through more than one divorce during your lifetime.

How well are your assets protected if you should divorce? How can you better prepare financially for your next marriage or your next divorce? Because divorce planning is so important in asset protection planning, you will find numerous protective strategies in this book.

Bankruptcy and creditor problems. What does it matter whether one litigant sues you for $100,000 or twenty sue you for $5,000 each? In either instance, your assets are in jeopardy to the tune of $100,000. You must know how to protect yourself against your creditors and the possibility that some day you may be bankrupt.

How can you legally and safely fortify your assets today so you lose the fewest assets if you must file bankruptcy tomorrow?

Here, too, the statistics are dismal. Over two million Americans are expected to file bankruptcy next year. Most of these debtors will lose everything. These are the people who could not foresee their financial problems or had too little time or know-how to protect themselves.

What if you lost your job? Or ran up unexpected medical bills? Can you be certain that you will escape future financial problems?

Paul, a poker pal, illustrates the vagaries of life. For years, Paul ran a successful construction company in South Florida. Paul was worth millions, yet never gave much thought to asset protection. Because he had plenty of liability insurance he assumed he was well protected. One of Paul's projects turned bad and his company went bust, leaving him personally owing a bank over six million dollars. When Paul was thrown into personal bankruptcy, he lost over four million dollars. Paul was only *one* of last year's statistics. You may be a statistic next year. To survive your own financial ups and downs with your wealth intact, you must plan your asset protection.

Tax problems. You know how easy it is to get into trouble with the IRS. Tax troubles are becoming increasingly common. Millions of hapless taxpayers are clobbered annually by audits and huge tax bills.

Once you owe the IRS, you will see how quickly

your assets can vanish. The IRS is now chasing about twenty million Americans who each owe the IRS at least $10,000. What will these tax delinquents lose? What would *you* lose should the tax collector knock on your door?

Government seizures. Here's another fast growing financial threat. You may not realize it, but federal and local enforcement agencies routinely seize billions in cash and property each year – without a trial. Even a minor drug violation or other minor infraction can cause your assets to be summarily auctioned.

So those are the dangers. There are others. Only with advance planning do you have a fighting chance to escape losing your assets. Adopt a defensive, realistic philosophy: Don't ask *whether* you will someday face financial danger, ask *when!*

Disaster Preparedness

The obvious conclusion is that you must anticipate trouble and build the strongest possible asset protection fortress today so you become as well protected as possible against tomorrow's possible financial crisis.

Timing is the key to successful asset protection. Protect yourself *before* you have trouble. You have far fewer options after you have a financial disaster. Since you are reading this book, you apparently recognize the possible dangers to your financial security. You have undoubtedly heard plenty of your own horror stories from those who lost their life savings, homes, or businesses only because they failed to prepare. You can't afford to be another statistic.

2

Building Your Financial Fortress

So whatever did happen to John and Millie Mathews?

On the downside, they lost their case. After several years of tumultuous litigation, John's ex-partner won a $700,000 judgment. With interest and costs, John ended up owing his ex-partner something over $850,000.

That's the bad news. The good news is that after several more months of wrangling, John settled the case by paying his ex-partner $45,000; this small sum, despite the fact that John and Millie had a net worth of over $3 million.

How did this favorable outcome come about? For one reason only: The Mathews had well-protected assets or what I call *untouchable* wealth.

John can tell you about it:

"I went through several tough months as my ex-partner's lawyer tried every way possible to collect on the judgment. But he always came up empty. Everything I owned was either fully mortgaged or protectively titled. About all I had exposed was a few thousand equity in my cars. I was more than lucky. Before I started my business I could foresee becoming a lawsuit target some day and that's when I had taken steps to protect myself. If I had not then thought defensively I would now be $850,000 poorer."

Asset protection can indeed make the difference between whether you keep your wealth intact and preserve your financial security or lose what you have worked a lifetime to amass.

Of course, the goal of protecting one's assets from life's inevitable risks and dangers is certainly not new. Raiders on horseback once pillaged and plundered treasure while brandishing menacing swords and lancets. The only defense was a secure fortress. That era is long gone, but little has changed. Nowadays the raiders are the lawyers who storm the courthouse with their Mercedes and Bentleys. With their Cross pens drawn, they are the new ransackers of our wealth. The only way to defend yourself against these legal knaves is to build the strongest possible fortress - your very own *financial* fortress.

It was a famous Chinese philosopher who once commented, "That which depends on me, I can do; that which depends on the enemy cannot be certain." That is the underlying philosophy of asset protection. You, too, must follow this tactical maxim if you are to become legally invincible and able to withstand the inevitable assaults on your wealth.

You Too Can Have Untouchable Wealth

John and Millie Mathews are not the only people who know how to effectively protect themselves by creating untouchable wealth. I have scores of clients with substantial wealth who have either completely sidestepped potentially devastating lawsuits or liabilities - or have settled their claims for mere pennies-on-the-dollar - only because they too had timely and intelligently protected everything they own…their home…savings…investments…real estate…business…cars…retirement accounts…etc., etc. They had virtually nothing exposed to adversaries or predatory attack.

Of course, successful wealth protection does not just happen. To effectively blockade litigants and creditors from grabbing your assets depends on a lot of 'ifs.'

You can achieve this important objective only…

- *if* you protect yourself well before trouble strikes.
- *if* you use the right strategies and employ the right tools for your particular situation.
- *if* you have the right professional advisor; one who can give you the right blueprint from which to build your *financial fortress*.
- *if* you make a real commitment to *sheltering* your wealth - the same commitment that you made to *building* your wealth.

In this chapter you will discover the more fundamental approaches to asset protection. In later chapters you will see the specific tools in greater detail and how they may apply in different situations.

Asset Protection Overview

Asset protection, in its simplest terms, is a strategy to title your savings, property, business and other assets in a manner that shields them from lawsuits and other creditor claims. More simply put, asset protection prevents your adversaries from seizing your wealth.

That asset protection has the goal to protect assets from litigants and creditors might seem rather apparent, but there is more to the definition.

John Mathews defines asset protection somewhat differently. "Asset protection - at least in my case - was a safety net. It doesn't guarantee that you won't get sued or run into other financial calamities; but if you do, you will lose few, if any assets. Without it you're in 'free-fall,' you're vulnerable and exposed.

If you have not heard much about asset protection before, it is because only America's wealthiest families were traditionally concerned with wealth protection. They were the 'deep pocket' defendants, those most frequently sued because they had significant wealth to lose. The Rockefellers, Kennedys and the other social elites of past decades have most relied upon partnerships, trusts, family corporations and a variety of other protective entities to privatize and lawsuit-proof their holdings; however, they seldom referred to their financial maneuvers as 'asset protection.' Undoubtedly, these same plans were also useful for tax avoidance and estate planning or in their case, 'dynasty planning.'

Of course, America's super-rich are no longer the only lawsuit targets. Every middle-income American, such as the Mathews, now has the same need to protect their wealth from lawsuits. With the fast-growing lawsuit threat, many more lawyers are seeking wealth protection for their clients, as they should. Unfortunately, too few attorneys emphasize this. This should not be surprising. Few, if any, law schools teach asset protection as a formal course (they too busily teach budding lawyers how to sue); and only recently have we begun to see professional seminars and books on the subject. As John Mathews observed, "Your lawyer may fight like hell to defend you against a lawsuit, but how many will tell you to shelter yourself in the event they lose the lawsuit? When lawyers walk the litigation tight-rope without the safety net, it is the client who pays the price when they stumble." John, of course, is absolutely right.

Benefits of Asset Protection

While the broad goal of asset protection is to provide you and your family lifetime security, the comfort that only comes from knowing that you cannot lose what you own, regardless of your financial or legal problems, a good asset protection plan achieves several other important objectives:

1. Discourage lawsuits

An important objective of asset protection is to *discourage* lawsuits from being filed against you in the first place. You can only achieve this when you can convince a potential plaintiff that they cannot seize your wealth, even if they should sue and win their case.

When you discourage a lawsuit, your asset protection plan simultaneously shields you from the oftentimes devastating costs of defending against the lawsuit. It is far better to discourage a lawsuit in the first place than to defend against the lawsuit and win. Once you are sued, you must still spend money, time and effort to "win," while preventing even one potential lawsuit can pay for your asset protection investment many times over.

Litigation has its economics. It is important to understand that before a potential plaintiff sues, he and his lawyer economically evaluate the case against you. They must attempt to weigh the costs of suing against both the odds of winning and the likely recovery based on your *exposed* assets. In other words, they must decide: *Are you worth suing?*

Not many prospective plaintiffs will sue if they doubt they can recover more than they will spend in the process or what the lawyer foresees spending on legal time. Even when you fail this economic test, you may nevertheless get sued because every lawyer knows that even the weakest lawsuit has some 'settlement value.' And they are right. The odds are that you will probably pay something to make the lawsuit disappear, perhaps because of privacy concerns, the costs of defending or the nuisance value. While you may consider this extortion and dislike lawyers and litigants because of it, it is, nevertheless, reality. That is how the system works.

Even when you have solid asset protection, some people sue 'vindictively.' They have a score to settle. There are other reasons why you may get sued. For instance, you may be a peripheral defendant in a lawsuit where the vulnerability of your wealth is not initially checked by the plaintiff because you are one of several or many defendants. Usually, it's only when you are the primary lawsuit target that your assets or ability to pay a sizeable judgment become a key factor in the lawsuit decision.

In sum, it is not whether or not you have sizeable assets that determines whether you are sued; it's whether your assets are *exposed*. If you want to avoid lawsuits, you must convince prospective plaintiffs that you have that *impregnable* financial fortress.

2. Negotiate favorable settlements

In those instances when you are sued, asset protection puts you in a far superior position to negotiate those pennies-on-the-dollar settlements. You negotiate from a position of strength because your opponent knows that you have nothing to lose and they have nothing to gain if they do sue. You can also think of it another way: If the lawsuit is how plaintiffs extort huge settlements, then asset protection is the great equalizer, the means to level the playing field.

Frequently a plaintiff will have no real fix on your financial situation until after you are sued and the attorneys can open a dialogue. That is when a good defense lawyer will begin to sell the proposition that you are essentially judgment-proof and therefore the case is best dismissed or settled for relatively few dollars. Settlement should be your attorney's objective early in the litigation process to avoid the lengthy, costly litigation process.

Few plaintiffs will blindly accept your representation that you are judgment-proof. They may demand financial affidavits or go through other means to verify your uncollectability.

There is also a psychology to settlement. We do not use an 'in-your-face' approach when discussing our client's asset protection. It is best to present the financial realities with more subtlety; but whatever the style of presentation the burden is on the defendant to quickly convince the plaintiff that the chances of recovery against him are small.

3. Reduce insurance costs

Good asset protection planning gives you more benefits. For example, I would not promote asset protection as a substitute for liability insurance, nevertheless certain high-risk professionals and businesses do find their insurance costs to be prohibitive, or liability insurance may not be available. Asset protection can then be either complementary to insurance coverage or serve as a substitute.

This does not suggest that you should forego liability insurance. While it is true that insurance may be costly and attract litigants; nevertheless, insurance is invaluable in any risk management program. To the extent insurance is cost-effective, it should be the primary defensive tool and asset protection should be secondary. The overriding strategy then is to focus the plaintiff on recovering only up to the policy and foregoing any further claim against the defendant - a goal more easily achieved when the defendant is in fact, well-insulated.

4. Improve financial planning

A good asset protection plan can also help you to save estate or income taxes, improve your estate plan or even lead you to better investments. Asset protection is an essential component of financial planning as I more fully explain in the next chapter.

From my observation, asset protection is typically the catalyst for improved estate and tax planning. It happens less often in reverse. In probably 80 percent of our cases, our asset protection plan was instrumental in helping a client achieve these other financial objectives.

5. Judgment-proofing

Obviously, the ultimate purpose of asset protection is to *safeguard* your wealth under a worst-case scenario - you are sued and lose. And the odds are even that you *will* someday lose a lawsuit. This is when you need well-protected assets; the moment your asset protection plan is put to the test.

This does not mean that one who is judgment-proof can cavalierly dismiss the problems that arise from a judgment. A plaintiff's lawyer may prove to be quite stubborn in his pursuit of even the most protected defendant. The plaintiff may nevertheless attempt to attach key assets and certainly has ample opportunity to drag the defendant through many more court proceedings to discover assets. Nor is it usually possible to fully protect every last asset. There is always that 'loose change' - those few assets that for one reason or another become exposed to the creditor.

More frequently, the benefit of asset protection is realized only after the plaintiff has won a judgment and has exhausted his collection remedies. There are those plaintiffs who will not settle until that point, notwithstanding earlier assurances by the defendant that he is indeed judgment-proof.

Still, even with the most formidable asset protection, every case has a settlement value even when the plaintiff has been unsuccessful in seizing assets. Few defendants relish the idea of a judgment hanging over their head for twenty or more years; and the plaintiff always has the option to petition the defendant into bankruptcy, even if it is for vindictive purposes. And a judgment does not enhance one's credit rating.

The ultimate success of an asset protection plan is not whether the plaintiff ended up with absolutely no recovery. In most of our cases our client paid 'something' to make the case go away. The true goal is to have the client assured that he will never involuntarily lose significant assets. When we review a case, we ultimately measure its success by asking ourselves "Was there anything more we could have done to achieve a better outcome." That's the litmus test of any plan.

The Three Pillars of Protection

Now, let's start with the basics. How do you protect assets? There are only three basic strategies. These are what I call 'The Three Pillars of Protection.'

1. The exemption laws. Own as many assets as possible that have some form of statutory protection from lawsuits and creditors (exempt assets) and own few or no assets that are not self-protected (exempt) assets.

2. Title your assets to a protective entity. These entities, in one or another manner, prevents your judgment creditors from seizing the assets titled to the entity.

3. Encumber or equity-strip your assets to reduce the assets economic value to the creditor.

That's it!

Nearly every strategy that you will discover in this book and that I use to judgment-proof clients rely upon one or more of these basic three strategies.

These are the legal concepts. Asset protection requires more. It is also about creating a defensible story and rationale for protectively titling assets; one that is less likely to be challenged by a creditor's attorney and more likely to be accepted as an arrangement not primarily intended to thwart a creditor's attempt to collect on his judgment. In sum, the defendant's financial arrangement must be viewed in its best light.

The Eight Asset Protection Firewalls

With these three over-arching concepts in mind, let's consider the eight specific tools that we most frequently use. I refer to them as 'firewalls,' because each in its own way and through different mechanisms serves to insulate assets from creditors. The firewalls include:

1. Federal and state exemptions (Chapter 5)
2. Co-ownerships (Chapter 6)
3. Corporations (Chapter 7)
4. Limited partnerships (Chapter 8)
5. Limited liability companies (Chapter 9)
6. Domestic trusts (Chapter 10)
7. Offshore entities (Chapter 11)
8. Debt-shields (Chapter 12)

Each firewall has its own unique characteristics; strengths and weaknesses, advantages and disadvantages, applications and instances where they would not be used. As with colors on the artist's palette; some may be used more than others, however, each is necessary for artistic perfection. That perfect portrait, however, only results from their right application.

Countless Opportunities

This does not suggest that every asset protection device can be so neatly categorized.

There are literally hundreds or even possibly thousands of variations on the theme. For example, there are scores of other entities that we could discuss, but most entities and strategies conceptually, at least, fall within one of these type firewalls. For example, limited liability partnerships and limited liability limited partnerships are variations on limited partnerships and limited liability companies.

Nor does every possible firewall fall within one category or another. For example, exposed cash may be used to buy a deferred annuity that will create an income stream many years hence. While the annuity payment may theoretically be claimable by the creditor, how much is it worth to a creditor who must wait years to collect?

Nor do I discuss every possible firewall. *So Sue Me* is not intended to be a technical treatise. Its job is to present the more common strategies. There are many more advanced methodologies that mostly combine legal and financial strategies. While these are invariably complex arrangements, they can provide the client with many financial as well as protective benefits. Asset protection is anything but a static specialty. Professional planners are always inventing new strategies and tactics to perfect the science and with the same diligence collection lawyers constantly try to find ways to pierce these more advanced plans. Many strategies in actuality are more financial than legal. For example, we now have a number of structured financial products (SFP's) that use complex arbitrage arrangements to effectively shift wealth between spouses who have different levels of liability exposure. We also use many insurance-based opportunities to shield wealth. Only the more common will be discussed here.

To balance the complex plans, we have many other protective maneuvers that are quite simple - even obvious. An example would be to use exposed cash to prepay certain expenses or repay favored creditors. Some of the best strategies are nothing more than common sense, particularly when the goal is to protect very modest wealth.

Layer Your Protection

The essence of asset protection is not to use only one device to protect a particular asset. No matter how safe or defensible we may believe a particular firewall to be; there is always the possibility that a creditor can find a way to pierce it. That is why we 'layer' our protection or use multiple firewalls. It is basically the 'belt and suspenders' approach to protection. Even if one firewall were to fail, we have others behind it, and always the opportunity to impose still others should the situation warrant.

The asset protection challenge is not only to know *which* firewalls to use but *when* to interpose additional firewalls as the creditor threat advances. You must always stay at least two steps ahead of any creditor in pursuit.

As you can see then, asset protection frequently evolves in stages. We have the *preventative* and *crisis* stage.

Hopefully, you will complete your plan before you incur liability. You should then only need a good preventative plan, or a basic first level of protection. This, of course, will not necessarily be your final plan if you are later sued, because your ultimate plan must give you all the safety you need against the particular threat. We would then add more firewalls as your specific situation requires, to make you as judgment-proof as possible *before* you walk into the courtroom. However, that's not necessarily the plan you would start out with.

Obviously, a crisis protection plan usually requires a more costly, complex plan than would a basic plan. That is why we layer firewalls *only* after there is a known legal threat. Until we know of a particular threat we cannot prescribe one best defensive position. How you will ultimately be protected will greatly be influenced by the amount and nature of the claim, the dynamics of the case, what the creditor will likely do to seize assets should he win a judgment; and other factors that we will soon discuss.

Cost-efficiency and the goal of simplicity are also reasons to begin with a basic plan. Not everyone gets sued. Nor is every lawsuit wealth threatening and even those that are may be covered by insurance or quickly disposed of through a reasonable settlement. Layering, then, usually progresses with the advance of the threat. To over-build a plan prematurely is to lose flexibility and to burden the client with needless cost and complexity.

Inevitably, you must create the plan with a high safety factor (no plan is 100 percent guaranteed). If you are early on with a legal problem, you want to know what your ultimate plan would be should it become necessary to go that far. My clients with lawsuits in hand always want to know what can be done to eventually achieve that safety factor. They must know what their firewalls will be, when we would add each firewall and how and why those firewalls work to insulate their assets. Understanding their ultimate game plan - not necessarily implementing the plan prematurely - lets my clients sleep well.

When you layer or combine firewalls, you exponentially strengthen the final plan, much as a plywood panel is substantially stronger than the sum of its component layers. To illustrate, the combination of the limited partnership, offshore trust, Nevis LLC and foreign annuity into one integrated plan interposes a collectively formidable firewall barrier. There are, of course, hundreds of layering possibilities. This is what asset protection planners refer to as *defense-in-depth.*

The Diversification Strategy

The deployment of assets in different protective baskets (layered entities) is still another axiom of good planning. Why put all your eggs in one basket? A creditor who must chase assets in several different directions is severely handicapped. And even if the creditor succeeds in recovering from 'one basket,' the wealth sheltered by the other 'baskets' remain safe.

Diversification is particularly important where more wealth needs protection. For example, a client requiring maximum protection for ten million in liquid assets may deploy this wealth into five separate protective baskets that may be quite dissimilar to each other.

It is this combination of layering or 'defense-in-depth' and diversification that creates the strongest shield. The trick is always to combine and diversify firewalls to create an insurmountable obstacle to block even the most determined creditor.

Counter Offensive Strategies

The best defense is a good offense. That truism applies to asset protection as well as to other conflicts.

There are a number of ways to impose liability on a creditor who attempts to seize assets. For instance, a creditor who obtains a charging order on a limited partnership or LLC interest may incur a tax liability. Or a creditor who commences litigation against a Nevis entity may be forced to pay a $25,000 bond. There are any number of liability-imposing features that act as quills on the porcupine. It makes pursuit that much less attractive.

Seldom do the counter-offensive capabilities of a particular strategy control its adoption but they may influence it. The goal is to present the creditor with a 'downside.' Now the creditor who is always uncertain about what he can gain from the asset chase suddenly realizes what he can lose.

Customize Your Plan

What should be apparent from all this is that there is no 'one right firewall,' 'one right strategy' or one right plan. Your plan must be customized to your own specific situation.

There is no such thing as a 'one-size' fits all. And that is a recurrent problem with both many 'so-called' asset protection planners as well as gullible clients who are either peddling or seeking that 'one quick fix' or 'magic bullet.'

For example, you will find planners who push Nevada Corporations as everybody's asset protection answer. Others suggest offshore trusts or limited partnerships for every client. Each is only one of many tools, but that's all they are. It may or may not be the right firewall for *you*.

Your planner must offer the entire range of possible firewalls because any one firewall occupies only one place in the planner's toolbox. No one firewall is *everybody's* lawsuit-proofing answer. Your planner must be adept at using *every* possible protective tool. Remember this.

Your planner must also offer both offshore and domestic (US-based) protective strategies (if you have a high net-worth, you probably need *both* a domestic and offshore component to your plan and your planner must skillfully provide both). Not every planner has this dual expertise.

Some planners protect only specific assets - and usually for self-serving reasons. That's how the planner makes money. For example, an insurance professional posing as an asset protection specialist may sell an accounts receivable factoring program to protect this one asset from lawsuits. They push their programs at seminars targeted to doctors and small business owners. The accounts receivable finances a life insurance policy for which the planner earns a commission. This factoring arrangement may or may not be sensible for a particular client, but even when it is, how do you protect your many other assets?

The point is that you need a planner who has the complete arsenal of protective tools. Anything less is to lessen your options and your protection.

Customizing the right plan requires the planner to consider several factors:

- your state laws
- the nature and value of the assets to be protected
- the liability (if any) to be protected against
- whether it is preventative or crisis planning
- your financial (estate planning, investment and tax) situation
- the strategies you would be most comfortable employing
- costs
- your personal situation (age, marital status, etc.).

It is the expert blending of these considerations into the one best customized plan for a particular client at a given point against a given danger that is the essence of good asset protection planning.

Keep Your Plan Updated

Finally, asset protection must be a continuous commitment. Frequently, people rush to protect themselves only when they are sued or anticipate a lawsuit. However, once the threat passes, they allow their plan to fall into disuse. That mistake can be costly.

Any asset protection plan is only your best plan at the given point in time it was first designed. However, time brings changes. Your finances, obligations and personal situations change, as will the laws, available strategies and possible firewalls. Obviously, your asset protection plan must also undergo change.

That is why asset protection planning must be a continuous and lifelong process. You must review your plan with your planner at least annually, and more frequently with each major event - a windfall inheritance, threatened lawsuit, relocation to another state, family change, etc. Each event triggers the need for an update. Only with continuous updates can your plan match your current situation.

Yes, it involves time, cost and effort to enjoy strong lifelong protection, but that is what I mean by your commitment to your own financial security. If your protection erodes because it is no longer your prime objective, you once again become vulnerable.

3

Ten Keys to a Great Plan

What distinguishes a *good* asset protection plan from a *great* plan - one that will give you the optimum benefits and is ideal for your particular circumstances?

I have reviewed many asset protection plans, and while there are an endless variety of possible plans (which explains why no two planners are likely to propose precisely the same plan); I nevertheless note that many plans can be improved if their planners had employed just a bit more thought.

Any great plan must do more than provide basic protection. The well-designed plan incorporates and satisfies many other considerations. Unquestionably, the planner must thoroughly understand the client's overall financial affairs and personal matters as well as have a good fix on the client's objectives beyond liability insulation.

There are also fundamental flaws that I see in plans. These errors may or may not compromise the safety of the client's assets, but they create adverse tax consequences, impose needless cost or complexity, or otherwise disrupt the client's other financial objectives.

So, how do you distinguish the *good* plan from the *great* plan?

Consider these criteria. They are what I call the *ten keys to great planning:*

Key # 1 - Protect Every Asset

It is axiomatic that an asset protection plan should insulate every important asset, but more than a few plans fail in this regard. They shelter only certain assets. Others remain exposed.

Why does this happen? There are several reasons. First, the client may overlook and not bring to the planner's attention such assets as intangibles (copyrights, patents, notes receivable, claims the client has against others, etc.). Second, you may also assume that certain assets are exempt or self-protected and take no further steps toward their protection. For example, we oftentimes see this with retirement accounts where a client erroneously assumed they had statutory protection. You should never assume that an asset is protected. Have your advisor confirm the protection of *every* asset. Nor should you think only in terms of protecting only your *personal* assets. If you own a business or professional practice, then its assets must also be protected.

For totality of protection you must also look forward and backwards. What *future* assets do your anticipate? (Inheritances, gifts, etc.). How can you protect *these* assets from creditor claims? Conversely, what major assets have you gifted or transferred over the past several years that may be reclaimed by a creditor as a fraudulent transfer? These questionable transfers must now be protected against foreseeable judgment creditors.

The point: *Every* significant *past*, *present* and *future* asset must be identified and sheltered by your plan. Anything less is only partial protection.

My web page (www.asgoldstein.com) offers a worksheet to help you inventory your assets. Estimate the value of each item, how each asset is presently titled (individually, tenants-by-the-entirety, joint tenants, tenants-in-common, in trust, etc.), and specify your ownership interest in any co-owned assets. Finally, list liens or encumbrances against each asset to determine the net equity that remains unprotected. Your planner will need this information.

Some planners recommend leaving sufficient assets exposed to give something to the creditor. I disagree with that philosophy. Why give the creditor any recovery? It only fuels their war-chest to attempt the recovery of other assets.

We may leave some assets of negligible value out of the plan if they cannot be cost-effectively protected. However, these same assets can seldom be cost-effectively recovered by the creditor.

Key # 2 - Start With a Flexible Plan

There is no one plan that is equally effective against every potential claimant. Asset protection is much like football. You need the right defensive line to block a particular offensive line.

For example, protecting assets against a routine civil lawsuit would likely involve a far different strategy than we would use to maximize protection against the IRS or a divorce. And how you might protect your assets against a small nuisance lawsuit would logically bear little similarity to one where it was the government or another powerful litigant who were chasing you for a significant amount.

First and foremost, your plan must best protect you

from any known or imminent threat; the danger that probably prompted you to seek asset protection in the first instance.

Beyond that, you cannot foresee your future troubles. That is why a good preventative plan should give you only the foundation or *basic* protection. You have the foundation. From there you would add the specific firewalls to counteract each specific threat as it occurs.

This requires flexibility or a plan that can be easily built upon or modified to meet these future situations. It is therefore important to understand the limitations of your plan and to consult your advisor whenever a new threat does appear.

Nor is there a 'standard' plaintiff even when lawsuits are comparable. We must somehow assess how far the plaintiff is likely to go to pursue recovery. This, of course, cannot always be achieved with great accuracy and therefore it is always best to overestimate your adversary.

We also want flexibility because a client's personal situation constantly changes and some modification to a plan is necessary almost on an annual basis to accommodate those changes.

There is also a constant stream of newer strategies and opportunities for asset protection. We then want to easily upgrade the plan.

Once a threat passes we may also want to partially dismantle the plan and return to the basic foundation. We eliminate excess firewalls which may be costly to maintain and may not be necessary against a future claimant. In sum, we try to build a 'modular' plan - one where components can be speedily added, deleted or changed.

Key # 3 - Keep it 100% Legal

Not too many years ago attorneys questioned the ethics

and legality of asset protection. That has changed. Only the most naïve lawyer would today question the legality of asset protection planning and fewer still could question its necessity.

Nevertheless, there can be a grey area between legal and illegal asset protection planning. A good planner will not rely upon secrecy, help you to conceal your assets, encourage you to commit perjury, violate tax laws, money launder, commit bankruptcy fraud or otherwise defraud your creditors. That's not what good asset protection is about. You want legal protection, not 'protective' strategies that can only get you into even bigger trouble. If you question the legitimacy of any proposed plan, seek the advice of another planner. There are too many perfectly legitimate ways to shield your wealth without the need to resort to questionable practices.

Too many people equate asset protection with secrecy - the concealment of assets - perhaps by titling the asset to privatized offshore entities or to some 'trusted' straw or stand-in.

We will talk more about this in the next chapter; but for now it is important to remember that secrecy is no longer a worthwhile tactic because your financial affairs cannot be fully privatized. The world today is too complex and aside from hiding money in a coffee can buried under the oak tree - virtually any financial transaction can be uncovered.

It is true that we may incorporate an element of secrecy into some of our plans and this may have value in discouraging a plaintiff from suing in the first place. However, a judgment creditor is entitled to honest answers about your finances and anything but honesty is perjury.

Most asset protection plans are tax neutral. They neither increase nor decrease your taxes. There are a few that can give you tax deferral. This doesn't stop some promoters from selling pure trusts and offshore entities for 'tax savings.'

You should be suspicious of any plan that supposedly saves you taxes. Have these plans reviewed by your CPA or tax attorney and obtain opinion letters.

Money laundering is another problem area. Transferring funds obtained by illicit means can give rise to money laundering charges. That is why your planner, banks and other fiduciaries who will be involved in your plan must follow certain due diligence or 'know your customer' rules. Rightly or wrongly, the government imposes this responsibility on us. Therefore, unless you have a clean background, proper identification and several reference letters, you may have trouble retaining a planner. And if a planner does not demand this background check it tells you something about the planner.

Key # 4 - Keep it Simple

For some planners, complexity is the hallmark of a great plan. I disagree. Simplicity is better.

Over-planning is a chronic planning mistake. While you want to layer as many protective firewalls as necessary, you can frequently accomplish an equal or even superior plan with less complexity. Not only may a simple plan give you good protection, but it will save you money. More importantly, the simpler your plan, the better the odds that you and other advisors will fully understand it. Nor does the simpler plan as frequently fall into disuse as one that is more complex.

The complex plan also incurs higher annual maintenance costs which may further encourage client disuse - particularly once the threat has passed.

That is why I prefer to start with the basic plan and add layers only on an 'as need' basis. Once the threat vanishes, we would disassemble to the basics.

There are many simple ways to protect assets -

converting non-exempt assets into *exempt* assets and debt-shields (encumbering the equity in your assets) are two highly-effective examples.

The goal is not to trade safety for simplicity; but to choose simplicity when a more complex plan gives you only comparable protection. The added marginal protection from a more complex plan must certainly equal or exceed its marginal cost.

I have hundreds of Florida clients whose wealth is sheltered by Florida's exemption laws. Most of these clients never need anything more complex. It is also easier to sell the efficacy of the plan to a creditor's attorney who will well understand that the family home in Florida is untouchable. Period. On the other hand, a complex plan can only give the creditors counsel reason to believe the plan is no stronger than its weakest link - and that he can find and break that link.

Above all, you must fully understand your plan. Regardless of its complexity, your advisor should explain the function of each component. If you cannot understand your plan, it is too complex.

Key # 5 - Keep it Cost-Effective

Cost is always important to the design of an asset protection plan. Though I refer to it as an 'investment,' no client seeks to spend more than is absolutely necessary to obtain protection. Therefore, economy and simplicity go hand-in-hand.

On one hand, you do not want to spend more than necessary to achieve a particular level of protection and on the other, you do not want false economy only to end up with a faulty plan.

Nor is it necessary to overspend on a plan. There are a good many low cost alternatives to more expensive structures and strategies. For example, the Nevis LLC (discussed in

Chapter 11) can oftentimes provide for superior protection to the offshore trust that may be several times as costly. And a number of judgment-proofing techniques (exemptions, tenancy-by-the-entireties, etc.) cost little or nothing to implement.

Cost, of course, is a function of both what you choose as your plan and who you choose as your planner.

While you may want to comparison shop different planners; it is important to understand that you cannot make accurate comparisons. For example, I am certain that a client may find an offshore incorporation service who could set up a foreign entity for slightly less than I may charge, but does his entity include the same protective features that I would include? Is he merely selling an entity or is he also providing legal advice concerning the entity - or whether that is your *right* entity? And does the offshore provider have forty years experience in asset protection? You cannot compare apples and oranges.

The lower price provider may prove to be no bargain. Is an offshore company organized by an offshore incorporation service really your best option? Are you simply buying protective entities or the expertise to know what structures and strategies should come together as your best plan? Again, the artistry metaphor; you need more than colors on a palette to create a fine painting. You must know how to apply them. That's what you pay for with an experienced asset protection specialist.

The better strategy is to compare the plans of different providers with comparable credentials and who will be providing a comparable scope of service.

A cost-effective plan also bears proportionality between the value of the assets to be protected against the cost of protection. How much can you justify spending to shelter

$100,000 in assets? How much more is justified for an estate worth ten or a hundred times as much?

Key # 6 - Retain Maximum Control

A common perception about asset protection planning is that for protection you must always surrender control over your assets.

That is sometimes true. However, it is frequently untrue. Much depends on the specific firewalls you use.

For instance, the limited partnership and limited liability company are two entities where you may retain complete control and the assets within these entities will remain protected. Similarly, you would retain control over exempt assets and assets titled between husband and wife as tenants-by-the-entirety.

On the other extreme, it would be fatal to your plan to retain actual or *defacto* control over a trust that you would depend upon for wealth protection. But even then, there are various control-retention techniques (discussed more fully in Chapter 11) that should allay most of your fears about delegating control to a third party.

A good plan strikes an optimum balance between safety and control, an objective not always easy for a planner to achieve because many clients stubbornly want to retain control over their assets, even when it endangers their plan.

While it is possible to achieve strong protection without sacrificing control, you will find that there are many ways to safeguard your assets even when you must entrust them to others. You gain considerably more planning options once you understand these control mechanisms and a plan can be customized for you that gives you greater control - or even complete control - while still adequately protecting your assets.

How much control you can safely retain in any given instance must, of course, be determined by your advisor and it is always wisest to err on the side of caution.

Oftentimes a debtor has little choice but to relinquish complete control over his assets to a third party (usually a professional trustee) if the asset is to remain safe from creditors. The client's discomfort with relinquishing control is abated by the reality that the other option is to keep the asset vulnerable. Which, then, is the less draconian alternative?

There have been a number of celebrated cases of asset protection plans - usually involving offshore trusts - that had gone wrong only because the client insisted upon retaining too much control.

The bane of the asset protection professional is this 'control' issue. It is most problematic in the planning process. It takes creativity to balance control retention with safety, particularly when the client is in crisis mode and the client insists upon retaining control. Certainly, education is part of the answer. A client who has greater confidence in the trustworthiness of the fiduciary will be more inclined to surrender control. But ultimately, the client must become comfortable with the arrangement; another alternative plan must be found or the client must be discharged because the planner can no longer bear responsibility for a plan that is unlikely to succeed.

Key # 7 - Match Your Plan to Your Other Financial Goals

Asset protection is one important financial goal; it is not your *only* goal. You also have estate planning, tax and investment goals. It is these four financial goals that must fit together into one well coordinated, integrated plan.

Asset protection should always be integrated with estate planning. Not surprisingly, many clients who come to me for asset protection have no estate plan, not even a simple will. Asset protection then spurs creation of an estate plan. Where the client has an estate plan, we must necessarily integrate the asset protection plan with his estate plan; which usually requires modifying the estate plan, at least to address the disposition upon death of the various entities we use for asset protection.

Integrating asset protection with estate planning can also give your arrangement a more 'innocent' purpose. This is particularly important when the planning is undertaken in the face of existing creditors. You want a plan that is more defensible, and it becomes more defensible when a judge sees the exercise as one undertaken to plan one's estate rather than to thwart one's creditors. You always want to present your financial affairs in the most favorable light.

We can do some very creative things when we combine asset protection and estate planning. And we can oftentimes improve upon the estate plan using some of the same entities that we use for asset protection.

A good asset protection plan may also introduce you to some legitimate tax savings or deferral opportunities. For example, we primarily use a limited partnership to shelter assets, but it may also save its partners considerable estate taxes. Of course, you must avoid the promoters who use asset protection as one more feature to peddle *illegal* tax schemes (pure trusts, etc.). And you must always ask your planner about the tax consequences of any proposed plan. As with estate planning, a good asset protection plan should help improve the client's tax position.

Your investment goals are, of course, a more distant objective from asset protection. However, even here clients through their asset protection plan, may discover new investment opportunities. It is all part of an integrated financial plan. We consider this commitment to financial integration so important that my firm has an integrated practice. We have in our office several financial and estate planning professionals for those clients who wish a comprehensive financial analysis and a more coordinated plan.

Key # 8 - Create a Comfortable Plan

You also have a great plan when you can enthusiastically accept the plan. Or at the very least, your discomfort should be reduced to a low level. For some people, the mere act of re-titling assets can be discomforting, particularly to those who are most comfortable with the status quo and most enjoy a life of financial simplicity.

More than anything else, however, it is relinquishing control, as we have already discussed, that is the major reason clients resist a proposed plan. We must then, if possible, maximize the control retention techniques (consistent with good asset protection).

Sometimes the planner cannot convince the client to accept a proposed plan because of client discomfort. We must then retrench to the next safest plan that the client will accept. There must be a psychological fit between the client and the plan. For example, my parents are from the Depression era generation. To them high finance is saving their money in the largest bank in town. How comfortable do you think they would be moving their lifelong savings to an offshore trust in some small Pacific Island with a trustee from the Isle of Man? You see the disconnect? Ultimately, both you and your planner must be comfortable with your plan.

The overly complex plan can also be unsettling only because the client doesn't fully understand the various components or how it all comes together. A series of circles and squares on a lawyer's legal pad may seem simple to the lawyer, but what does a client know about limited partnerships, offshore trusts or captive insurance companies? Nothing. A good planner educates the client as part of the planning process. In fact, that is one reason why I wrote this book and several other books on asset protection. It is also why I invite my clients to attend my *Wealthsaver* seminars. My clients must understand what we propose to protect their wealth. An educated client is a comfortable client.

Key # 9 - Contain Liability

Asset protection must do more than protect particular assets from creditors. It is equally important for the plan to *contain* liability or insulate the client personally from business and other external liabilities and limit creditors to one (or the fewest number of entities).

Essentially, this strategy deploys assets in different baskets so a creditor can target the least amount of assets. For example, a plan that shelters a business owner's personal assets is incomplete unless the plan simultaneously contains or limits creditors to the assets of the specific business entities. Similarly, a great plan maximizes the concept of *transference*, or the shifting or sharing of liability to a third party.

Many of the strategies in this book are useful to contain or minimize liability. Review the chapters that discuss corporations and limited liability companies for examples of its application.

Key # 10 - Build a Plan That Works

Everything else is meaningless if your plan fails to achieve its primary purpose - to protect your assets.

No planner can guarantee the absolute safety of their

plan (and you should be wary of any planner who does); however, you want at least reasonable certainty that your assets can sustain a creditor attack, should it occur. Ultimately, you want your assets as close to 100 percent lawsuit-proof as legally possible. Anything less is *not* a great plan.

I was a pharmacist before I became an attorney. In my former profession I dispensed sleeping pills. In actuality, my business has not changed. I am still in the sleeping pill business; only now I compound the strongest possible asset protection plan which allows my clients to sleep soundly.

You cannot sleep soundly if you have only questionable protection. You must know how you will build protection - if it becomes necessary - so that you are always one or two steps ahead of a creditor. When you understand why you *can't* lose your assets you have a *great* plan!

4

Fraudulent Transfers and Other Fatal Blunders

In asset protection planning, there are many more things that you can do wrong than you can do right. The big blunders that I see time and again are mistakes that can cause you to lose your asset protection and possibly get you into big trouble are: (1) Fraudulent transfers (2) Titling your assets to a 'straw' and (3) Concealing your assets.

Fraudulent Transfers

Fraudulent transfers are the most frequent mistakes in asset protection planning and it can be your costliest mistake because it gives you illusory protection.

Every state has laws against fraudulent transfers. Some states follow the *Uniform Fraudulent Conveyance Act (UFCA),* and others subscribe to the *Uniform Fraudulent Transfer Act (UFTA).* However, I use the terms *fraudulent transfer* or *fraudulent conveyance* interchangeably since their provisions are so similar.

These fraudulent transfer laws allow a judgment creditor to unwind transfers previously made by a debtor with the result that the fraudulently transferred property can then be seized by the creditor. In other words, given certain circumstances, the courts will invalidate and revoke a prior sale, gift or other transfers by a debtor. Whatever assets the debtor sold or gave away for less than fair value are re-transferred to the debtor to the benefit of the judgment creditor. The obvious effect of a fraudulent transfer is that it may partially or totally destroy your asset protection plan.

For effective asset protection you must safely title your wealth *beyond* the reach of your creditors. Fraudulent transfers are dangerous obstacles to that goal since your creditors can nevertheless unwind or reclaim a fraudulently transferred asset even when it is no longer titled in your own name. Judgment creditors attempting to seize a debtor's wealth frequently invoke the fraudulent transfer laws to seize assets previously transferred by the debtor. The fraudulent transfer may be to a spouse, family member, friend, corporation, partnership, trust or any other third party. The creditors' success on their fraudulent transfer claim chiefly depends upon whether the creditor can convince the court that the transfer was simply a last-ditch effort to defraud the creditors.

With your asset protection plan designed by a good asset protection specialist, you should be able to convince the court that any transfers that you made were not fraudulent, and thus defeat any creditor attempt to recover previously transferred assets. If you fail in court, however, you lose the very protection that your plan was intended to provide. Whether you successfully defend against a fraudulent transfer challenge is often the true test of an asset protection plan.

You should think of asset protection planning as a vaccine, not a cure. The best way to avoid potential fraudulent transfer claims is to protect your assets *before* trouble strikes. Once you have a liability or are sued, many of the protective strategies in this book will no longer be effective, just as a vaccine is of no value once you are afflicted with a disease. That's why the strongest asset protection plan is always *preventative,* planning against *future* liability.

You may have hurriedly transferred assets after you were sued or became aware of a possible creditor claim, or you may have thoughts about sheltering your assets from your creditors by gifting them to friends or relatives with the tacit understanding that they will dutifully return your property once your financial problem ends. These are typical knee-jerk reactions to legal troubles, but they seldom work. They may even get you into even bigger trouble.

That's the bad news. The good news is that because a creditor can as a matter of law recover fraudulently transferred assets does not necessarily mean that a creditor always makes such an attempt. From my experience, few fraudulent transfers are recovered by creditors because comparatively few judgment creditors diligently discover the fraudulent disposition of assets. Another reason is that what is owed the creditor, or the value of the transferred assets, may be too small to justify the creditor's time and expense to pursue recovery, or there may be too many competing creditors. A recovery effort by any one creditor would not be worthwhile if the creditor must share the recovery with the other creditors. In other instances, the procedural obstacles to recovery are too great. For example, offshore asset protection imposes many procedural barriers that may make it too costly and time-consuming to attempt recovery. While a creditor may have legal recourse as a *theoretical* remedy, it is not always a *practical* remedy when the creditor has too many firewalls to hurdle. A creditor's *legal rights* to reclaim fraudulently transferred assets becomes academic when the creditor won't assert those rights as a matter of practicality.

Nevertheless, it's faulty planning to base your asset protection upon the mere hope that a fraudulent transfer won't be discovered or acted upon by a judgment creditor. The best asset protection plan is one where your creditor *can't* recover your assets as a matter of law and *won't* attempt recovery as a matter of practicality, even if the creditor believes a transfer to be fraudulent.

Fraudulent Conveyance Law

There are two types of fraudulent transfers: (1) Fraud in fact or *actual fraud,* and (2) Fraud in law or *constructive fraud.*

With actual fraud cases, it must be proved that you actually *intended* to hinder, delay or defraud your creditor. This, of course, is usually difficult to prove directly as the creditor must either prove your state of mind, or alternatively, you must admit your fraudulent intent. However, courts do look for certain *badges of fraud* from which fraudulent intent can be inferred. These 'badges of fraud' include:

- Transfers to close family members or friends
- Secretive transfers
- Transfers for less than fair value
- When the debtor continued to use or possess the property after the transfer
- Concealed assets
- A transfer that occurred when the debtor incurred a large debt or may have anticipated a lawsuit
- Transfers that impoverished the debtor and left him unable to pay his debts.

However, the fact that a creditor can prove one or more of

these 'badges' does not necessarily mean that the court will conclude that the transfer was fraudulent; these 'actions' only infer fraudulent intent and can help persuade a judge of fraudulent intent. In themselves, they are not fraud. Your creditor must still prove fraudulent intent. On the other hand, a court can conclude that a challenged transfer was proper, even with one or more of these badges. For example, any presumption of fraud may be overcome when the transfers can be justified as achieving a business, investment or estate planning objective rather than an attempt to avoid a debt due a creditor.

Because actual fraud cases are so difficult for creditors to prove, even with a showing of badges of fraud, creditors more often invoke *constructive fraud* claims to unwind fraudulent transfers. Constructive fraud is a gift or sale of property that:

1) is for less than fair value (or *fair consideration*)
2) in the face of a known or probable liability
3) leaves you insolvent.

Notice that with a constructive fraud claim a transfer can be ruled fraudulent, even when you act innocently with no intent to hinder your creditors. However, a creditor who challenges your transfer must still prove all three elements. Let's look at them more closely:

1. A gift or sale of property for less than fair value: In constructive fraud, cases your creditors must first prove that you made the transfer for less than fair value. While a lack of consideration is obvious when the debtor merely gifts his assets, proving a sale was for less than fair value can sometimes be difficult to show, because courts define fair consideration subjectively.

Generally, fair consideration is defined as that price which a reasonably prudent seller would obtain when selling his or her property through commercially reasonable means. This price, however, need not necessarily be the fair market value. Fair value depends largely on the type property. For example, stocks or bonds of publicly traded corporations have a readily ascertainable fair value because it is listed daily on the public exchanges. If a debtor transfers his publicly traded stock for less than its quoted daily price, then the sale would be for less than fair value and thus a fraudulent transfer, at least to the difference in value.

Other assets are more problematic to value. For example, what is the fair value of real estate, shares in a privately owned business, antiques, vehicles, or other assets? Fair consideration for these assets, as determined by a court, may be considerably less than fair market value as viewed by a creditor. What if the debtor does not have adequate time to find a buyer willing to pay a higher price, or wants to sell for less for fast cash? Courts have ruled that real estate sold for 70 percent of its appraised value satisfies the fair value test. Other difficult-to-value items, such as jewelry or a closely held business only requires the courts to consider all the relevant facts to determine reasonable value. It is always subjective.

2. A gift or sale of property where there is liability: Even when a creditor who challenges a transfer can demonstrate that the asset was sold for less than its fair value, the creditor must next show that the transfer was made with a *present* liability in existence. A present liability means that you cannot safely transfer your assets for less than fair value to protect them against future *probable liabilities.* But you can safely make such a transfer to protect your assets against future *possible* *liabilities.* Again, we can't always easily differentiate between *probable* and *possible liabilities.* Courts consider the facts of each case. When did the act occur that created the liability? When did the debtor first realize that he might have liability for that act? Finally, when did the transfer occur? As you can see, courts reach different conclusions as to whether a liability was *probable* or *possible* at any point in time.

The prevailing definition of a '*present* liability' is one that occurs from the moment you have a creditor (incurred a liability). Later asset transfers can be challenged. For example, if you sign a lease today and gift your assets tomorrow, your landlord can probably recover your gifted assets should you later default on your lease. Notice that you didn't have to be in present default on your lease for the transfer to be fraudulent. And it's immaterial whether or not you were yet sued. The critical date is when the liability arose, not the default or lawsuit date.

Here's another example, assume that you're a surgeon and negligently leave a sponge in a patient. You are unaware of it and so too is the patient. The following month you gift your assets for estate planning purposes. Two years later the patient discovers the malpractice and sues you. If the patient wins a judgment can she then recover the transferred assets? I believe that the patient would prevail and recover your assets. Notice, it wouldn't matter that both you and the patient were unaware of the possible future claim when you transferred your assets because fraudulent intent is not required for a 'constructive' fraudulent transfer claim. What is significant here is that you never know what claims can arise from the past, and thus any transfer that you make for less than fair value since that date can put you on the wrong end of a fraudulent transfer claim.

3. A gift or sale of property that leaves you insolvent: Now, let's finally suppose that your creditor can show that your transfer was for less than fair value and that you made the transfer when there was a probable liability. The court, even in those circumstances, will not unwind the transfer unless the transfer left you insolvent, which means that you then have too few remaining assets to pay your existing debts as they come due. More simply, you cannot pay your creditor because you impoverished yourself.

When you review these three factors of a constructive fraudulent transfer claim, you still have hundreds of unanswered questions. For instance, would it be a fraudulent transfer to exchange non-exempt assets for exempt (protected) assets of equal value? What if you have no present creditor, but transfer your assets when you have a foreseeable creditor (i.e. you expect to sign a lease)? We can go on and on. The point is that the fraudulent transfer laws are quite complex and they create a vast gray area of uncertainty as many transfers are neither clearly fraudulent nor conclusively non-fraudulent. It takes a seasoned asset protection specialist to best understand the complexities and nuances of the fraudulent transfer laws and to determine whether a transfer is likely to be unwound by your creditors and the courts.

Case Examples

Now that you have this background on fraudulent transfers, let's sharpen your judgment with a few case examples:

Case 1: Suppose Mark guaranteed a $500,000 business loan from his bank. Shortly thereafter, and while his bank note was in good standing, Mark gifted his assets to his children for estate planning purposes. Several months later, Mark's business unexpectedly failed and the bank sued Mark on the note. Were Mark's gifts to his children a fraudulent transfer?

Answer: Yes. There was no consideration paid for the assets since the assets were gifted. The transfer also rendered Mark insolvent and with no assets to pay the bank. This case highlights this question: Was the bank guarantee a *present* liability? The loan certainly created a contingent liability, but could Mark reasonably foresee the failure of his business and the need to pay on the guarantee? I believe that the fact that the liability existed (a signed guarantee) would probably be sufficient for the court to rule it a fraudulent transfer.

Case 2: Bob resides in Florida and transferred his home to his sister as trustee in trust for Bob's minor children. Florida residences are fully protected by the state homestead laws and therefore exempt from lawsuits. When Bob transferred his home to the trust, Bob had a $200,000 lawsuit against him and no other assets to satisfy the claim. Was this a fraudulent transfer?

Answer: Bob's transfer of his home in these circumstances would not be a fraudulent conveyance because Bob's creditors could not seize the home *before* the transfer since it was already fully homestead protected. Therefore, Bob's transfer of the home never prejudiced the creditor. A creditor cannot assert a fraudulent conveyance unless their right to the asset is hindered by the transfer.

Case 3: Assume Linda owned $500,000 in non-exempt (unprotected) assets and, facing several lawsuits, exchanged these assets for $500,000 in exempt or legally protected property. Would this be ruled a fraudulent transfer?

Answer: This case has an uncertain outcome. Some courts would rule that it is not a fraudulent transfer because there is a fair value exchange, notwithstanding that the assets received are safe from creditors while the transferred assets were exposed. Another common argument here is that there was no 'transfer' to another party.

Asset protection plans frequently convert non-exempt or unprotected assets for protected, exempt assets, but not all courts agree on whether this is a fraudulent transfer. You must examine *your* state laws and cases. This again underscores what I consider the major difficulty with asset protection planning: Courts are inconsistent and frequently reverse their positions, which adds uncertainty concerning the safety of many asset protection plans. Your attorney must thoroughly research recent cases in your state to more accurately predict a court ruling on any asset transfer that can possibly be challenged.

Case 4: Assume Sam deeded his $500,000 home to a friend to partially repay a $700,000 debt?

Answer: This transfer probably would withstand creditor challenge because repayment of an existing debt is considered fair consideration for a transfer. For instance, Sam could have instead repaid his friend's $700,000 debt, and this would not have been fraudulent. Property transferred or mortgaged to one creditor to fully or partly satisfy or secure an existing debt is not fraudulent, even when the encumbrance is to the detriment of other creditors. It is true that the unpaid creditors would have the right to petition the debtor into bankruptcy within three months of the transfer to set aside the mortgage as a voidable preference under bankruptcy law, but that does not make the mortgage voidable as a fraudulent transfer.

Case 5: Before filing bankruptcy, Henry transferred his property to his new wife who, in return, promised to care for him in his later years. Is this a fraudulent transfer?

Answer: Whether this transfer is fraudulent would depend upon whether the transfer was made before or after a particular debt in question. Such a transfer made *after* debt could be set aside as fraudulent because the consideration contemplated *future* services, not services previously or simultaneously rendered. However, the property could not be recovered by later creditors (those which arose after the transfer) since they could not argue that the transfer hindered or delayed their rights to collect; they were not creditors at the time of the transfer. While this is the general rule, here, too, there are exceptions.

Now you better understand what a creditor must prove for a court to rule a transfer (as either actual or constructive fraud). In practice, to defend a client's transfer, we need only prove one essential factor is missing. The court must then, as a matter of law, conclude that the transfer was not fraudulent. For instance, we may successfully show that there was no fraudulent intent, that the client received fair value, there was no probable liability at the time of the transfer, or that the transfer did not leave the client insolvent. If so, we win the case.

The Statute of Limitations

Your creditor must also challenge a fraudulent transfer within your state's statute of limitations. In most states it is four years after the transfer, or one year after actual discovery of the transfer could have been reasonably made by the creditor, whichever date is later.

Under this rule, you can see that a fraudulently

transferred asset is never completely safe because a creditor can always argue they only recently discovered a transfer that may have occurred years earlier. This would then give the creditor one more year to set aside the transfer.

States that follow the fraudulent conveyance statutes generally impose a strict five-year statute of limitations. Later claims are disallowed regardless of when the creditor discovered the transfer. Check your state laws to find when your creditor's recovery claims become time-barred.

Fraudulent transfer actions are frequently initiated by a trustee in bankruptcy who will claim the bankrupt fraudulently transferred assets before the bankruptcy. Bankruptcy law gives the trustee two years from the first meeting of creditors to commence a fraudulent transfer claim. Moreover, the fraudulent transfer must have occurred within the year preceding bankruptcy. However, this does not make earlier transfers necessarily safe. The bankruptcy trustee can instead sue under your state's fraudulent transfer law rather than under bankruptcy law since the state has the longer statute of limitations. That's why it is important to delay filing bankruptcy for as long as possible if you have questionable prior transfers.

Creditor Remedies

A judgment creditor who asserts a fraudulent transfer has several remedies. The judgment creditor can ask the court to:

- Set aside the transfer and restore the title to the original owner debtor for seizure by his creditor.
- Enjoin further transactions, encumbrances or depletion of the asset (freeze the asset) pending the outcome of the fraudulent conveyance case.
- Award damages from the transferee and supplemental

damages from the transferor (the legal costs to recover the asset).

- Appoint a receiver over the conveyed asset, if the asset is likely to disappear or be dissipated.
- Recover from the debtor the proceeds received from transferring the property (but the creditor cannot void the sale to a subsequent good faith purchaser who paid fair value).

While these and other remedies are available to a judgment creditor, the courts, to the extent practicable, usually only attempt to restore the creditor to his position before the fraudulent transfer. Whether this remedy can be practicably accomplished, of course, depends largely on whether the transferee still holds the asset and whether it has since been altered, destroyed or sold.

Litigants who have not yet won a judgment generally *cannot* commence a fraudulent transfer claim; this is a remedy for *judgment creditors*. Nor can *pre-judgment creditors* usually attach assets or restrain a defendant's rights to transfer assets, even if the transfer is fraudulent. The plaintiff's remedy is to attempt recovery of the asset under the fraudulent transfer laws after the creditor wins his case.

Moreover, the law does not obligate a lawsuit defendant to hold his assets for the benefit of their creditors, notwithstanding common belief to the contrary. Justice Antonin Scalia, in a recent US Supreme Court case, announced, "A creditor has no cognizable interest in the assets of a debtor prior to obtaining a judgment. Anyone can transfer their assets all day long until the sheriff shows up on a Writ of Execution pursuant to a court order."

Further, contrary to popular misconception, a fraudulent transfer is not a crime. A fraudulent transfer only defines a civil remedy, which simply divides irreversible transfers from transfers that can later be reversed by the courts. Neither the transferor nor transferee usually become subject to criminal penalties. In most cases, there is ample opportunity for a defendant's attorney to argue that the transfer at issue was not fraudulent for all of the reasons I noted previously. Even in those cases that a defendant loses, all a court can do is to grant the creditor the noted remedies - essentially, to unwind the transfer.

The essence of a fraudulent transfer was well articulated in a recent Florida Supreme Court case:

"A fraudulent conveyance action is simply another creditor remedy. It is either an action by a creditor against a transferee directed against a particular transaction which, if declared fraudulent, is set aside thus leaving the creditor free to pursue the asset, or is it an action against a transferee who has received an asset by means of a fraudulent conveyance and should be required to either return the asset or pay for the asset. A fraudulent conveyance action is *not* an action against a debtor for failure to pay an amount owing from a prior judgment and does not warrant an *additional* judgment against the same debtor because of the fraudulent conveyance. A fraudulent conveyance action is not a lawsuit against a transferor debtor, but it is an action against the property or the transferee holding the property."

Nevertheless, attorneys should not encourage clients to make transfers that are fraudulent or could bring criminal sanctions. The objective should be to design a plan that, even in the most extreme case, can be justified as a non-fraudulent transfer applying one or more of the noted defenses.

Of course, attorneys walk a fine line. On one hand, an attorney has a duty to defend his client's wealth as aggressively as possible. On the other hand, counsel cannot step over the line and encourage unethical or illegal practices. The asset protection attorney's constant dilemma is to define that fine line on any particular case. Reasonable attorneys also differ in their viewpoint. For that reason, some attorneys will accept a particular case while others would decline. An attorney's sensitivity to potential fraudulent transfer actions also help define the strategies an attorney may use to protect their clients' assets.

What is clear is that it is not necessarily too late to take defensive measures once a lawsuit is filed. It is true that you have fewer options than if you had undertaken advance planning, but even the most dire situation has its solutions. Again, to quote the US Supreme Court, "A debtor [who is sued] need not be like a deer frozen in the headlights of an onrushing auto. The debtor still has it within his rights the opportunity to attempt to put his wealth beyond harm's way."

Clearly, the safest path is to protect yourself before you have problems. You then have many more planning options and less risk that your transfer will later be challenged. Unfortunately, too many clients already immersed in litigation or debts are advised by their attorney that it is too late to protect themselves because a lawsuit has begun or is threatened. This is poor advice, and it is hardly different than a doctor advising a patient that it is too late to try to save him because he has already contracted a disease. Yes, you may have less desirable wealth-saving alternatives once you have a claim against you, and you may need to go to greater lengths to safely shelter your assets, but you *do* have options and strategies available to you.

Avoid Fraudulent Transfer Claims

Your goal is to avoid fraudulent transfer claims. Therefore, it is important to not only know some law, but also apply some common sense. For starters, avoid the badges of fraud. They only invite suspicion and undue inquiry. Your transfers must pass a creditor 'sniff' test. Other points to remember:

- **Protect your assets before you have a liability.** There cannot be a fraudulent transfer if you transferred your assets before you incurred the liability. This is why we constantly counsel clients to become judgment-proof *before* they encounter financial or legal problems. Your safest strategy is to be liability-free when you protect your assets.

- **Make small, incremental transfers.** These attract less notice than sudden transfers of major assets. Nor should you transfer all or even most of your assets to one transferee. When your eggs are all in one basket, they are vulnerable. Widely scatter your assets. Your creditor is then forced to file numerous fraudulent transfer lawsuits, requiring considerably more cost and effort.

- **Avoid insider transactions.** Transfers to family members, friends or close business associates are suspicious. Even completely innocent and fair value transactions can appear suspicious to courts and creditors. It is best to use non-family members as trustees, corporate officers or fiduciaries for any entities to which you transfer assets.

- **Document that your transfer was for innocent purposes**. A transfer should not have the obvious goal of sheltering your assets from present creditors. Your attorney's correspondence, for instance, may instead show that you were engaged in estate planning when he prepared your irrevocable trust. Documents that recite an innocent legal purpose for the conveyance can be persuasive to a court who may otherwise see another motive.

- **Carefully document** whatever consideration you receive for your property. What services were performed? Why are they worth their stated value? Did you borrow money? Do you have cancelled checks, or can you otherwise prove the validity of the debt?

- **Avoid circumspect actions.** Selling your home? Don't stay on as its tenant. People seldom buy homes to rent. Selling your business? How will your creditors view your staying on as its manager? Selling your boat? Don't keep it at *your* dock. You get the idea.

- **Verify the value of your property** to establish fair consideration. For example, have your home appraised to prove that you are selling it for close to its fair market value. Are you selling another asset for a low price? Photographs or appraisals may show defects or other reasons to justify the low price. Assume the value of significant, recently transferred assets will be questioned by your creditors. Be prepared.

- **Choose your transferees carefully.** What if a creditor challenges your transfer? Will your transferee defend the transfer? A friendly 'straw' who holds title to your property may not act as you want when *he* is sued. If your transferee quickly surrenders your asset or otherwise fails to cooperate in defending the case, you lose your assets by default. Transferees to questionable transfers must also realize that your creditor may later sue them, and they must be willing to defend against such a claim.

- **Never publicize your transfers.** Why alert your creditors if you do rearrange your financial affairs?

This only encourages your creditors to move more swiftly to protect *their* rights.

- **Employ multiple asset protection strategies**. Why deed your home to a third party when you can also mortgage it to a 'friendly creditor,' which then requires your creditor to contest both the transfer *and* the mortgage. Challenging both transactions may be too ambitious and expensive a proposition for your creditor.

- **Don't overplay your hand.** It is not always wise to be completely judgment-proof. Creditors who are forced to search too strenuously for some assets to recover may target your more valuable assets. A less valuable asset is better bait if a creditor 'goes fishing.'

'Straw' or Nominee Owner Deals

You may conclude that your easiest and safest option is to title your assets to your spouse, a trusted friend, or a relative, particularly if you sense that they are a lower lawsuit risk.

Many of my clients come to me proposing precisely that arrangement. For example, one physician client argued, "I no longer worry about malpractice lawsuits. I titled everything to my wife, and she won't get sued." Can an asset protection plan be that simple?

Other 'straws,' of course, may also own your property. Friends or other relatives are the most likely candidates. Whatever their relationship to you, your assets are still titled to someone else. Of course, the real deal is that you own that asset, but for lawsuit protection, you no longer want it titled in your name. You believe that your asset is safer titled to a third party.

There are obvious pitfalls to such arrangements. First, we already discussed the pitfalls of fraudulent conveyances where you gift your assets to friends and relatives with the tacit understanding that they will return the assets once the danger passes. We are talking here about titling your assets to somebody *before* you have creditors.

You cannot assume that whoever is entrusted to hold title to your property is necessarily safer than you from lawsuits and creditors. Your nominee may have their own marital problems, tax troubles, creditors, or lawsuits. When straws hold title to your assets, *their* creditors and ex-spouses can claim *your* assets titled in *their* names. Plenty of people lose their assets not to their own creditors, but to their nominee's. For this one reason alone you should never title your asset to a third party nominee.

When a spouse acts as the straw the drawbacks are less severe, and sometimes it is sensible to title assets to a less vulnerable spouse. Still, even this raises problems. Suppose you own a million dollar home and title the home and your other assets to your wife for protection on the expectation that your wife *won't* get sued. This arrangement may create estate planning and estate tax disadvantages. With your assets titled in *both* your names, you and your spouse could more advantageously plan your estates. For instance, you could then use credit shelter trusts to maximize your death tax credits. With your interest titled to your wife, she has only her estate tax exemption. The balance of her estate will be taxed and this may cost your heirs thousands more in estate taxes. When assets are titled to one spouse it often creates a lopsided estate plan with the loss of tax planning options.

Nor are assets titled to one spouse necessarily safe from creditors of the other spouse. Even when the liability arose *after* the debtor's assets were titled to his or her spouse, the creditor can argue that the debtor-spouse retains an equitable or beneficial interest in at least half the property. For example, the creditors can argue that there is a constructive or resulting trust; namely, that the spouse who holds title is in actuality a trustee for the debtor-spouse. This argument is likely to succeed when the debtor-spouse's money was used to buy the property, or his or her income paid the mortgage, maintenance, and upkeep on the property. When most of the money that is invested in the asset came from the debtor-spouse, then under these circumstances the property is not really property of the other spouse. When the debtor-spouse's assets can be traced to property, his creditors can assert claim to that property. Nor should you gamble on further litigation by presenting these sloppy issues. The best plan is a totally defensible asset protection plan, free of such possible challenges.

The tax problems are more significant when the parties are not married. For example, I had a stubborn client who told me, "I'm not married, and I own this expensive Los Angeles real estate. I worry about lawsuits, so I titled my property to my 87-year-old mother, who has never been sued."

Whenever you gift or transfer property without consideration, it is a gift. This man made a taxable gift to his mother. Gifts between spouses aren't taxable; however, gifts to others, including mothers, are gift taxable. He inadvertently incurred a huge gift tax as a consequence of that transfer. Moreover, my client's real estate is now part of his mother's estate. When she dies, what assurance does my client have that his mother will bequeath him back his property in her will? Indeed, she may instead bequeath his house to him *and* his siblings. His mother will have her own taxable estate and will pay a 55-60 percent estate tax on the *son's* house when she bequeaths it back to him. Can you imagine a more dangerous way to 'safely' title assets?

You must be particularly careful about straw deals if you file bankruptcy. Bankruptcy fraud convictions are common. It does not pay for a bankrupt to hide assets with others. A bankruptcy trustee or court, who concludes that you hid your assets with a straw, can easily make a case for bankruptcy fraud which is a very serious crime.

Finally, how do you know that you can trust your straw? You can't afford to be trusting. I have seen it all; parents who stole entrusted assets from their children; brothers who double-crossed each other. Your best friend could soon forget that *your* asset is not really *his!* Forget straw deals. There are far safer ways to protect your assets.

Secrecy and Concealment

That brings us to the third big blunder: Confusing secrecy or concealing assets with asset protection. Secrecy has less to do with asset protection than with discouraging lawsuits. This is the chief function of financial privacy. You cannot rely upon secrecy because your judgment creditor can compel you to disclose your finances under oath, so you cannot rely on secrecy when you are under oath. If you truthfully disclose your assets, you destroy your secrecy. If you lie to conceal your assets, you commit perjury. Your goal is *legitimate* asset protection, a plan that gives you the ability to fully disclose your every asset, confident that they will stay safe from your creditors. Remember: A judgment creditor is entitled to full and honest answers about your present and past assets. Secrecy does not protect them.

It is not only a judgment debtor who must answer questions concerning his or her assets, but also the spouse. Spousal communication ordinarily is confidential; however, this marital privilege does not extend to proceedings to discover assets. In most states, a creditor can interrogate a non-debtor spouse about the debtor spouse's financial affairs. This rule prevents using the marital privilege to conceal assets from a judgment creditor. Therefore, probable creditor inquiries should be reviewed with your spouse before any asset discovery deposition to ensure both correct and consistent answers. Another tactic is to tell your spouse as little as possible about your finances.

A judgment creditor can force you to disclose your financial information in many different ways. In some states, your creditor can examine you in court through depositions or interrogatories, or can request that you produce documents. They can subpoena records and information from third parties.

A judgment creditor searching for assets has many ways to find them. They may review loan or credit applications, bank records, tax returns, court cases (such as prior divorces that disclose assets), or insurance policies. The paper trail can be revealing. Computer technology makes everyone's financial life an open book.

With asset protection so common a financial goal and with the techniques to achieve secrecy so sophisticated, both judgment creditors and prospective litigants now hire professional asset search firms to find hidden assets. Sometimes they are hired to reveal whether a prospective defendant has sufficient assets to make a lawsuit even worthwhile. These firms efficiently track asset transfers from those with judgments against them, hoping to uncover assets that may be reachable by their creditor clients.

For less than $1,000, your creditor can obtain a very accurate financial profile on you. Forensic accounting firms who are involved in larger cases customarily trace millions in assets, even the most deviously and secretively deployed wealth. Don't play the 'hide the assets' game. Your creditor will probably find your assets.

Part 2

Strategies and Tools

5

Self-Protected Wealth is Safe Wealth

Is it possible to owe creditors $32 million and still live like a king?

Absolutely. If you're O.J. Simpson.

No, I'm no fan of O.J. Simpson (and no, he is not one of my clients); nevertheless, O.J. is a great case study on how to create self-protected wealth.

Consider how O.J.'s fabulous Miami home is fully protected under Florida's homestead laws. His six-figure annual pension is also judgment-proof, thanks to federal laws. His insurance can't be touched by his creditors under Florida law, and as the head of the household, O.J.'s earnings can't be garnished, no matter how much he earns.

O.J.'s firewalls are the numerous and formidable state and federal laws that automatically protect certain assets from lawsuits, bankruptcy and creditors. You don't have to be O.J. to fortify your assets with the same firewalls. Many Americans can just as advantageously use their homestead laws, wage and pension exemptions, bankruptcy exemptions and the array of other protective laws that the federal and state governments have enacted to help you protect certain assets.

However noble their goal, how much protection against lawsuits these laws provide you varies between states. You may find the exemption laws to be extremely valuable in your planning, or you may find them virtually meaningless. Their effectiveness chiefly depends upon the type of liability you need protection against, as well as where you reside.

Let's begin with a word of caution: Maximizing your protection under the federal and state exemption laws can seem like a simple task, but it is sometimes tricky. You need professional assistance to be confident that these laws will fully protect your assets in your specific circumstances.

Homestead Protection

For many Americans, their home is their most valuable asset. You are probably already somewhat familiar with your state laws that partly or fully creditor-protect your home. Possibly you have assumed that you couldn't lose your home in a lawsuit because it is 'homestead protected,' and you may be right. Or wrong. You see, the homestead laws run 'hot and cold.' Some state homestead laws *totally* protect your home; however, in most other states, their homestead laws do little or nothing to shield the home from creditors. While forty-five states feature homestead laws, they vary greatly in the home equity they protect.

Will your state's homestead laws safeguard your home? First, understand what is meant by 'homestead.' The homestead laws apply only to your home or primary residence. However, not every property that you might consider to be your 'home' qualifies. The homestead exemption relates only to real estate that is your primary residence – property that you own *and* occupy. Specific 'residences' that qualify for homestead protection chiefly depend on each state's statutes and court interpretations.

For example, not every state homestead-protects cooperatively owned apartments. Your state homestead protection may shelter single-family homes but not duplexes, triplexes or other multi-unit structures where you occupy only one unit. Your state may not shield a mobile home or houseboat that you occupy as your 'home.'

Such unique situations make interesting cases. One case involved a client who lived on a 48-foot yacht anchored in Miami's Biscayne Bay. The question was whether the boat was homestead protected under Florida law. One Florida court earlier ruled that a houseboat would be homestead protected as a 'home,' but would this decision extend to a yacht? Would the court possibly distinguish between a houseboat intended primarily to be used as a residence and a craft designed primarily for cruising? We never got our answer. Rather than gamble on an uncertain ruling, we took other steps to protect our client's boat. This case illustrates that the state laws do not always cover such fine points.

Other restrictions may limit your homestead protection. For example, while Florida protects an unlimited home equity, it only protects those residences within a certain acreage. For example, Florida protects homes on up to one-half acre of land.

Once you determine that your home qualifies for homestead protection, you must then ask how much home equity your state protects under its particular laws. The answer is usually 'not enough.' The majority of states only lawsuit-proof somewhere between $5,000 and $50,000 in home equity, and five states have absolutely no homestead protection. Massachusetts is one of the more protective states, with an exemption up to $300,000; however, California and several other states also boast six-figure exemptions. When you consider today's rapidly escalating real estate values and the large equity that many people now have in their homes, you can see that states with a small homestead exemption give you worthless asset protection.

If you are fortunate enough to live in Texas, Florida or one of several other states that protect an unlimited equity, your home has the strongest possible firewall. A multi-million-dollar Texas or Florida home is safe even in bankruptcy! O.J.'s fully homestead-protected Florida home is more than his personal castle. It's also his financial fortress.

To what extent do homestead laws protect the equity in your home? Compare the statutory protection to the equity in your home. Subtract all mortgages from your home's fair market value. For example, if you have a home worth $300,000 with a $150,000 mortgage, then your equity is $150,000. If your state homestead laws shelter only $20,000 in equity, $130,000 in equity remains vulnerable to lawsuits or creditors.

There are procedural requirements. Every state also imposes its own requirements to claim homestead protection. Some states require their residents to file a declaration of homestead in a public office. Other states impose a short residency period before they grant homestead protection. The point is that you cannot simply assume that your home is protected. Have your attorney show you how to comply with your state's procedural formalities to claim homestead protection.

In certain states, only the head of the household can claim homestead protection; however, most states allow either spouse to do so. If you are married, be careful. Sometimes when both spouses file homestead declarations, their cross-declarations cancel each other out. Again, that's why your asset protection attorney should guide you on the technicalities for filing your homestead declaration.

There are other potential traps. For instance, in some states - such as Florida - you lose your homestead protection if you title your home to a living trust (and probably any other trust). Yet tens of thousands of Floridians have been advised by their estate planners to title their home to their living trust to avoid probate, but these Floridians then lose their homestead protection. Unfortunately, few of these people realize their homes can now be lost to their judgment creditors.

Your homestead exemption cannot shield your home from every creditor. Generally, homestead laws only protect the home from debts that arise *after* you claim your homestead protection, although some states also homestead protect the home from debts that arose *before* you claimed homestead protection.

There are also various creditors who can also override your homestead protection and seize whatever equity you have in your home. These creditors include:

- The IRS and other federal agencies: If you owe federal taxes or are sued by the SEC or the EPA, for example, you can lose your home to the government, regardless of where you reside.
- Do you owe state taxes? Your homestead laws may or may not protect your home from the state tax collector. Laws vary between states.
- Spouses in a divorce or family members who challenge their inheritances can also override the homestead laws.
- Plaintiffs suing you for intentional torts (libel, fraud, deceit, etc.) are not usually blocked by homestead.

- Mortgages or deeds of trust, voluntarily granted to your creditors as collateral, are unaffected by homestead. These lenders still have full recourse to your home.
- Other creditors unaffected by the homestead exemption include those where you specifically waive your homestead protection (such as for a mortgage).

There are also a few minor disadvantages with homestead protection. For example, you may encounter minor legal complications when you sell or refinance your home after you declare homestead. As a procedural formality, your bank or buyer may then require that you temporarily lift your homestead exemption for the transaction to close. These and other minor potential procedural inconveniences should not, however, dissuade you from claiming your homestead protection.

The far greater problem with homestead protection is that it often creates illusory security. For example, if you now have $30,000 or less in home equity and a $30,000 or greater homestead exemption, your home is *now* fully protected. How well protected will your home be in the future, though? With each passing month you build equity (assuming your home is appreciating) while you simultaneously reduce your mortgage. Should you be sued years down the road, you may have a substantially greater equity that would then be lost.

Because of its limitations, homestead exemptions are seldom sufficient to fully protect the family home. One recommended solution is to refinance your home so that the combined mortgages *and* your state homestead exemption leave no equity for a lawsuit plaintiff to seize.

It's also important to know that if you do live in a state with an unlimited homestead exemption, a judgment creditor cannot attach your home, cloud its title, or in any way impede your sale or refinancing of the property. Your home is completely immunized against the judgment creditor. Nevertheless, there are tips to turn your homestead protection into the strongest possible firewall:

- Are you married? Let the spouse who is most vulnerable to lawsuits file the declaration, so the protection shields that spouse.

- Do you reside in a state with an unlimited (or large) homestead exemption? If you're concerned about lawsuits, take your exposed cash and buy a more expensive home. Or improve your present home. Or reduce your mortgage. (You can always refinance once the lawsuit threat passes.)

- Do you own multiple homes? File the homestead declaration for the home that has the most equity exposed if you can realistically show that you live in that house with the intent to make it your permanent domicile. Your homestead status may be challenged, so be prepared to prove your legal address. Is this the address on your tax returns? Is this where you receive your mail? Is this the address where you are registered to vote? Is this where you spend most of your time?

- Consider moving to a state with an unlimited homestead exemption such as Florida or Texas. This follows a common asset protection tactic: Convert *non-exempt assets* into *exempt assets*.

Let me illustrate this strategy with a short story. One of my clients, a St. Louis builder, invested heavily in commercial real estate. Harry was a partner in a major condo project and personally guaranteed a bank note for over $5 million.

When Harry realized that the project would tank because of a downturn in the economy and the local real estate market, he tried to insulate himself in anticipation of the project failing.

Harry had substantial assets exposed. His St. Louis house had a huge equity and negligible homestead protection. He also owned over $2 million in other assets. After consultation, Harry now has an asset protection plan. He had always wanted to move to a warmer climate, and now was the time.

Harry liquidated his major non-exempt assets (stocks, bonds, his St. Louis home and his $400,000 boat). With the sale proceeds he bought a beautiful Palm Beach mansion, which for the next several years became Harry's home. Harry paid taxes as a Floridian, filed an affidavit of domicile and a declaration of homestead on his Florida home, and, of course, thoroughly enjoyed his weekends and vacations on Florida's famous golf links. He maintained a small St. Louis apartment while he completed his real estate project. Yes, Harry's project eventually went bust and the bank predictably sued Harry on his guarantee. A year after buying his expensive Florida home, Harry filed Chapter 7 bankruptcy to rid himself of the bank guarantee.

Although the St. Louis banker's loss was considerable, the bank never challenged Harry's bankruptcy. Harry's bank debt was completely discharged while his Florida home was fully protected by Florida's generous homestead laws. Once free and clear of the bank debt, Harry entertained thoughts of 'cashing out' and moving back to Missouri - if he could only give up his golf games!

Harry's case isn't unusual. Hundreds or even thousands of beleaguered debtors relocate each year to more 'debtor-friendly' states - usually Florida or Texas - to redeploy their vulnerable wealth into one or more assets protected by the laws of these states. Usually their money finds its way into an expensive home with their total net worth now fully homestead protected home equity. It can be a great strategy. If you can see your way to relocating your family to somewhere with great weather and even greater laws for beleaguered debtors, then welcome to sunny Florida! Your asset protection solution may be as simple as trading your vulnerable wealth for a Texas or Florida home with gold doorknobs and platinum plumbing.

Safeguarding Retirement Plans

After your home, your retirement plan is probably your next most valuable asset. Is it lawsuit-proof? How much of your retirement accounts can you afford to lose to a creditor? What portion of your retirement is safe? More importantly, what can you do to shield your retirement accounts if they are now exposed?

For asset protection purposes, we divide retirement plans into (1) ERISA-qualified plans and (2) all other (non-qualified) retirement plans (such as Individual Retirement Accounts).

An *ERISA-qualified plan* is a retirement account that meets the requirements of the Employee Retirement Income Security Act of 1974 (ERISA), a law enacted specifically to protect the rights of employees enrolled in benefit plans sponsored by their employers or unions. A key requirement of ERISA is that the pension plan be structured as a spendthrift trust – one that prohibits the beneficiary from gifting, anticipating, or encumbering the plan's principal or income.

The most common qualified retirement plans are profit-sharing plans (defined contribution plans); pension plans (defined benefit plans) and 401K plans. These are plans in which the employee makes voluntary contributions to the plan.

For many years preceding 1992 there were mixed court decisions as to whether these plans were creditor-protected. Then a US Supreme Court decision, *Patterson v. Shumate*, solidified the protection for ERISA-qualified pension plans. The Court ruled that ERISA-qualified plans cannot be claimed by creditors, whether in bankruptcy, by lawsuit, or through other means. This decision applies to *all* ERISA-qualified pension and profit-sharing plans. Public pensions (those funded by state or federal government) have always been protected from creditors.

Is your pension plan ERISA-qualified? Generally, the answer is yes. If both the company owners and at least one other employee is covered under the plan, then it is most likely ERISA-qualified. If you are uncertain whether your plan is ERISA-qualified, have your asset protection lawyer or plan administrator review your pension documents.

Several court decisions have somewhat eroded the protection granted retirement accounts under the *Patterson* decision. There are a growing number of cases where the plaintiff successfully argued that the 401K did not fully comply with IRS/ERISA regulations, and the plan was thus unprotected by ERISA. Such disqualified plans were then only afforded whatever protection other non-qualified plans had under state law.

Generally, Keogh plans with multiple participants have the same lawsuit protection as ERISA-qualified pensions. Most likely, your Keogh plan is lawsuit-proof. However, sole-participant Keogh plans are more vulnerable. The courts routinely allow creditors to seize sole-participant Keogh funds because the beneficiary/debtor can voluntarily withdraw the funds and the beneficiary/debtor is his own trustee; therefore no one other than the debtor would be affected by the seizure.

In most states, IRAs are significantly less secure than are ERISA-qualified plans and Keoghs. An IRA is a custodial account set aside for its owner, who can withdraw the funds at any time. Since IRAs have neither 'spendthrift' provision nor trustees, there is no federal protection for IRAs. Also, because the owner can liquidate the IRA (frequently with a tax penalty), the courts have routinely ruled that the owner's creditors should have the same access to the funds. Other non-qualified plans include Simplified Employee Pension (SEP) accounts, Roth IRAs, and single-owner qualified plans.

How safe are non-qualified plans today from lawsuits and creditor claims? There is no one answer because these plans do not enjoy blanket federal lawsuit immunity as do ERISA-qualified plans. Instead, their protection depends solely upon state law. As with other state exemptions (homestead, insurance, wages, etc.), state laws vary. For example, several states fully protect non-qualified accounts, but many others afford them no lawsuit protection. However, most states at least partially protect non-qualified plans. Their protection may be either for a statutory minimum amount (i.e., $50,000) or for such amount as a court deems necessary for the debtor's support. There may be other limitations or restrictions under your state statutes.

Some states protect only those accounts held in trust, but do not protect distributions to a beneficiary. If your state laws are silent on this point, then review your state court decisions.

Are you planning bankruptcy? Retirement accounts reasonably necessary for the support of the debtor are usually protected in bankruptcy. Several important cases have ruled that IRAs should be afforded the same full bankruptcy protection as qualified retirement plans, even when state law provides no exemption. Still, these decisions are far fewer than are the opposing decisions. Generally, bankruptcy courts shield IRAs only to the extent that they are immune under the debtor's state law. Nor are Roth IRAs necessarily as protected as IRAs. Many states have yet to amend their laws to extend the same statutory protection to Roths as they did for IRAs. You may have this same problem with SEP-IRAs.

This uncertainty leads to one conclusion: Your IRAs and other non-qualified plans must be carefully reviewed by your asset protection or bankruptcy lawyer. You can't *assume* that your plan is automatically protected. You may be wrong.

Whether your retirement plan is lawsuit-proof depends upon several factors:

- Whether your plan is qualified under the Employee Retirement Income Security Act (ERISA)
- Whether state law exempts your non-ERISA plans (i.e. IRAs)
- Whether your plan is a pension or welfare benefit plan and whether it is in payment mode
- Who your creditor is, and
- Whether you are in bankruptcy.

Fortunately, through several key strategies, you can shelter even an *unprotected* retirement plan. Following are some options.

1. Keep Your Money in Your Pension Plan

Think carefully before rolling over your pension plan into a self-directed IRA. If you roll over your ERISA-qualified funds into a self-directed IRA, and reside in a state that does not fully protect IRAs, you then reduce or possibly even eliminate your creditor protection. Of course, you may not have the option to leave your retirement account in your employer's 401K plan, or you may particularly want to direct your own investments through an IRA. The rollover decision should be primarily an investment decision; however, consider asset protection when you make a rollover decision.

One client made this terrible asset protection blunder several years ago. Frustrated by the excessive administrative costs charged to his partnership's pension plan, Jim wanted greater returns by rolling his pension plan into an IRA so he could day-trade his own funds.

Unfortunately, what Jim didn't realize was that while his pension plan was lawsuit protected, his new IRA account was unprotected and shielded by neither federal nor state law. When Jim was later sued on a bad business deal, he lost most of his $500,000 IRA.

2. Rollover Your IRA Back into a Qualified Plan

Just as it may be smarter for lawsuit-proofing purposes to keep your retirement funds in an ERISA-qualified plan, it may be wise to roll your IRA back into a qualified plan – assuming that your IRA was originally a rollover from an ERISA-qualified plan. Or, why not create your own new qualified plan? For example, we set up a number of zero percent money purchase plans that are fully IRS compliant, ERISA-qualified, *and* creditor-proof.

Similarly, if you have a pension plan that is not fully protected (such as a single member plan) and you add one or more beneficiaries, you now have a creditor-protected plan.

3. Invest Your IRA in an FLP or LLC

Another favorite strategy is to invest an unprotected IRA, SEP-IRA, or deferred compensation plan into a family limited partnership (FLP) or single member limited liability company (LLC). Your retirement funds then have 'charging order protection' as I more fully explain in the chapters on limited partnerships and LLCs. One technicality: Your plan custodian must agree with this arrangement. It is also possible that the transfer may be recoverable by a present creditor as a fraudulent transfer. Therefore, don't rely on this strategy if you have an *existing* creditor. However, a single member LLC can frequently be an excellent investment vehicle for your retirement funds, and you may be the designated manager or investment advisor for your IRA.

4. Invest Your IRA Offshore

When you need even stronger protection, move your retirement funds offshore. Your accounts have considerably more protection than they would by investing in family limited partnerships or LLCs.

Here you have two options: (1) You can move your retirement account into a sub-trust of a foreign asset protection trust (FAPT), or (2) arrange for your fund custodian to invest your IRA in an offshore LLC.

The first alternative, using an FAPT for retirement fund protection, is both complex and costly. You can also inadvertently disqualify your plan unless it is done correctly. Another FAPT drawback is that appreciating sub-trust assets may not be tax deferred.

It is usually preferable to invest IRAs into a single member offshore LLC. It is certainly simpler and less costly than an offshore trust. Essentially, your retirement plan sets up a Nevis or Isle of Man LLC with the appropriate protective provisions (see Chapter 11). Your IRA custodian would transfer your retirement funds to the foreign LLC in exchange for full ownership of the LLC. Your plan then has *no* funds within the US subject to creditor claims. Instead, now your retirement account only owns the membership interest in the foreign LLC, which is subject only to the charging order remedy. You may be the investment advisor (and even a co-signatory on the foreign LLC account) until you have a judgment creditor, when you would surrender control. Until that time, you can also safely reinvest the foreign LLC funds in US investments. As you will see later, a US court cannot compel you or the custodian to turn over the funds in the foreign LLC because the foreign LLC owns the funds and the foreign manager and the custodian control the funds.

Do you have an IRA over $100,000 and reside in a state that doesn't fully protect IRAs? Consider this foreign LLC strategy. Here's one impediment: Few US custodians are familiar - and hence comfortable - with this offshore strategy. We have several qualified custodians who can readily implement this foreign LLC strategy.

5. Terminate Your IRA and Protect the Proceeds

When your IRA is creditor exposed, your most practical solution may be to terminate your IRA, pay the tax (and any early withdrawal penalty), and protect the proceeds as you would cash or other liquid assets. Plan dissolution is certainly the most economical option when you have a relatively small IRA and you can't justify more complex and expensive protection.

6. Invest Your IRA in an Exempt Annuity

Annuities are frequently fully exempt from lawsuit seizure even in those states that do not completely protect IRAs. In such cases, you may safely invest your IRA in annuities, although we do not ordinarily recommend that our clients buy annuities through an IRA because it only duplicates the tax deferral advantage. However, buying a self-protected annuity can be sensible when asset protection is your primary goal.

7. Relocate to a State That Fully Protects IRAs

If you own a large, unprotected IRA and have foreseeable legal problems, then it may also be sensible to relocate to a state that fully protects IRAs. This is essentially the same strategy as homestead 'shopping' for the most protective jurisdiction to shelter your home.

As a final thought, why not use your retirement plan as your safe haven for any extra cash if your retirement plan is fully creditor-protected? Yes, there are limitations on how much you can put into your retirement plans for tax deferral purposes, but you can always invest more *after-tax* dollars in a lawsuit-proof plan. When you reach whatever you can invest tax-deferred annually into your retirement plan, you can pay the tax on the excess contributions, which would nevertheless be protected by your plan.

Protecting Wages and Other Income

A judgment creditor seizes paychecks through *wage garnishment*. However, the amount a creditor can claim from a paycheck is limited by both federal and state laws that fully or partially protect wages.

As is true with the other state exemptions, each state affords wages a different degree of protection. Texas and Florida - always debtor-friendly states - fully exempt wages from creditor garnishment. Florida fully protects the wages of the 'head of the household - presumably the family member with the larger income. However, New York, as another example, shelters 90 percent of their citizen's wages. Only ten percent (in the aggregate) can be claimed by a debtor's creditors.

As with the homestead laws, there may be state

requirements with which you must comply in order to protect your wages. For example, your state may require you to separate wages into 'wage exemption or 'wage earner' accounts and not commingle your wages with other unprotected funds.

Even if you reside in a state with less wage protection, the federal Consumer Credit Protection Act (CCPA) nevertheless limits the amount a creditor can garnish from your wages. And the Federal CCPA overrides state laws that provide less wage protection, so you can at least count on the protection of the CCPA, and possibly greater protection if your state laws are more restrictive. The CCPA limits the amount of wages a creditor can garnish to the lesser of (1) 25% of the debtor's disposable income per week (*disposable income* is the net paycheck after deducting federal and state withholding and FICA taxes), or (2) The amount by which your weekly disposable weekly income exceeds 30 times the federal minimum hourly wage.

Exempt (protected) income cannot be garnished once you receive it, provided that you keep it segregated.

How can you avoid garnishment? You have options. One is to form a corporation and direct your income to the corporation. For tax purposes, you can draw out the money as a loan. While this simple strategy has been used by many debtors to temporarily shield their non-exempt wages from creditors, it is seldom a practical, long-term solution.

A less common but equally protective wage protection strategy is to make a wage assignment to a 'friendlier' creditor who would then periodically 'loan' you your money. Wage assignments must be in writing and in force before your other creditors obtain their garnishment order.

How protected are welfare payments to welfare recipients? Can they be seized by creditors? They are exempt in most states; but again, the laws on welfare funds are hardly uniform. Many states only partially protect welfare payments and other states give them no protection, even to such common public assistance programs as Aid to Families with Dependent Children (AFDC). As with wages, welfare payments are no longer protected once they are received and commingled with non-welfare funds or converted into other non-exempt assets.

Public assistance payments such as aid to the blind and aid to the elderly and disabled are generally protected. Creditors cannot garnish these payments, provided the debtor segregates these payments from their non-exempt funds. Exempt proceeds used to acquire non-exempt assets always lose their protection.

What about Social Security and disability income payments? Are they lawsuit-proof? Because Social Security is not considered a pension under the Employee Retirement Income Security Act (ERISA), it is not federally protected. Therefore, whether your creditors can seize your Social Security check depends upon your state's laws. The IRS, of course, can always seize Social Security payments, but as a policy matter seldom do.

There are exceptions to these exemption laws. For example, the Child Support Enforcement Act of 1975 overrides federal and state income exemptions to enforce alimony or child support orders. Therefore, alimony and child support payments are generally not exempt from garnishment by either the payor's or recipient's creditors. Support payments also have a limited exemption in certain states.

Life Insurance and Annuities
May Be Your Safest Investment

Buying annuities or insurance may be a simple way to shelter your investments from creditors. Every state partly or fully creditor-protects life insurance. The life insurance exemptions have been adopted since as early as 1841 to protect the financial stability of an insured's dependents without the need for state support. However, life insurance is important for more than its lawsuit protection. Life insurance can also, in many circumstances, be an excellent investment alternative. While life insurance is generally seizure exempt (and likely will remain protected well into the future), the states are not uniform in their protection of insurance and annuities. Here's what to look for:

- Does your state shield the entire policy proceeds from the policyholder's creditors?
- If your state does not fully protect the entire policy, what amount does it protect? Arizona, for instance, exempts only the first $20,000 of insurance proceeds.
- Does your state protect the policy proceeds? Does the protection depend on whether the policy beneficiaries are the policyholder's spouse, children or other dependents?
- Does your state exempt all life policies (term, universal, whole life, etc.)?
- Does your state protect a policy's cash surrender value as well as the policy proceeds? If your policy has a substantial cash value, then see your state exemptions to determine how much of the cash value is protected.
- Also remember: A policy purchased with fraudulently transferred funds can be unwound by the courts, as they can unwind other fraudulent transfers.

Essential to any asset protection plan is the irrevocable life insurance trust (ILIT).

If your insurance beneficiaries have present or potential creditors, your policy has a cash value, you have IRS problems, or you reside in a state that doesn't fully protect insurance, then set up an ILIT. As I explain in greater depth in Chapter 10, an irrevocable life insurance trust fully lawsuit-protects both the policy proceeds and the cash value from your creditors and your beneficiaries. With the ILIT, you can also save significant estate taxes if you anticipate a taxable estate.

Annuities are similarly protected by the same state laws that protect insurance, but an annuity may or may not be an appropriate investment for you. This is a question you must ask a good investment advisor or financial planner. You should base your decision to buy an annuity chiefly as an investment, not for asset protection.

Still, I have many clients who enthusiastically buy variable annuities. Some are at least partly motivated because annuities are lawsuit-proof in their state. As with insurance, however, you shouldn't allow asset protection to be the primary factor when buying annuities. They offer both advantages and disadvantages, as do any other investments. If annuities make financial sense for you, then you can obtain even greater protection when you buy certain foreign annuities.

Swiss annuities, in certain circumstances, provide full creditor protection (including protection against divorce, the IRS, and bankruptcy) if your spouse or descendents are the beneficiaries (or a third party is an irrevocable beneficiary). Other countries similarly creditor-proof their annuities and life insurance products. Two favorites are the Isle of Man and the Bahamas. Annuities from Isle of Man insurance companies excel for several reasons. First, their exemption laws are even more protective than Switzerland's. You can find several S&P Triple A rated underwriters in the Isle of Man, and their annuities also have exceptionally attractive investment features.

More Lawsuit-Proof Assets

Many other assets that you now own are undoubtedly safe from lawsuits and bankruptcy. Some common examples include: burial plots, wedding rings, household furniture, and autos (up to a stated value), tools of your trade, livestock, farming implements, funds under 529 plans and similar college programs and gifts under the Uniform Gifts to Minors Act.

The possible list of exempt assets continues. State exemption statutes can make for fascinating reading. Massachusetts, for instance, is a throwback to more politically incorrect times. The Bay State's laws still exempt 'one wife' from creditor seizure. Of course, you can find husbands who would wish otherwise.

Sheltering Exempt Property Proceeds

If you sell or refinance exempt property, will the proceeds remain safe from your creditors? For example, if you sell your fully homesteaded home, how can you safely shelter the proceeds?

You have several options. You can directly transfer the proceeds from one exempt asset to another. For example, with the protected proceeds from the sale of a homesteaded home, you may buy an exempt annuity. You might apply the proceeds to some other safe harbor, such as a limited partnership or an irrevocable trust that would keep it safe from creditor seizure.

Every state protects the proceeds derived from selling or refinancing an exempt asset. Some states protect the assets either for a specified time (set by statute) or for a reasonable time (determined by the courts). However, if they are to maintain their protection, the exempt funds must remain segregated so they do not lose their source identity.

Exemption Law Limitations

The exemption laws won't shelter otherwise protected assets against your most dangerous creditor – the US government. The IRS and other federal agencies, such as the SEC, FTC, and Health Care Financing Administration (HCFA), etc., can ignore every other law that protects assets from other creditors. For example, the IRS can seize a Texas or Florida home, notwithstanding their strong state homestead laws. Similarly, state laws that shelter annuities, insurance, wages, IRAs, and other assets offer no protection against the IRS or other federal agencies. What assets are protected from the IRS? Only those few assets the IRS allows you to keep. Moreover, your state exemptions may or may not be protected from state claims.

Exempt assets are not safe in divorce, either. For example, a divorce court can award your spouse a share of your otherwise protected retirement account under a Qualified Domestic Relations Order (QDRO). Similarly, family law courts can seize exempt assets to enforce child support orders.

Even when an asset is *generally* self-protected under your state law, you cannot assume that it is protected against *your* creditor in *your* particular circumstances. You can't rely on generalities. Again, a knowledgeable attorney is invaluable.

Convert Vulnerable Wealth into Self-Protected Wealth

You see the obvious strategy: Maximize your protection by converting whatever non-exempt (or unprotected) assets you have into exempt or self-protected assets. If you have the good fortune to live in such debtor-friendly states as Florida or Texas, you have options. You could 'jurisdiction shop' and relocate to a state with laws more protective than the state where you now reside.

Another possibility is to exchange assets with a liability-free spouse. Your strategy here is to transfer to your spouse any unprotected assets that you own in exchange for *protected* marital assets of equal value.

Transforming non-exempt assets into exempt assets has its dangers. Whether by statute or case law, certain states deem such conversions to be fraudulent transfers against existing creditors, even when it is a 'fair value' exchange. Florida, for instance, has a (seldom enforced) general anti-conversion statute. Florida also has specific statutes that deny protection for insurance and annuities acquired with the proceeds from non-exempt assets purchased *after* you have a creditor. Conversely, this tactic of converting vulnerable wealth into exempt assets - even against existing creditors - may be permissible in other states.

In my view, Texas is the most protective state. Texas specifically sanctions by statute the conversion of non-exempt assets into exempt assets. For instance, you can safely buy a Texas home with your cash and file bankruptcy the following day. Your home remains protected by Texas homestead laws. Such conversions, then, are generally safer in Texas than in Florida, although Florida has been the more popular state for protection. This imagery probably has more to do with Florida's great beaches than a thorough understanding of its laws. Florida is then second best to Texas.

Plenty of O.J.-type stories abound in both Texas and Florida, but it's not only the O.J.-style debtors who flock to Florida and Texas to escape their creditors. While these two states offer many good options for wealth protection through their generous exemption laws, there are hundreds of ways to protect your wealth under other state laws - if you creatively apply these exemption laws.

Here are some good examples:

- A Texan debtor obtained a second mortgage to 'equity-strip' his family's non-homestead vacation home. The proceeds reduced his mortgage on his primary home, which was fully homestead protected.
- Expecting a big lawsuit, another savvy Texan 'cashed out' her vulnerable mutual funds and used the money to buy fully protected annuities and life insurance.
- Before starting another risky business venture, a Florida chiropractor made her brother a co-trustee on her sole participant - and hence vulnerable - Keogh plan. This instantly immunized her Keogh from lawsuits.
- A Massachusetts businessman sold his homestead-protected home for financial reasons just before he was hit with a major lawsuit. The sale proceeds were used to buy another exempt asset – in this case, Swiss annuities. We replay the tactic: When you sell or refinance an exempt asset, shelter the proceeds in some other exempt asset.

Even when it is practical and feasible to redeploy your wealth into exempt assets, this strategy won't always work if you are already sued. For successful planning you must have full confidence that your 'exempt' assets are indeed sheltered under your state laws. This takes more than a cursory review of your laws. You must also understand the many nuances, and case decisions that may compromise your plan.

6

Co-Ownership Opportunities and Traps

Do you co-own property? I am not referring to the co-ownership of legal entities, such as corporations or LLCs, but situations where you and others directly title assets in your own respective personal names.

Those who own property too seldom contemplate the potential liabilities they can incur from their co-ownership arrangement. They do not always consider whether their co-ownership arrangement aids or impedes protection of assets from their personal creditors.

An example may be two business partners who buy commercial real estate and title the property in their own names as tenants-in-common. If someone becomes injured on the property, who has liability? How could these co-owners have more intelligently titled their property to reduce their personal exposure? What if one co-owner files personal bankruptcy or loses a lawsuit and has a major judgment creditor? What more could have been done - and *should* have been done - to safeguard the debtor-partner's interest in the property?

Consider the situation of an elderly mother with a middle-aged daughter. The mother wants to leave her savings account to her daughter when she dies and she wants her daughter to have access to the account should the mother become disabled. The mother sets up a joint account and titles the bank account in both her name and her daughter's as joint owners. The mother logically reasons that when she dies, the money automatically passes to her daughter without the necessity of probate. It sounds sensible, but does the mother realize the potential pitfalls and liabilities of a joint bank account? What if the daughter is sued or encounters her own creditor problems? What if the daughter has tax troubles or divorces? Poof! A healthy chunk of the savings accounts would then belong to someone else.

Married couples may see co-ownership as the simplest, most natural way to title their marital property, but they, too, must ask themselves the same questions: Will co-owning their assets expand their respective liability? Will they gain more or less lawsuit protection? How solid is that protection? Aside from asset protection, will co-ownership help or hinder them in achieving their other estate and tax planning objectives?

This chapter helps you take a hard look at whether - and when - you should co-own property. It also explores the potential dangers and alternatives.

Co-Ownership Basics

Before you can understand the risks and benefits of the various types of co-ownerships, you must know how each co-ownership is created and functions. Unless noted otherwise, these ownership arrangements can apply to personal property (bank accounts, stocks and bonds, motor vehicles, copyrights, partnership interests, etc.) or real property (land, homes, condos, buildings, etc.). These ownerships are called *tenancies*. 'Tenancy' in this context does not suggest leases and tenants, but a form of co-ownership.

Following are the basics of each type co-ownership:

1. Tenancy-in-common:

- Each co-owner owns a fractional interest in the property (i.e., if there are three co-owners, each owns a one-third share).
- Each co-owner can transfer or mortgage his or her share of the property without the consent of the other co-owners.
- A co-owner can bequeath her ownership share.
- Tenancy-in-common is the *default tenancy* for unmarried co-owners. Unless you specifically designate another type of ownership in the title or transfer documents, the law assumes that it is a tenancy-in-common.

2. Joint tenancy:

- Each co-owner owns an *undivided* interest in the property (i.e. if there are three co-owners, each owns an undivided share of the entire property).
- Each co-owner can transfer his interest without the consent of the others. If one joint owner transfers his interest, this severs the joint tenancy and the new co-owner becomes a tenant-in-common with the previous joint owners. For example, there are three owners of a property in joint tenancy - A, B, and C. Each owns an undivided one-third share. If joint tenant A sells to a buyer, then the buyer becomes a tenant-in-common with joint tenants B and C; however, B and C, between themselves, remain joint tenants.
- When a joint tenant dies, his or her share automatically

passes to the surviving joint tenants. Ownership shares cannot be passed on through a will. This is called the joint tenant's *right of survivorship*. Under the previous example, if C later died, B would automatically inherit C's one-third interest. B would then own two-thirds of the property as tenant-in-common with the buyer, who would own a one-third share.

- Most states require joint tenancy to be created by a written agreement. You will see the words *joint tenancy, jointly, jointly with the right of survivorship, joint tenants with the right of survivorship* (JTWROS), or similar verbiage. In some states joint tenancy does not automatically carry the right of survivorship; this survivorship right must be expressly stated within the documents.

3. Tenancy-by-the-entirety:

- This form of co-ownership is available in about half the states. In these states, only a husband and wife can co-own assets as tenancy-by-the-entirety. Tenancy-by-the-entirety is thus a special joint tenancy reserved for married couples. As a form of joint tenancy, it also carries the right of survivorship; that is, the surviving spouse automatically inherits the deceased spouse's share.
- Neither spouse can sell, transfer, or mortgage the property without the other's consent.
- The tenancy-by-the-entirety remains intact until both spouses agree to change the form of ownership, divorce, or one spouse dies.
- Several states that permit tenancy-by-the-entirety restrict it to real estate, such as the marital home. Other states allow a married couple to own any form

of personal property and real estate as tenancy-by-the-entirety.

Tenancy-In-Common

Because each co-owner in a tenancy-in-common (or *tenant-in-common*) owns a divided fractional share of the property, this arrangement creates serious lawsuit dangers and, reciprocally, no creditor protection. There are many examples to illustrate the risks for tenants-in-common. For instance, if you and your friend John are tenants-in-common and own an apartment building, each of you can sell, gift, or mortgage your half share of the building without the consent of the other. You are thus essentially 'partners' in the business of renting apartments, collecting rents, maintaining the premises, etc., and the building provides you both with an income. Someday you expect to sell the building for a hefty profit.

Since you and John are tenants-in-common, you each own a separate share in the building, which is distinct from the interests of the other tenants-in-common. Your personal creditors cannot claim your co-owner's interest and, conversely, if John is sued (for a reason unrelated to the building), John's creditors could then only claim *his* half interest in the building. Your half remains safe from John's creditors. While this outcome may seem acceptable, particularly if you see yourself as the *safe* co-owner, a tenancy-in-common can nevertheless cause you plenty of problems.

One big risk is that your co-owner(s) creditors can force a sale of the *entire* property to satisfy your co-owner's personal debts. Since your co-tenant, John, can transfer his share of the tenancy-in-common property without your consent, John's creditor can 'step into his shoes' and similarly force the transfer of his interest. You may possibly negotiate to buy your co-owner's interest to avoid the forced sale of the entire property, but this is not always practical; you may not have the money. Should the court force the sale of the entire property, you will nevertheless lose the property, although you will recover your half share of the net proceeds from the forced sale.

Suppose John's creditors do not force the sale of the entire property, but instead bid for and claim John's half-interest in the property. The net result is that you now have a new partner - John's creditor! It can and does happen.

You can see that John's financial problems can cause you serious problems, and your problems can become John's headache.

More importantly, how safe is *your* ownership interest from your own creditors when you own property as tenants-in-common? You already know the answer: Just as John's creditors can seize his interest, your creditors can seize *yours*.

This is why co-owning property as tenants-in-common is too risky. If you or your co-owner has financial problems, you can easily lose control of the property or you might lose significant money. Avoid this trap. Later chapters show you many superior co-ownership arrangements to title assets through various protective entities. If you insist upon titling assets as tenants-in-common, then at least make certain that your co-tenants are financially secure; otherwise you risk a forced sale, a new co-owner, or losing control of your investment.

Aside from the vulnerability of your co-ownership interest, an even bigger pitfall is that tenancy-in-common *expands* your liability. What if John accidentally injures somebody through his negligent management of the co-owned property? Who gets sued? Both you and John, of course. Since you co-own the property, you essentially created a general partnership. Should the plaintiff win a $5 million judgment - or an amount that exceeds what the property or John is worth - then who pays? *You*, of course. As co-owners, you and John have joint and several liability for any liability that arises from co-owning the property. The bottom line: Never own property directly as tenants-in-common.

Joint Tenancy

Joint tenancy is a particularly popular form of co-ownership. Several key features distinguish it from tenancy-in-common. One such feature is its right of survivorship. When one joint tenant dies, the jointly owned property automatically passes to the surviving joint tenant(s). Jointly owned property then passes *outside* a will, and thus avoids the expense and delay of probate. Because joint tenancy avoids probate, many financial and legal advisors recommend to their clients the joint tenancy form of ownership. Unfortunately, these advisors don't always tell their clients the many ways that joint ownership can hurt them. In my view, joint tenancy is nearly always a mistake because it significantly increases lawsuit risks, frustrates sound estate planning, and at the same time, provides little or no lawsuit protection.

For starters, jointly owned property, whether personal property or real estate, creates the same lawsuit and creditor risks as does tenancy-in-common. In some circumstances you can have greater exposure. Generally, you also have the same lack of protection as with tenancy-in-common. Your personal creditors can seize only your interest in the co-owned property. You also have about the same tenancy-in-common risks. If your co-owner(s) has legal or financial problems, creditors can claim that interest in the property and become a co-tenant in common with you, or alternatively the creditor can force a sale of the entire property to recover the debt owed by your co-owner.

However, joint ownership has an added twist. It puts you in a 'winner takes all' game. You 'gamble' that you will survive your co-owner (joint tenant). Because jointly owned property automatically passes to the surviving joint tenant(s), if the liability-free tenant dies before the debtor tenant, the entire property automatically passes to the debtor, and the entire property can then be claimed by the debtor's creditors.

For example, if you and John own the building as joint tenants, and you die, John's creditors could then levy or seize the entire building. Your family would have no further ownership claim to the building.

Of course, the alternative outcome in this 'winner takes all' game is that if the safe co-owner (you) survives the debtor co-owner (John), you own the entire building free of John's creditors. This may be one advantage with joint tenancy: It is you who may win the game.

Joint tenancy also impairs good estate planning. For instance, if your estate plan is to gift your property at your death to your friends, you would normally provide for this in your will or living trust.

Joint tenancy may frustrate this estate planning objective because whatever property is jointly owned instead passes automatically by rights of survivorship to your surviving joint tenant(s). This automatic transfer occurs the instant you die. Your will or living trust would be totally ineffective in disposing of any jointly-owned property. Any beneficiaries that you designate in your will or trust to inherit your share of jointly owned property are effectively 'disinherited' since the property instead goes to the surviving joint tenant(s).

I see this avoidable tragedy every day because many people do not understand this survivorship feature about joint ownership, nor do their advisors always inform them.

A prosperous plumber, Pat, was in his late 60s when he married for the second time. Shortly after his marriage, Pat transferred his Pennsylvania home, Arizona winter vacation condo, and a $2 million stock portfolio into joint tenancy with his new wife. Six months later, Pat died. Who now owns his home, condo, and stocks? His new wife, of course. His three children and eight grandchildren inherited nothing, although Pat's last will bequeathed several of these assets to them.

Mildred, a retired widow living in Florida, set up a joint bank account with her daughter in New Jersey. Despite my advice, Mildred insisted upon this arrangement in case she got sick and could no longer write out checks for herself. Also, she wanted joint tenancy to avoid probate. I explained to Mildred how she could more safely accomplish her objectives by preparing a durable power of attorney to give her daughter signing authority on her checking account, and that a living trust would be the right way to avoid probate. Mildred was stubborn. How safe is Mildred's $300,000 joint account now that her daughter is divorcing?

Many intelligent, well intentioned people get stuck in these same dangerous joint ownership arrangements because they don't fully realize its inherent risks. Many people do not even know how their assets are titled. Those who decide upon joint ownership to avoid probate or for its other perceived benefits seldom see its downside dangers.

As with tenancy-in-common, another problem is that joint tenancy owners are jointly and severally liable for any debts or liabilities arising from the co-owned asset.

How are your assets titled? Do you own property jointly or as tenants-in-common? Then see a lawyer - fast!

Tenancy-By-The-Entirety

Tenancy-by-the-entirety is a special type of joint tenancy

reserved for husbands and wives in twenty-five states, chiefly in the eastern part of the country.

Some states that recognize tenants-by-the-entirety provide about the same creditor protection as with joint tenancy; that is, very little. However, assets titled to spouses as tenancy-by-the-entirety in many other states enjoy comparatively strong protection from their creditors and lawsuits.

The more protective states generally provide that a creditor of only *one* spouse cannot claim that debtor-spouse's interest in property owned by the married couple as tenancy-by-the-entirety (T/E). However, a common creditor to *both* spouses can claim tenancy-by-the-entirety property. For example, if both the husband and wife guaranteed a bank note, that bank could claim the couple's tenancy-by-the-entirety property. If only one spouse was sued on a debt incurred alone by that spouse, then property owned by the couple as tenants-by-the-entirety would be lawsuit-protected from that one creditor. You can see the value of this protection.

Does your state provide T/E protection? Check my website www.asgoldstein.com. If T/E protection can adequately protect you, then discuss with your attorney whether to re-title any property that you co-own with your spouse as tenancy-by-the-entirety. Your attorney can tell you whether assets titled as tenancy-by-the-entirety in your state are sufficiently shielded without additional protection. Also, bear in mind that when you die, tenancy-by-the-entirety property automatically passes to your spouse; you cannot then bequeath these assets to other beneficiaries. If this is not your intention, then avoid tenancy-by-the-entirety for those specific asset(s).

There is no uniformity throughout the states on tenancy-by-the-entirety laws. Florida and New York both have exceptionally strong tenancy-by-the-entirety laws. Many clients from both states rely chiefly on their tenancy-by-the-entirety laws for lawsuit protection. For instance, an attorney-client recently sailed through bankruptcy with over $1 million in assets titled to himself and his wife as tenants-by-the-entirety. The assets remained untouched by the bankruptcy trustee because his solvent wife (who was not herself in bankruptcy) shared none of his liabilities.

However, some erosion is occurring with tenants-by-the-entirety protection. For instance, several recent bankruptcy cases have ruled that a bankruptcy trustee *can* claim the tenants-by-the-entirety interest of the bankrupt spouse. Whether the trustee can then force a sale of the debtor spouse's property depends on a balancing test: How much will the creditors benefit from a forced sale versus what the injury would be to the non-debtor spouse? Moreover, several appeals court decisions have allowed the IRS to seize a tenants-by-the-entirety interest owned by a delinquent spouse taxpayer, even when the spouse had no tax obligation.

You cannot always title *any* property as tenancy-by-the-entirety. Some states limit tenancy-by-the-entirety protection only to real estate. Others further limit its creditor protection only to the family residence. Florida and New York again exemplify two states where you can title any asset as tenants-by-the-entirety.

In those states where tenancy-by-the-entirety provides adequate lawsuit protection, a couple may choose to title virtually everything they own as tenancy-by-the-entirety. I have many clients who have so-titled not only their home, but also their investments, family business, etc. However, we would not have them title their vehicles or other liability-producing assets as tenancy-by-the-entirety (or in any other form of co-ownership), because both spouses would then become liable in the event of an accident.

Unfortunately, most tenants-by-the-entirety states have laws that only partially lawsuit-protect certain assets. Massachusetts, as one interesting example, protects the family home from the creditors of one spouse for as long as the other spouse resides there, but not thereafter. As you can see, tenancy-by-the-entirety laws create patchwork protection. You must know precisely what the laws in your state protect, and also their exceptions and limitations.

Tenancy-by-the-entirety, of course, is hardly foolproof even in those states where it seemingly provides broad protection. For example, if you own property with your spouse as tenants-by-the-entirety and your spouse unexpectedly dies while you have a judgment creditor, you, of course, would then automatically own the entire property, which could be seized by your creditor.

Divorce similarly extinguishes tenancy-by-the-entirety protection. Arguably, you would expect divorcing spouses to remain sufficiently amicable to transfer tenancy-by-the-entirety property to another protective entity before they finalize their divorce (particularly if one spouse has creditors), but this doesn't always happen. I have had cases where a divorcing spouse's creditors had that window of opportunity to seize the debtor-spouse's share of previously protected T/E assets immediately following a hostile divorce. Ex-spouses don't always cooperate in asset protection planning.

It is most important to remember to avoid tenancy-by-the-entirety if it is not your intention to bequeath your property to your spouse. For instance, if you are in a second or third marriage and want to bequeath your assets to your children, then tenancy-by-the-entirety defeats this possibility, as does joint tenancy.

Despite its shortcomings, tenancy-by-the-entirety can, in some states and in some circumstances, give you reasonably good protection. Married couples *should* seriously consider tenancy-by-the-entirety: (1) When the couple intends survivorship rights to the asset; (2) When the spouses have low liability risk, and do not generally incur significant joint obligations; and (3) When the couple is reasonably young and has less concern that one spouse may unexpectedly die and leave the property exposed to the surviving spouse's judgment creditors.

If you and your spouse own property jointly in a state that recognizes tenancy-by-the-entirety, and if your assets are not now otherwise protected from your own and your spouse's creditors, then consider re-titling your assets as tenancy-by-the-entirety. You will have survivorship rights plus asset protection.

Protecting Community and Separate Property

Nine states follow community property law: Arizona, California, Idaho, Louisiana, Nevada, New Mexico, Texas, Washington, and Wisconsin. Each state's community property laws have important differences in the construction or interpretation of their laws. If you live in a community property state, then review with your attorney precisely how your state laws work. Focus on the specific rights that creditors have against both community and separate property. Therefore, I necessarily speak in generalities; your community property state may follow somewhat different rules.

Community property essentially gives each spouse a one-half interest in the community property. Community property is any property, including personal property, that is acquired by *either* spouse during their marriage, other than inheritances or gifts made only to that one spouse. Conversely, property acquired by either spouse before marriage or after divorce (or *permanent separation,* depending on the state) remains that spouse's *separate property.* Similarly, debts incurred before or after marriage are *separate debts.* Those incurred while married are *community debts*, provided they benefit the couple. Most debts are construed as marital debts, even debts incurred by one spouse.

For example, Harry and Wilma, husband and wife, marry in 1995 and divorce in 2005. Harry's boat, which he owned since 1994, remains his separate property as does his inheritance from his father, which he received in 1997. The loan on Harry's boat dating back to 1994 also remains his separate debt. Whatever Harry earns as an accountant during their marriage becomes community property, as does the antique car he acquired in his name in 1997.

Couples frequently use transmutation agreements to legally convert community property into separate property and vice versa. However, to avoid problems, a transmutation agreement must be carefully drafted according to state law and closely followed by both spouses. A transmutation agreement essentially provides that: "This specified property – and any property that I acquire hereafter is mine alone and [that] property – and any property that you hereinafter acquire is yours." Thus, the agreement divides present community assets as well as the future assets of each spouse into separate property. The effect of this arrangement is that the creditors of each spouse would then only have recourse to the separate assets belonging to that debtor-spouse. This, of course, is a safer arrangement than allowing a creditor to seize assets co-owned as community property.

In concept, a transmutation agreement can accomplish the same outcome as a prenuptial agreement, except that you can enter into a transmutation agreement *before* or *during* the marriage; a prenuptial agreement must be executed before marriage.

I have many married clients who live in community property states, and I frequently have them sign transmutation agreements to divide their community property into separate property. Why foolishly give one spouse's creditors access to the other spouse's assets?

To prepare a transmutation agreement when you have present creditors, requires some care. Dividing assets into separate assets after you have an *existing* creditor may be considered a fraudulent transfer. A *present* creditor who is unsatisfied from the debtor-spouse's assets may then claim assets fraudulently transferred to the non-debtor-spouse as separate property. Timing is critical. Sign your transmutation agreement *before* you incur liabilities, and record your transmutation agreement in your public registry to provide public notice of when the agreement was completed and that it remains in full force.

The next question concerns what assets a creditor can levy, lien, or seize in a community property state. The answer depends chiefly on the type of debt the creditor is enforcing (whether it is a community or separate debt) and the type of property the creditor is claiming (whether it is community or separate property). It is frequently difficult to distinguish between community or separate assets and debts, and these issues often become contested in court. Nevertheless, there are general principles: The separate creditors of one spouse can claim that spouse's separate property. Separate creditors can also usually claim community property, as well as the separate property of the other spouse, if the debt was for necessities (food, shelter, clothing, utilities, etc.) or in instances when the debt benefited both spouses.

Community creditors (creditors of both spouses) can claim community property. In certain states they can also claim either spouse's separate property. For example,

California's community property law and most community property states employ a system that is most favorable to creditors. Creditors under their rules may satisfy their debts from property over which the debtor-spouse has management control. For instance, in California, a creditor may then seize both the separate property of the debtor spouse *and* the community property, since both spouses presumably have equal management and control over the community property. Of course, you may have a different result in other community property states.

How safe community and separate property remains from creditor claims is frequently cloudy. Usually, *both* spouses' separate and community property are vulnerable. If you live in a community property state, protect both your separate *and* community property. Also keep separate property apart from community property and uncommingled, or you may lose half of your separate property to your spouse (through divorce) or to his or her creditors (during the marriage).

Co-Owning Assets Can Increase Liability

Any co-ownership expands liability. For example, if you jointly own an auto or boat and have an accident, both you and your co-owner share liability, regardless of who caused the accident. Consider the case of my 83-year-old client who accidentally rocketed her car through a K-Mart window and seriously injured several shoppers. She will now be sued for millions. To compound the problem, the car was titled to both her and her husband, so her husband is now co-defending the lawsuit. Because her husband owns substantial assets, he may someday be forced to pay a hefty settlement, despite my best efforts to protect his assets. Although the couple own much of their property as tenants-by-the-entirety, this won't protect them because both spouses are being sued by the same plaintiffs.

In addition to the non-existent (or at least questionable) asset protection - as well as the expanded liability - from these various co-ownership arrangements, you have other possible co-ownership disadvantages:

- When one co-owner dies, the IRS may try to tax the entire value of the jointly owned property for estate tax purposes, unless the surviving co-owner can prove his contribution, the entire property will be subject to estate taxes (this applies only to property co-owned by non-spouses).

- Co-owners cannot always transfer their ownership interests without the consent of the co-owners. This restriction can prevent the timely transfer of property, whether for asset protection, estate planning, or any other reason (i.e., you want to sell or gift your interest). For example, one optometrist client is now struggling to keep his small optical chain alive. If he fails, he will be sued for $400,000 on SBA loans. His major asset is a one-third interest in a million dollar commercial property that he co-owns as tenants-in-common with his two uncles, yet I cannot convince my client's uncles to re-title the property so that *everyone* is safer. After all, nobody's chasing *them!* We now have to use more costly procedures to protect his one-third interest.

- One co-owner's death can temporarily impede the other owner's use of the asset. For example, jointly owned bank accounts are sometimes frozen throughout the probate process, which can take years. In another example, a client owned valuable waterfront property with a partner as tenants-in-common. Unexpectedly, the partner was hit with a $700,000 IRS tax lien, which clouded the title to the entire property. The property cannot be sold until the IRS claim is resolved, and who knows how long that will take.

Everyday problems with co-ownerships arise only because people *don't think*. You must ask those important questions when you decide how to title your assets.

You can overcome almost every disadvantage that comes from personally co-owning assets by titling collectively-owned assets to a protective entity - whether a corporation, limited liability company, or limited partnership. It's part of the overriding strategy: Never own assets in your own name - and never in your own name together with others.

7

Inc. Yourself

The chief purpose of a corporation is to insulate personal assets (or the assets of other businesses) from the debts of the incorporated business. The corporation is a comparatively poor entity to hold or protect personal assets.

There are two major drawbacks with using the corporation as a personal asset protector: (1) When you transfer assets to and from the corporation, you create tax consequences, and (2) Personal creditors can seize the shares that you own in the corporation, as well as any obligations due you from the corporation. The limited liability company (LLC) and limited partnership (LP) overcome these corporate disadvantages and so play a far more important role in personal asset protection planning.

The ABCs of INCs

It is easy to understand the concept of a corporation and how you can most effectively use this for asset protection.

A corporation is a legal entity that is authorized to

conduct business or own assets as though it were a natural person. However, unlike a natural person, a corporation has a perpetual existence. It is owned by shareholders who invest in the corporation and share in its profits.

The mere mention of a corporation usually brings to mind Microsoft, General Motors or some other Fortune 500 company, yet more than 25 million corporations are owned by individuals or families to operate their own small businesses. They may also use corporations for other tax, estate planning or asset protection purposes. Many more people each year now discover the advantages of owning their own corporation. Incorporating is a small expense and brings big dividends. Here are some important features of a corporation:

- **Created by state law.** Each state sets its own requirements to establish and maintain a corporation. Some state laws, however, are more corporate-friendly than others.

- **Distinct legal entity.** You should understand that a corporation is a separate legal entity; it is separate in every way from its shareholders. For example, the corporation enjoys the same constitutional rights as a natural person. Similarly, assets titled to a corporation are owned by the corporation, not its corporate shareholders.

- **Limited liability of shareholders.** This, of course, is the key benefit of incorporating. A corporation protects the personal assets of its stockholders, officers, and directors from the debts of the incorporated business. Since a corporation is a legal entity distinct from its shareholders, its shareholders have no personal liability for the debts of the corporation. Shareholders can only lose their investment in the corporation (what they paid for their shares or loaned to the corporation) if the corporation is sued, cannot pay its debts or files bankruptcy.

- **Unlimited existence.** Unless the corporate articles state otherwise, the corporation can last in perpetuity. A stockholder's death does not terminate the corporation.
- **Centralized management.** Shareholders do not manage the corporation. Its board of directors, elected by the shareholders, set corporate policy. Daily operations are the responsibility of the corporate officers, who are appointed and supervised by the board (although the president may be elected by the shareholders).
- **There can be any number of shareholders.** Shareholders own the corporation and elect the board. The board of directors must have at least one director, although some states require more. One individual can, in most states, be the corporation's only shareholder, director, and serve every requisite office (president, secretary and treasurer).

In Business? Incorporate!

If you go into business by yourself, your choice is between a sole proprietorship, corporation or limited liability company (LLC). If your business has more than one owner, your choice is between a general partnership, corporation or LLC. (While you can always operate through a limited liability company, which I will discuss in a later chapter, for now, let's consider the LLC the same as a corporation as a liability insulator.)

Before I make my case for the corporation, let me first make my case *against* a sole proprietorship or general partnership. Let's begin with definitions.

A sole proprietorship form of organization exists when you operate your business without creating a formal legal entity such as a corporation or LLC. When you operate your business as a sole proprietorship, there is no legal separation between you and your business. You have personal liability for *every* business debt.

It is amazing in these litigious times that so many small businesses still function as sole proprietorships. Consider that four out of five small businesses fail within their first several years, and you can see that their owners needlessly gamble their family's financial security on the success of their venture. When their business fails, as most will, their owners will likely end in financial ruin as their business creditors grab their personal assets.

The general partnership is an even more dangerous form of business organization because the general partners are jointly and severally liable for every partnership liability. Partners in a general partnership can easily lose their personal wealth to creditors if the business or the other partners have too few personal assets to satisfy the partnership obligations. You can lose *your* wealth even if your partner created the liability.

As you can see, a major disadvantage with both the sole proprietorship and general partnership is that they create 'inside out' liability. Creditors of the proprietorship or partnership can go 'outside' the business to satisfy their claims from the owners' personal assets.

There is also 'outside in' exposure. An owner's personal creditors can seize his business assets to satisfy his personal debts. In the case of the general partnership, a partner's personal creditors can force the liquidation of the partnership to claim his equity in the business.

In contrast, a corporation is a separate legal entity distinct from its shareholders since the law looks upon the corporation as a separate person. That is why a corporation (or LLC) can protect your personal assets from the inevitable debts and lawsuits against your business. Because your corporation is its own legal entity, you as its shareholder, director or officer are not liable for the debts or lawsuits against your corporation. If your corporation is sued or cannot pay its debts, you lose *only* your investment in the business; your other assets remain safe. That is why the corporation is such a powerful wealthsaver.

Business owners frequently start their ventures as sole proprietorships or general partnerships and become concerned about losing their personal assets only when their business is sued or heads towards bankruptcy. Are you that business owner? You may still have the opportunity to avoid personal liability. Incorporate your business and transfer the assets of your proprietorship or partnership to the corporation. Your corporation then reduces the debts for which you have personal liability. While it may incur new corporate debts, however, these new debts are corporate obligations for which you would have no personal liability.

If you presently operate an unincorporated business, you should incorporate *before* you get into financial trouble. The smartest strategy, of course, is to incorporate before you start your business.

No business is too small to incorporate because no business is safe from lawsuits. Obviously, the larger enterprise has more need for corporate protection if only because it is a larger lawsuit target, but still no business, no matter how small or seemingly safe, is immune from legal and financial disasters.

Here is why I say *no* business is safe. Mrs. Humphrey, a wealthy widow from my own neighborhood, enjoyed spending her weekends selling imported dolls at a local flea market. However, not long ago Mrs. Humphrey sold a defective doll. A customer's three-year-old daughter punctured her eye by dislocating the doll's arm, exposing a large nail. Mrs. Humphrey is now defending herself (and her not insignificant wealth) against a $5 million product liability claim.

Had Mrs. Humphrey incorporated her tiny kiosk enterprise it would be her corporation, and not her, who would have the liability; Mrs. Humphrey's personal assets would not be in jeopardy. Why *didn't* Mrs. Humphrey incorporate? It was her accountant who discouraged her. "You don't need a corporation. Why spend money to incorporate to run a nickel-and-dime weekend business?" Bad advice! Had Mrs. Humphrey spent a few bucks to incorporate, she would not be worried sick about losing everything she owns. Incorporating is your *best* insurance.

More Corporate Advantages

The limited liability that the corporation provides its shareholders is certainly the one key reason to incorporate your business. However, a corporation can give additional benefits that are not always available with other entities:

- Employees can participate in corporate profits and defer their income in corporate retirement plans.
- Corporations frequently enjoy lower tax rates than individual taxpayers.
- Tax brackets may be split among several corporations, or you can multiply your tax deductions within the same corporation.
- Social Security payments are 50 percent deductible to the corporation.
- Trusts, limited partnerships, LLCs and other

protective entities can own a C corporation.

- It is frequently possible to consolidate the income and losses of one corporation with those of other corporations to reduce your overall income taxes.
- Corporate shares can be donated to maximize your deductible charitable contributions.
- Certain tax deductible fringe benefits may be available only through a C corporation.
- When you liquidate your corporation, you may advantageously defer or reduce your capital gains tax.

Saving Taxes with an S Corporation

The S corporation gives you the same limited liability protection as does the C corporation. Business owners frequently select S corporation designation to avoid the double taxation of a regular or C corporation. However, because the S corporation is taxed as a partnership or proprietorship (depending upon the number of owners), many people erroneously think that the S corporation similarly loses the limited liability feature of the C corporation. This is not so. Consider only the tax factor when you decide whether to choose S or C corporation status. This decision is best left to your accountant.

You will find it far easier to lawsuit-proof your stock ownership in a C corporation than an S corporation, because the S corporation must be owned by natural persons. C corporations, limited partnerships, LLCs and other legal entities, with few exceptions, cannot own shares of an S corporation. This gives you far fewer options to protect your S shares from your personal creditors. The S corporation has other key features:

- The S corporation has pass-through taxation. Corporate profits are taxed only once when they 'pass through' to the shareholders. The S corporation is thus taxed as a proprietorship or partnership. The corporation itself is not taxed, but its owners are.

- The S corporation is limited to 75 shareholders, and all shareholders must be US citizens or residents.
- The S corporation must be organized under US law, have only one class of stock and may not own 80 percent or more of the stock of another corporation.

You request S corporation status from the IRS. You can also change from C to S corporation status, within certain rigid IRS guidelines.

Corporation or Limited Liability Company?

An LLC is a similar entity to an S corporation since the owners of both entities enjoy limited liability and both entities can be taxed as a proprietorship or partnership. An LLC member's risk is also limited to his loss of investment. However, a chief asset protection advantage of the LLC over the S corporation is that the LLC affords you more ownership options. For example, your LLC can be owned by a family limited partnership (FLP), a trust, another corporation, etc. S corporation shares cannot be owned by these entities. Their stock ownership is restricted to individuals. Both estate and asset protection planning become more difficult with S corporation shares.

More importantly, an ownership interest in an LLC is considerably more creditor-protected than are shares in an S corporation, which can be easily seized by a stockholder's personal creditors. A member's interest in an LLC is creditor-protected in the same way a partnership interest in a limited partnership is protected. A member's personal creditor is limited only to a charging order against the LLC interest, which gives the creditor only the right to receive distributed profits due the debtor partners.

There are still a few advantages of an S corporation over an LLC: (1) An S corporation can be more tax advantageously acquired by another business; (2) S corporation owners pay employment taxes only on *their* salaries, while LLC owners pay employment taxes on *all* profits; and (3) State taxes may be lower for an S corporation.

Professionals and Professional Corporations

Although not all states allow professions a choice between professional or corporate structures, physicians, dentists, accountants, lawyers, architects and many other professionals may conduct their practice through a professional corporation. However, the limited liability partnerships (LLPs) are also becoming a popular organizational alternative. The number of professional corporations (PC) and professional associations (PA) rapidly grew in numbers during the 1980s when, in those pre-tax reform days, a professional could invest more money into corporate pension plans. Few professionals organized professional corporations for liability protection because there were then far fewer malpractice lawsuits. Moreover, professionals traditionally had less concern than business owners about everyday vendors and business debts because they were service providers who incurred few commercial liabilities. Although they knew that they could still be sued personally for malpractice even if they had an incorporated practice, professionals then, as now, viewed malpractice insurance as their traditional liability shield.

Today, the professional corporation is a far more protective tool for the professional. True, a professional can still be personally sued for negligence, but the professional corporation insulates against any personal liability that may arise from an employee's or associate's negligence, as well as contract claims, employee lawsuits, etc. It would be the corporation - not the professional - who would be sued because the corporation would be the employer of a negligent employee or the party responsible for the obligation.

Still, a surprising number of legal, accounting and physicians' groups continue to operate as general partnerships or loose-knit associations. These firms would greatly benefit from incorporating. The professional corporation would insulate each professional from the unlimited personal liability they can now incur because of their organizational structure.

I spend a large part of my time designing safer organizational arrangements for professionals. For example, we may have each professional in a group organize their own professional corporation. Their respective corporations would then form a partnership with each corporation as a partner. If the partnership incurs a liability, the creditors' recourse would be against the partnership assets, and this limits recovery to the assets of the respective partner corporations. In this way each professional's personal assets remain safe.

The professional corporation is not always the professional's best organizational choice. A business corporation may offer the professional one major advantage over the professional corporation: The professional need not own a business corporation, as they must with the professional corporation. A business corporation may be owned by the professional's spouse, another protective entity (such as an LLC, trust or limited partnership), or in some other way that shields the corporate ownership. Other organizational options include the limited liability partnership (LLP), which is particularly suitable for attorneys and accountants.

In certain states a professional can use either a professional or business corporation; much depends on the specific profession. For example, chiropractors can frequently use a business corporation, although medical doctors are usually limited to the professional corporation by state medical regulations.

Maintain Corporate Protection

Merely operating a business through a corporation does not always mean that some corporate creditor won't try to sue you personally to collect a defaulted corporate debt or try to hold you personally responsible for some corporate mishap. Corporate creditors do sue their owners personally.

These corporate creditors try to pierce the corporate veil to get to their owners' personal assets. They usually claim that their owners are only alter-egos of their corporation. Can they succeed? Possibly, if the owner does not follow basic corporate formalities.

It is not difficult to correctly operate a corporation or any other legal entity. Your one goal is to always treat your entity as independent from you personally and any other entity. If you don't, your corporate creditor can successfully argue that you and your corporation are indeed one and the same and you lose corporate protection. You can avoid such trouble by respecting your entity:

- **Don't commingle assets:** Operate your corporation as a distinct entity, one separate from you personally in every respect. For example, document whatever assets you transfer between you and your corporation. Record all transactions on both your personal and corporate records. Document financial transactions between related corporations or other entities.
- **Sign your corporate documents as a corporate agent:** If you operate through a corporation, your

legal documents should say so. Disclose your corporate name and title alongside your signature on all documents.

- **Operate each corporation autonomously:** Do you own multiple entities? The officers or directors of related corporations should occupy different positions, conduct separate corporate meetings and maintain separate corporate books.

- **Keep adequate corporate records:** Business creditors frequently pierce corporations when their records fail to properly document key corporate actions. Record every major director and shareholder vote. You can find inexpensive software to help you instantly prepare your corporate records without a lawyer.

- **Don't voluntarily dissolve your corporation:** If you voluntarily dissolve your corporation, you lose your corporate protection. Pay all corporate taxes and franchise fees. Keep your corporation in good standing. Do not voluntarily dissolve your corporation if it has outstanding debts, or these corporate debts automatically become your personal obligations as its corporate stockholder.

Observe all corporate formalities. Does your corporation have its own business address? Telephone number? Do you have cancelled corporate checks to show that your corporation pays its own expenses? Does your corporation have the necessary business licenses? Checking and bank accounts? Each compliance point establishes your corporation as a legitimate entity - one separate from you as its owner.

Creditors who try to pierce the corporate veil on the basis that the corporation is only a stockholder's sham alter-ego has a difficult burden. Courts only reluctantly dismiss a corporation's important liability protection unless its owners flagrantly ignore corporate formalities.

I usually find a business creditor's lawsuit against the corporate owner to be only an effort by the creditor to force the business owner to defend the lawsuit or settle. That's when you need a combative attorney, someone who will countersue the creditor *and* his attorney for frivolous bad faith litigation.

Incorporation as a Total Shield

If you are in business, then incorporating is an absolute must if you want *outside* protection; your only other option is the LLC. While incorporating does not give you complete protection from *every* business creditor, incorporation is nevertheless an important first step to protect yourself against nine out of ten lawsuits.

- **Incorporating protects you from tort claims and business debts.** You shield your personal wealth from the most common lawsuits against your business when you incorporate; for example, negligence claims (slip-and-falls, car accidents, etc.) or claims by employees (responsibility for the acts or omissions of your employees, employment discrimination, etc.). You also shield yourself from corporate contract claims and debts if you did not personally guarantee the contract or debt.
- **Incorporating protects you from customer claims.** Incorporating usually protects you against claims from selling goods or services to your clients or customers. This includes product liability claims, negligence, breach of warranty and employee's malpractice lawsuits, which often bring huge jury awards.

- **Incorporating won't protect you on personally guaranteed debts**. Those conducting business with a corporation often require that an officer (i.e. president, vice president, etc.) or principal stockholder sign a personal guarantee on the corporation's debt. For example, a landlord may want the owner's personal guarantee on a corporate lease for business premises. If your corporation breaches the lease, the landlord can then sue the owner personally on the guarantee. Debts guaranteed personally for your corporation override corporate protection.

- **Incorporating won't protect you when you personally cause the harm.** If you personally caused the harm for which someone sues, you are not protected by the corporate shield. For example, if you negligently drive the corporate car and cause an accident, the victim can sue both the corporation and you, because you were personally negligent. Similarly, a physician would be personally sued for his own malpractice, notwithstanding that he was employed by an incorporated group practice.

- **Incorporating won't protect you as a corporate officer.** This is true for certain tax liabilities and other governmental claims against the corporation for which officers and even directors, in some circumstances, have statutory responsibility.

Avoid Corporate Guarantees

To the extent small business owners guarantee their corporate obligations, it obviously reduces the usefulness of their corporation as a liability insulator.

Major debts, particularly bank loans, inevitably require the small business owner's personal guarantee. However, you can sidestep guarantees demanded by most other creditors (as well as escape liability on existing guarantees) with some common sense and a tougher attitude.

If one supplier demands your guarantee, then find others who won't make your guarantee only another bargaining point for credit. You can locate prospective suppliers who will extend to your corporation at least limited credit without your personal guarantee. That is why I say that when one supplier demands your guarantee, find a more lenient supplier.

However, understand your creditor's concerns. Try to reduce his risk. You can then more successfully convince your creditor to forego your guarantee. For instance, a supplier who refuses to extend your corporation $20,000 on credit without your personal guarantee may risk $10,000. Perhaps the supplier will accept alternative collateral or a security interest on business assets instead of your personal guarantee or a guarantee from an affiliated corporation.

If you must sign a guarantee, then negotiate for a partial guarantee that limits your exposure. Insist that your creditor cancel your guarantee once your business establishes its own good track record for prompt payment.

Here's another cardinal rule: never guarantee an existing debt. Why should you? You gain nothing. Yet, once a business falters, creditors plead, promise, threaten and cajole for the owner's personal guarantee. It would be foolish, however, to risk personal assets to secure an already shaky corporate obligation. Nor can you assume that your business will someday pay its obligations. Companies seriously in trouble seldom fully pay their debts.

Your partners, of course, should sign the same guarantees that you sign. Note that if your partners are less wealthy than you, your creditor will chase you for payment. Creditors pursue the deepest pockets. You want a partner whose pockets are as deep as yours.

If you have already signed numerous personal guarantees, there is a way to extricate yourself from these obligations. To begin, verify which obligations you guaranteed. Many businesspeople do not know which debts are guaranteed. The guarantee may have been part of an original order form or credit application. Ask every creditor whether they have your personal guarantee and request copies.

Next, terminate outstanding guarantees. You can always revoke guarantees for future credit and you should revoke your guarantees to avoid further liability. Also, do not forget to cancel outstanding guarantees for future purchases when you sell your business.

If your business is in financial trouble, you want to float your floundering business while you fully pay any personally guaranteed debts before your company fails or secure your guaranteed creditors with a mortgage on the business assets. Your guaranteed creditors will be paid from the liquidation of the business before the non-guaranteed creditors. This greatly reduces the odds that you will someday be forced to pay these debts from your own pocket.

Your final objective is to negotiate releases from outstanding guarantees. Here you need bargaining power. For example, a creditor who is owed $20,000 may accept $20,000 in return merchandise, or $10,000 in cash, or a mortgage on business assets in exchange for canceling your personal guarantee. Do you owe your bank $500,000? Perhaps they will tear up your guarantee if you agree to help the bank recover more than they could on their own when they liquidate your business. Secured lenders typically need the business owner's cooperation to maximize their recovery. Bargain your cooperation for those concessions that reduce or eliminate your personal exposure.

Of course, some creditors or lenders who hold your guarantee won't release you for your cooperation. Will this same creditor respond to less friendly overtures? For example, threatening Chapter 11 may forestall foreclosure and this would not necessarily be to your creditor's advantage. You have many bargaining chips to coax creditors to cancel guarantees. Use the 'carrot and stick' approach. It works when you deal with guaranteed creditors.

If you personally paid a guaranteed corporate debt, you also can indemnify and reimburse yourself from your corporation. Set up properly, you can have your corporation give you an indemnification and a security interest on its assets to secure this indemnification. You then have a priority right to be reimbursed from the corporation before your unsecured creditors get paid. Bankruptcy courts frequently set aside 'insider' mortgages when the business goes bankrupt within the year, so you want to secure yourself earlier or liquidate your business without bankruptcy in this instance.

Why a Corporation Should Not Shelter Personal Assets

This chapter so far primarily discussed *outside protection* or personal asset protection that a corporation can provide you if you operate an active business; but now let's return to the idea of using your own passive corporation to safeguard your personal assets. This is *inside protection*.

For a corporation to give you inside protection, you must transfer your personal wealth to the corporation. You would no longer personally own your boat, car, paintings, etc.; your corporation does. Your personal creditor could not directly claim the assets owned by the corporation. However, they could seize your corporate shares. That's the problem. Whatever ownership interest you have in the corporation, your creditor could seize and control. If you own a controlling interest, your creditor would indirectly control your corporation's assets. This shows that you can never safely use the corporation alone to protect personal assets. *You must use it in combination with other asset protection tools* to adequately shield your assets.

Nevertheless, a corporation can provide temporary shelter for personal assets. For instance, in one memorable case, a client transferred $100,000 to a Nevada corporation only two days before a creditor won a sizeable judgment against him. Had my client kept the bank account titled in his own name, the creditor would have immediately levied the account. With his funds temporarily titled to a corporate account in another state, the creditor would first have to go through discovery before the creditor could find and seize the corporate shares. Of course, this gave us ample time to create a safer repository for his money.

In sum, the problem with using a corporation to protect personal assets is that you literally 'chase your tail.' While your assets are no longer exposed, your shares are now vulnerable.

For asset protection, you must find ways to protectively title your corporate shares. They cannot be owned by you personally. You have options:

- **Married? Transfer most or all of the corporate shares to your less vulnerable spouse, who would then control the corporation.** One obvious problem with this solution, of course, is that you no longer control the corporation. Consider whether this arrangement meets your personal, estate planning or divorce-proofing objectives.

- **Title the shares with a family limited partnership (FLP)**. For example, the husband and wife may become the general partners and control the partnership assets. They may also be the limited partners, or other beneficiaries such as children, friends, charities, etc. may be the limited partners. As the general partners, the husband and wife would then *control* the partnership that owns the corporation, which in turn would own the assets. Indirectly, the husband and wife, of course, control the assets, but they would not *personally* own the assets nor the shares of stock of the corporation that owns the assets. Since the assets are now owned by the corporation, they cannot be claimed by the couples' personal creditors, assuming that the transfer of the assets to the corporation were not fraudulent.

- **Transfer the corporate shares to an irrevocable trust set up for your children or other beneficiaries.** For example, the husband and wife may become the co-trustees and manage the trust that controls the corporation. The couple would indirectly control the corporate assets without directly owning the corporation shares.

- **Title the shares to an LLC.** As with a limited partnership, a member's personal creditor cannot seize a membership interest in the LLC. Again, you must beware of fraudulent transfer laws if you now have creditors.

- **Title the shares to an offshore trust or Nevis LLC.** Both the offshore trust and foreign LLC can well protect your corporate shares. Combine the offshore trust with the limited partnership as the corporate shareholder to substantially strengthen the arrangement. Titling shares of a US-based corporation to an offshore company also 'privatizes' your ownership; however, a judge can force you to surrender your shares in an offshore corporation to your creditor. Therefore, this plan is not recommended, although it is a common arrangement.

- **Title your shares as tenants-by-the-entirety.** If you co-own your shares with your spouse in a state that adequately protects corporate shares, then tenancy-by-the-entirety may give your stock ownership sufficient protection when only one spouse has creditors.

Each of these strategies is illustrated in other chapters, but for the moment, understand that for your personal corporation to protect your personal assets, you cannot directly own the corporate shares. You must layer your protection with trusts, limited partnerships or other protective entities as the owner of your corporate shares.

Also, when *inside* protection is your goal, then you want a *passive* personal corporation. A corporation that engages in business will incur liabilities and you risk losing your personal assets that would be owned by the corporation to any business creditors. Another danger is that corporations used primarily to hold personal assets create serious 'holding' corporation tax problems. C corporations are subject to double taxation. While S corporations are only singly taxed, they cannot be owned by a trust, partnership or any other protective entity. More importantly, the IRS heavily taxes passive income of holding corporations.

As you can see, there are tax traps. Before you set up a corporation for 'inside' protection, review the idea carefully with your accountant for its tax consequences. You will soon understand why limited partnerships, limited liability companies and other entities better protect your personal assets.

To avoid corporate shares from seizure by creditors, many debtors camouflage their ownership interest. Diligent creditors can usually identify corporate shareholders by examining corporate books, tax returns, licensing applications, public records, etc. You can more easily conceal an ownership interest using a Nevada or Wyoming corporation - two states that allow for bearer shares. Unless you actually possess the bearer shares, you can truthfully deny ownership. If you have already incorporated elsewhere, then your corporation may be owned by a Nevada or Wyoming corporation, or a foreign corporation in an offshore privacy haven can be your parent company. International business corporations (IBCs) in several jurisdictions also allow bearer shares, or you can register the shares to a nominee 'straw.' Of course, you will need your lawyer to guide you on these strategies so that you do not commit perjury or incur tax problems concerning your corporate ownership. For less visibility and connection to the corporation, resign as a corporate officer or director. Officers or directors of closely held corporations are suspect as having some ownership or financial interest.

'Poison' Your Corporate Shares

When creditors are in hot pursuit, you can quickly sell any publicly traded stocks or bonds, but what do you do as a stockholder of a privately owned corporation? How can you easily or quickly sell your shares? The answer is that you probably can't. Still, you can make your shares nearly worthless to your creditors.

- **Impose transfer restrictions on your shares.** Corporate restrictions on the transfer of shares generally won't prevent creditor seizure; however, restrictions can discourage a less aggressive or knowledgeable creditor. Restrictions on transfer must be reasonable to be enforceable, but creditors won't usually incur the cost or effort to challenge even unreasonable restrictions.

- **Assess your shares.** If your shares are not fully paid or if the shares are assessable by the corporation, then a creditor who seizes your shares takes them subject to your obligation to pay the assessment. Obviously, a potential assessment by the corporation reduces the value of the shares to your creditor by the amount of the potential assessment. An 'assessment' can be a particularly effective 'poison pill,' and I frequently include 'assessment provisions' in corporate documents as an anti-creditor device.

- **Issue irrevocable proxies.** A proxy is an assignment of your right to vote your shares. For example, you may issue a proxy to a relative, etc. A creditor who seizes your shares cannot vote your shares because the voting powers have been irrevocably assigned to the proxy holder. This, too, will significantly lessen the stock's value to the creditor, since the creditor would gain no voting rights in the corporation. If you are sued, you may exchange voting shares for non-voting shares, which will also be of less value to creditors.

- **Dilute your stock ownership.** Why allow a creditor to seize a controlling interest in your business? If you own a controlling interest, dilute your ownership. If and when it becomes necessary, you can have the corporation sell additional shares to other family members or to family controlled entities (trusts, limited partnerships, etc.). A creditor who seizes a minority ownership interest in the corporation cannot, of course, control the corporation. As a minority stockholder, the creditor only has the right to vote his or her shares and await whatever dividends may be declared. It is sometimes wise to spread the stock ownership in a family owned corporation between family members so that no one family member owns more than 49 percent of the voting shares. The by-laws would empower the remaining 51 percent to control the corporation.

- **Pledge your shares.** Another option is to pledge your shares as collateral to a friendlier creditor. If the amount borrowed approximates the value of your shares, your creditor will chase shares with no equity. Chapter 12 shows you many ways to create a friendly mortgage and encumber your shares.

Check Nevada for Incorporating

Corporations are creations of state law, and state laws differ, so there may be advantages and disadvantages of incorporating in a particular state. How do you decide where to incorporate? If your corporation operates an active business in only one state, then it is probably best to incorporate in that state where you will do business. If you set up an out-of-state corporation, it must register as a foreign corporation in your home state. This subjects the corporation to your home state laws, and to some extent it will nullify advantages of incorporating elsewhere.

If your corporation will not operate a business (a passive corporation) or if you have flexibility as to where to incorporate, then Delaware is a good choice. Most of America's largest corporations are Delaware corporations. Many more corporations, particularly smaller corporations, are organized in Nevada, which has been America's 'Incorporation Capital.'

Nevada's corporate laws are better than Delaware and all other states, except Wyoming, whose corporation laws follow those of Nevada. The following are advantages of Nevada incorporation

- Delaware taxes corporate profits while Nevada is tax-free. Delaware is more costly tax-wise if you expect big profits.
- Nevada won't share tax information with the IRS. Every other state, including Delaware, exchanges information.
- Delaware has a franchise tax, but Nevada does not.
- Delaware requires extensive annual disclosures. (Stockholder meeting dates, business localities outside Delaware, number and value of shares issued, etc.) Nevada requires only a current list of officers and directors.
- Nevada corporate stockholders may hold anonymous bearer shares.
- Nevada's corporate officers and directors have far broader protection than do Delaware's. For example, Nevada corporations can eliminate or limit the personal liability of officers and directors for breach of fiduciary duty (other than improper dividend payments). Nevada also has a shorter statute of limitations to sue for improper dividends and offer more opportunities for director indemnification. Delaware director indemnification is at the court's discretion; in Nevada it is an absolute right.
- Nevada allows for broader indemnities to others who incur liability on behalf of the corporation. The use

of insurance trust funds, self-insurance and granting directors a security interest or lien on the corporate assets to guarantee their indemnifications are a few examples. For asset protection purposes, the absolute authority of corporate officers and directors to lien the corporate assets to indemnify themselves gives them a priority claim over their corporate assets without the need to prove an exchange of funds. This strategy can be critical for asset protection. Delaware and every other state will invalidate such self-serving legal arrangements. Absent fraud, a Nevada board of directors' decision concerning such financial arrangements is conclusive and cannot be voided by the courts.

- Many astute business owners now set up Nevada corporations, so you find many firms who can offer complete incorporation and resident agent services to their nationwide clients. Order *How to Establish and Operate Your Own Nevada Corporation* (Garrett Publishing) to learn how to quickly and inexpensively form your own Nevada corporation. For faster, more comprehensive service, call Nevada Corporate Planners (888-627-7007). They are a superb and ethical Nevada corporate formation firm that provides a wide range of corporate and small business services.

8

Lawsuit-Proofing With Limited Partnerships

More astute Americans than ever are forming limited partnerships (LP) to shelter their wealth. There are several very good reasons for the popularity of limited partnerships. The limited partnership ensures continuous succession of property ownership and control over the assets between generations while protecting this wealth from lawsuits, creditors, and to some extent, gift and estate taxation. The versatile limited partnership has helped thousands of families maintain their wealth with optimum protection. Few other legal entities can match the limited partnership's advantages or its many benefits.

The limited partnership, or family limited partnership (FLP), although it need not necessarily involve family members, is not a new entity. The limited partnership's long tradition in asset protection, tax and estate planning began in 1916 when the states first adopted the Uniform Limited Partnership Act (ULPA), now revised in some states as the

Revised Uniform Limited Partnership Act (RULPA). This long history characterizes the limited partnership's stability, predictability and dependability for achieving so many wealth preservation objectives.

If you attend seminars or read books about asset protection, you will unquestionably discover that the family limited partnership is the cornerstone to many wealth preservation plans.

I organize hundreds of family limited partnerships each year, and I have yet to have a limited partnership fail in protecting a client's assets. That's a strong endorsement for the limited partnership.

If you want to lawsuit-proof your personal assets, you, of course, have a choice of organizational entities to achieve your legal and financial goals. Each entity type has its own unique characteristics and features, and selecting the best entity involves many considerations.

Your range of choices will, of course, also depend greatly upon the intended purpose of the entity. For instance, if the limited partnership is to conduct business, you must evaluate it against the sole proprietorship, limited liability company and corporation.

If your goal is tax reduction, estate planning or asset protection, then you must weigh the limited partnership against various trusts, limited liability companies and other methods to safely title these assets. Alternative entities may be preferable to the limited partnership in certain circumstances.

You must consider many factors as you evaluate each possible entity. Compare their advantages and disadvantages and decide which are most important to you.

Limited Partnership Fundamentals

A limited partnership has at least one general partner and one limited partner. The limited partnership's general partner(s) have the same rights and liabilities of a partner in a general partnership, namely the right to manage the partnership. They also have unlimited personal liability for the partnership debts. The limited partners, on the other hand, have no managerial authority and their personal liability is limited to their investment in the partnership. In terms of insulation from partnership debts, limited partners have essentially the same protection as corporate stockholders.

However, stockholders in a corporation can lose their corporate shares to their personal creditors. In contrast, a partner in a limited partnership cannot lose his interest in the limited partnership to his personal creditors. Later I explain this point in greater detail, but for now, you can see the significant creditor protection advantage that the limited partnership offers.

General and limited partners in a limited partnership may contribute money, assets or a service, or a combination in return for their partnership interest. The general partner also has complete authority to run the limited partnership.

If the limited partnership can incur liability, then the general partner should be a corporation or LLC. A creditor of the limited partnership can then only pursue the assets of the corporation or LLC as its general partner. The assets of its stockholders or members would be safe. The corporation or LLC, owning only a nominal interest in the limited partnership, would only have modest exposure, and whatever assets the corporation or LLC owns can be protected through other asset protection strategies. A corporation or LLC general partner owned and managed by limited partners does not change the situation, because the corporation is a party separate and distinct from its principals.

Limited partnerships operate like general partnerships

except that they have limited partners. A limited partner contributes cash or other assets to the partnership and receives distributions based on his or her partnership interest. The limited partner, however, has no direct control over the partnership or its assets. Historically, the limited partner was the 'silent' partner, or the partner who did not want his or her identity revealed and did not want to run the company. Instead he or she simply wished to passively invest in the business and receive a profit.

Today's limited partner need not remain anonymous, but contributes assets to the business and still has no significant say in the affairs of the company. In exchange, the limited partner receives distributions from the partnership and enjoys limited liability. A limited partner's assets cannot be claimed if the company loses money or incurs debt.

While a limited partner cannot give orders or directives to the general partner, a limited partner can provide advisory opinions. The limited partner's name should not be part of the partnership name, nor can the limited partner in any other way create the inference that the limited partner manages the business, although he or she is, in fact, an owner. A general partner may also be a limited partner. In this instance, the individual has unlimited liability arising from the role of general partner.

Limited partners can access the partnership's financial records to the extent that corporate shareholders have the right to inspect corporate records. Limited partners also have the right to other information, such as documents filed with the state and any amendments, copies of the original partnership agreement and any amendments, a list of partners, their addresses, contributions, shares in profits and losses, all partnership income tax returns and any records of the business that are not considered proprietary information.

General partners must furnish the limited partners with the information needed to complete their federal and state income tax returns. Unless the partnership agreement provides otherwise, no limited partner may be required to make additional contributions to the limited partnership, and no limited partner in any way has priority rights over any other limited partner. Most importantly, the limited partners have certain voting rights specified in the partnership agreement or under the Uniform Limited Partnership Act (ULPA).

Forming Your Limited Partnership

To prepare a good limited partnership agreement, you need the right assistance. A qualified attorney is essential to prepare an agreement that meets all governmental standards as well as your own personal needs and requirements.

The best attorney is not necessarily your lawyer cousin or your racquetball partner; find a specialist. Friends and business acquaintances who have recently formed partnerships or corporations may provide referrals, as can the local division of the American Bar Association.

Each partner should consult their own attorneys as you may have conflicts of interest when one professional represents multiple parties. While you may trust your partners, you seldom share the same needs and goals. Your attorney must protect *you*.

To create the limited partnership, you must file with the state a certificate of limited partnership, also called a certificate of organization or registration statement. Once approved, the state issues a charter or other document acknowledging its formal existence.

Most states have their own form of certificate that can be obtained from the Secretary of State's office. Several states have no form, but require you to file your own prepared certificate containing certain points:

- Name of the limited partnership
- Address of the partnership
- Name and address of the general partner
- Name and address of the resident agent
- General activities or purpose of the limited partnership
- Mandatory dissolution date.

Some states require additional information, so you should check your state's requirements. The certificate normally does not list the limited partners, nor is the limited partnership agreement filed as a public record.

Once your certificate of limited partnership has been filed and approved, you apply to the IRS for an employer's identification number (EIN) by completing and returning Form SS-4 to the IRS. If you already have an employer identification number for a retirement account or because you have had employees prior to registering as a limited partnership, you nevertheless need a new number because the limited partnership is a new entity. You may also need a tax identification number from your state; check with your state tax department. The simplest way to obtain your number is to telefax the SS-4 application to the IRS. This should bring you a number within a week, as opposed to four or more weeks when the application is mailed.

Once the limited partnership obtains its taxpayer (SS-4) number, it should open its own bank accounts and set up recordkeeping. It is important to remember that funds and other assets belonging to the limited partnership must be kept separate and apart from your own funds as well as funds belonging to other entities because it is viewed in the eyes of the law as a legal entity separate and apart from the owner(s).

Hence, to avoid potential IRS problems, you must maintain separate records for the limited partnership separate from your personal affairs. As a rule, however, it is not necessary to maintain an elaborate bookkeeping system. Separate bank accounts and bookkeeping that clearly show what you and the limited partnership separately earn and pay out are usually sufficient. A local bookkeeper or accountant can easily set up a convenient accounting and tax system for your partnership.

Transferring Assets to Your Limited Partnership

There is a difference between the assets your limited partnership *can* own and what assets it *should* own. The limited partnership is not an ideal entity to hold certain assets, although it would be legally permissible. There are many considerations when you select which assets your limited partnership should own.

If the limited partnership has a specific business purpose, then the limited partnership should own only those assets necessary to fulfill that function. For example, a limited partnership organized to develop real estate should not own unrelated assets, such as personal investments. Obviously you would not use a limited partnership to own your own assets with a number of unrelated partners. Here you would invest only in proportion to the other partners, usually cash or other assets to be utilized to further the business or investment interests of the partnership.

Your limited partnership can possibly protect all, or at least a significant percentage, of your wealth. For instance, your limited partnership can own:

- Cash
- Stocks, bonds, and other investments
- Vehicles
- Real estate

- Antiques, art and collectibles
- LLC memberships
- Other limited partnership interests
- Intangible assets (copyrights, patents, etc.)
- Claims against others
- Notes/mortgages/other obligations due you
- Beneficial interests in trusts
- C corporation shares.

As a rule, your limited partnership should only own income-producing or appreciating assets, which is ostensibly the reason for setting up your limited partnership.

Under S corporation rules, the limited partnership cannot own S corporation shares. It also should not own annuities, because you would then lose their tax deferral status.

Your limited partnership also cannot own IRAs or other retirement accounts; however, your retirement account can invest its funds in your limited partnership, which then protects your IRA.

A limited partnership should not be used to operate a business since the general partners would incur liability for the partnership debts. The corporation or limited liability company is preferable to operate a business.

Also, do not title your home to a limited partnership. A creditor can argue that your home is not an 'investment or business related' asset, and this could persuade a court to disregard your limited partnership. You would also lose two tax benefits that are yours when you personally own your home; the deduction on mortgage interest and the capital gains rollover. Still, some limited partnership promoters recommend titling the home to a limited partnership. Generally, that's poor advice. There are better alternatives for protecting your home - for example, transferring it to a single-member limited liability company would be preferable.

Use Multiple Limited Partnerships

Multiple limited partnerships can maximize your asset safety. Even when the limited partnership is your best organizational choice, don't title all your assets to the same limited partnership. Segregate your assets within multiple limited partnerships. If one limited partnership encounters financial or legal problems, it won't jeopardize the assets titled to the other limited partnerships. Remember the axiom, 'Never put all your eggs in one basket.'

Separate safe or 'no risk' assets from liability-producing or 'at risk' assets. For example, you may title surplus cash, stocks, bonds and mutual funds within one limited partnership because they are 'no risk' assets. They may decrease in value, but they will not create liabilities or creditor problems that would jeopardize these assets.

Commercial properties belong in a separate limited partnership because they are 'at risk' assets that can create liability. For example, a tenant who sues for negligent maintenance of the building has recourse against the assets held by that specific limited partnership. You would not want to expose your 'no risk' assets to this potential litigant.

I have clients who have deployed their assets amongst ten or more separate limited partnerships. Individuals with extensive commercial property holdings often prefer a separate limited partnership for each property to decrease their exposure as much as possible. Some large property owners have many limited partnerships to match their separate properties. However, it is generally preferable to title investment real estate to limited liability companies which are better liability insulators.

How the Limited Partnership
Creditor-Proofs Your Assets

The limited partnership has become the cornerstone for protecting domestic (US-based) assets for several reasons. With the limited partnership, you can maintain complete control over your assets as the general partner and indirectly own the assets through ownership of a limited partnership interest. Correctly drafted, assets transferred to the limited partnership become fully protected and beyond the reach of any future creditor, including the IRS and other governmental claimants. Most asset protection attorneys share my view that the limited partnership is generally the most advantageous domestic entity for protecting assets which it is why it is the foundation for safeguarding assets situated within the United States.

When considering the limited partnership for asset protection, the two central questions are:

- How does a limited partnership protect assets?
- How much protection does a limited partnership provide?

To answer these questions, you must understand the specific rights and limitations of a partner's personal creditor when that partner's assets are protected through ownership in a limited partnership. Generally, a creditor of a limited partner can attempt to seize only three types of assets:

- the limited partnership interest
- any profits or distributions payable to the limited partner
- those assets previously transferred to the limited partnership by that debtor-partner.

Let's examine each possibility:

1. Seizure of the Limited Partnership Interest

A creditor of a limited or general partner cannot seize his limited partnership interest. A judgment creditor of a limited partner can only apply to the court for a charging order against the limited partnership interest. The charging order only gives the creditor the right to claim any profit or liquidation proceeds payable to the limited partner.

The charging order does not make the creditor a substitute partner, nor does it give the creditor any partnership rights except to claim profits or distributions payable to the debtor-partner. For example, the creditor cannot sell or auction the partnership interest, nor can the creditor vote as a limited partner or even inspect the partnership books. In sum, the creditor becomes only an assignee of the limited partnership interest for the purposes of collecting any profits or distributions voted by the general partners and actually paid to the limited partner.

The charging order's central purpose is to protect the partners that are not involved in the debts of the debtor-partner from any undue interference in the affairs of the partnership by that creditor. This is distinguished from a typical corporation where a shareholder's creditors can force the sale of the debtor-shareholder's shares with the buyer becoming a successor stockholder with all the rights of a stockholder. This one distinction makes the limited partnership useful for safeguarding wealth.

2. Seizure of Profits or Liquidation Distributions

If the creditor's right to claim distributed profits or liquidating proceeds due the debtor-partner is his sole remedy, how practical is that remedy? Consider its limitations.

First, partnership profits can be illusive, particularly when the limited partnership is family-owned or the interests of the partners are closely aligned, as is the case for most limited partnerships.

Second, the decision of distributing profits belongs exclusively to the general partners. The creditor cannot force a distribution.

Thus, the limited partnership can simply defer any profit distributions until the charging order creditor loses patience and settles; nor will this deferral strategy necessarily deprive the debtor-partner access to partnership funds. The debtor-partner may accept loans, salaries, consulting fees or payments for other assets he may sell to the limited partnership. The debtor-partner can also divert profits to other interconnected entities that may transact business with the limited partnership, and thus become a protected conduit for partnership earnings. These funds would not be subject to the charging order because they are not a distribution of profits or proceeds from liquidation.

Third, you can structure your limited partnership to allocate a higher percentage of the profits to the other partners, who nevertheless may own a lesser percentage of the partnership. Thus, you may own, for example, 90 percent of the limited partnership but be entitled to only 10 percent of its profits. This 10 percent would be the only vulnerable profit distribution. Indeed, the opportunities are endless to defeat the creditor from ever receiving partnership profits. A creditor awaiting profit distribution can be in for a long, frustrating, profitless wait.

Of course, the ability to frustrate a creditor may not be so easy if you are only a minority limited partner in a limited partnership with hundreds of investors and an unaffiliated general partner whose interests and agenda may not parallel that of the debtor-partner. Should a partnership generate a constant and substantial profit stream, the creditor's charging order may produce payment. The debtor-partner's only option would then be to sell or encumber his partnership interest or assign future partnership profits to another protected entity - perhaps another limited partnership under his control.

Thus, a creditor is in a far better position when the debtor-partner cannot control or influence the distribution of profits, such as when the limited partnership includes large numbers of unrelated partners. A 2 percent debtor-partner who receives consistently large cash dividends will lose those dividends to a charging order creditor, and, in this instance, the limited partnership becomes far less advantageous an asset protector.

In fact, few creditors ever get a charging order for one good reason: The charging order creditor becomes automatically liable to pay the taxes on all partnership profits allocable to the debtor-partner - even when the creditor receives no payment or profit distributions from the partnership.

Consider the plight of a creditor holding a charging order against a limited partner with a 50 percent partnership interest. Assume that the partnership earns $100,000 in a particular year, with $50,000 allocated to the debtor-partner, who would normally pay the taxes on this $50,000. Instead, the charging order creditor assumes the partner's tax liability, whether or not he receives the distribution. A creditor in a 35 percent tax bracket thus has a $17,500 tax bill each year the charging order is in effect and the debtor-partner has similar allocable profit. Meanwhile, because no profits have been actually distributed, the creditor has a $17,500 tax liability and still has received no cash. Conversely, the debtor would enjoy $50,000 tax-free retained earnings within the limited partnership.

Under IRS Revenue Rule 77-137, the tax obligation becomes entirely the obligation of the charging order creditor and the creditor, not the debtor-partner, receives the K-1 reported to the IRS. Some states even prohibit a charging order creditor from releasing the charging order without the consent of the debtor-partner - a consent the debtor-partner with taxable income may understandably withhold. Thus, the charging order cannot reasonably be seen as an effective weapon, but more realistically as a device that can give the creditor only a tax bill instead of a payment.

3. Recovering Assets Transferred to the Limited Partnership

A third possible remedy is for the creditor to ignore the charging order remedy and instead attempt to set aside any prior transfer of assets from the debtor to the limited partnership. With these assets no longer in the partnership, they would then be unprotected and subject to creditor seizure.

This is frequently a far more threatening possibility than the dangers from a charging order, and creditors often recover assets fraudulently transferred to the limited partnership. Of course, a creditor cannot directly claim limited partnership assets because the assets no longer belong to the debtor-partner, but are owned by the limited partnership under a tenancy-by-partnership. That is why if the creditor is to obtain access to the assets, he must first rescind the prior transfer to the partnership as a fraudulent transfer.

Creditors do, of course, have remedies when assets are fraudulently transferred to a limited partnership or any other party. For example, if you owe a creditor $100,000, you might transfer $70,000 in cash to the limited partnership so that the creditor cannot seize your cash. This could constitute a fraudulent transfer and the cash may be recoverable from the partnership (or any other transferee) by the creditor.

The result, nevertheless, is far from certain. Much depends upon how you structure your limited partnership. For instance, if you and your wife each contribute $70,000 and each obtain in exchange a 50 percent partnership interest, then the court may agree that the transfer was a 'fair consideration' exchange because you now own one-half of a limited partnership with assets worth $140,000, or an interest mathematically equal to your original $70,000. However, if you and your wife each contributed $70,000, but you obtained a disproportionately smaller partnership interest - or no interest, then you essentially 'gave away' at least part of your money, and at least that portion would be recoverable by your present creditors.

Many debtors overlook this point and hurriedly transfer their assets to the limited partnership for a disproportionately small partnership interest because they want little or no interest subject to a creditor's charging order. They probably also overlook the fact that the creditor would pay the larger share of the taxes on partnership profits if they had owned more. This is always poor planning, because a present creditor can then successfully argue that the transfer was without fair consideration and thus a fraudulent transfer.

Even when the consideration is fair, it does not guarantee that a court will not set aside such a transfer made against a present creditor. Many courts find that merely impairing a present creditor from collection is sufficient to constitute a fraudulent transfer, even when the consideration (the limited partnership interest) has a value corresponding to the value of the asset transferred.

Because the law on this point varies between states and individual cases, you cannot assume that any transfer to a limited partnership made against a present creditor is safe. The limited partnership provides more protection than keeping it titled in your name, but appreciably less protection than would an offshore trust or some other foreign structure that keeps the asset beyond the reach of US courts and any practical opportunity to recover. While liquid assets can be physically transferred offshore and placed beyond the reach of US courts, we have different problems when the assets must remain US-based, as with real estate. Here, when the limited partnership offers questionable protection, the only remedy is to sell or fully encumber the assets and move the proceeds to an offshore trust or comparably protective structure.

Still, from the debtor's position, the limited partnership shields the partnership assets from all but the most determined creditor. A creditor must overcome numerous barriers before he can recover assets. As a practical matter, few creditors choose to pursue a partnership interest or assets conveyed to the partnership unless the claim and the corresponding assets are exceptionally large.

The Limited Partnership as a
Personal Liability Protector

The limited partnership protects limited partners against the debts of the partnership. This remains true, however, only if the limited partners do not actively participate in the management of the partnership as outlined previously, yet it is easy for a limited partner to overstep his bounds and thus incur liability for partnership debts. Therefore, limited partners should fully understand the prohibited activities if they are to remain personally immune. Here the limited liability company has a decided advantage: its members can freely involve themselves in company affairs without jeopardizing their personal immunity.

General partners are liable for all debts of the

partnership, including all tort and contract claims. Therefore, individuals should not become general partners when the partnership has 'liability-producing' assets or activities. In this instance, they may form a corporation or limited liability company - with minimal assets - to serve as the general partner.

Bankruptcy and the Limited Partnership

A common question is whether a limited partner will lose his limited partnership interest in bankruptcy. The general answer is no. The bankruptcy trustee obtains only the charging order remedy of an individual creditor. However, the trustee may claim any paid-in capital contribution that the bankruptcy partner is entitled to withdraw. Of course, the limited partnership agreement should be carefully reviewed by an insolvent partner, well in advance of bankruptcy.

A general partner's bankruptcy does not transfer the managerial authority to his bankruptcy trustee. Nevertheless, the bankruptcy can, in numerous ways, cause disruption to the smooth or continuous management of the partnership and, therefore, the general partner contemplating bankruptcy should be replaced in advance.

Combining Limited Partnerships and Offshore Trusts

For maximum asset protection, it is often recommended that the limited partnership interests be held by an offshore asset protection trust. Family members can be the general partners and thus control the partnership assets. Upon any threat to the partnership or its assets, the partnership can simply liquidate. Since the offshore trust would own 95 percent or more of the partnership interest, it would receive a corresponding share of the partnership assets upon liquidation. Obviously, the partnership proceeds entrusted offshore would enjoy considerably greater protection. Moreover, since the trust owns the limited partnership interest, it would not be subject to a charging order from creditors of any family members involved in the arrangement.

Nine More Ways to Maximize Limited Partnership Protection

Aside from the many pointers already discussed, there are several other strategies to bolster the asset protection from limited partnerships:

1) The limited partnership agreement should give the general partners full discretion to withhold distributions of profits for purposes of future investment.

2) The agreement should also specifically restrict the transfer of a limited partnership interest without the consent of the general partner and/or a majority of the limited partners.

3) The agreement should further prevent a limited partner from withdrawing capital contributions without partner consent.

4) The agreement should also carefully specify that a creditor of a limited partner becomes only an assignee of the limited partner's interest and acquires no partnership rights other than the right to distributions.

5) A particularly effective strategy is to have a limited partnership agreement allow the general partner to 'assess' the limited partners for a further contribution and to extend this obligation to any charging order creditor.

6) 'High-risk' family members should own a smaller partnership interest, but always proportional to the

asset contributions to avoid gift tax consequences or claims of fraudulent conveyance. The agreement should also give the 'low-risk' family member a disproportionately high percentage of the profits.

7) Limited partners may also consider granting an 'option to purchase' the partnership interest back to the limited partnership. Issued well in advance of a creditor claim, it can be an effective way to divert partnership interests.

8) Spouses may consider holding their limited partnership interests as tenants-by-the-entirety in the states where this type of tenancy is recognized. This further protects the interest from creditors of any one spouse.

9) When investing in a large, non-controlled limited partnership or limited liability company, title ownership in a family limited partnership to protect the distributions that you may not be able to avoid.

A well drafted limited partnership agreement can be a formidable barrier to any creditor.

I have few war stories to tell you about limited partnerships. In my many years of practice, I have had only two experiences with charging order creditors. The first case involved a creditor with a $700,000 judgment against my client, who owned a 45 percent limited partnership interest; his family owned the remaining interest. Although the partnership had about $3 million in assets, the creditor sat with his charging order for over two years and never collected a dime in profit distributions. Eventually he settled for $50,000. It wasn't a bad outcome.

My second case was more interesting. The creditor was the IRS (yes, a limited partnership is equally effective against the IRS). I never expected the IRS to get a charging order against the limited partnership interest owned by my client and his wife (who had no tax liability). The limited partnership had a $60,000 net income, so my client would have $30,000 in taxable income. We sent the tax liability (Form K-1) to the IRS as the substitute taxpayer for the husband. In essence, the IRS had to pay itself the tax on the husband's $30,000 'phantom income.' A crazy story? Sure, but it makes my work fun. We never again heard from the IRS.

How to Structure Your Family Limited Partnership

There are typical limited partnership structures for families. Most often, mom and dad form the partnership and contribute various income-producing or business assets in exchange for their respective partnership interests. They can initially receive a small interest in the partnership as the general partners. As such they equally control the partnership, just as they previously controlled the contributed assets. Mom and dad may each also receive, as limited partners, the remaining majority interest in the limited partnership (general and limited partners can be the same parties and both can own an interest in a limited partnership). Thus, mom and dad enjoy exclusive, equal ownership and control of the partnership - and thus the assets contributed to the partnership - just as they enjoyed their assets when titled in their own names. The one difference is that their assets are now fully protected from creditors.

There are many other ways to structure a family partnership. Perhaps dad has many creditors, so mom becomes the general partner. It would not be to dad's advantage to be a general partner when his creditors could interfere in the partnership. Mom and dad could form a corporation or limited liability company, which would be the general partner in the partnership - a particularly good choice if the partnership can incur liabilities for which the general partners are liable.

They may subsequently transfer their limited partnership interests. They can gradually gift their limited partnership interests to their children, to a living trust or some other entity, which may also own a part of the limited partnership. Since the limited partnership structure is flexible, the family limited partnership works very well for estate planning and adapts itself perfectly to a systematic gifting program.

As stated, a most attractive tax feature of the family limited partnership is its ability to spread the tax burden between the partners any way you choose. For example, general partner dad in a high tax bracket could contribute large amounts of money to a partnership while retaining only a small interest, but full control. The tax burden for this contribution would thus be spread to the limited partners - the kids - who own the majority interests in the partnership.

Combining trusts with limited partnerships makes for a powerful family asset protector. However, combining a trust with a limited partnership is a much more complicated structure than using either one alone. A legal or financial consultant should arrange the structure to fully protect your family's assets.

Combining the family limited partnership with the living trust frequently provides a superior estate plan. The partnership, as owner of the family assets, provides asset protection and discounted valuations for estate tax purposes. The limited partnership interests owned by the partners' respective living trusts allow the partners to bequeath their partnership interest while avoiding probate.

In structuring this arrangement between spouses who own the partnership, it is assumed that they will take advantage of the unlimited marital deduction. Upon the grantor's death, the family trust becomes irrevocable, succeeded by two internal trusts: a credit-equivalent bypass trust and a marital trust. This strategy essentially transfers the estate tax liability to the surviving spouse's estate, thus deferring the estate tax.

The customary probate complexities and costs are avoided when the partnership interests are owned by living trusts. Delays in completing probate are avoided and creditors need not be notified, allowing disposition economically, quickly and efficiently.

Reducing Estate Taxes

The ability of the limited partnership to reduce estate taxes is its most formidable tax benefit. Assume that an individual has, upon his death, cash in the amount of $3 million and that the estate tax exemption is $1.5 million. The estate tax would then be levied on the $1.5 million balance. If these same assets were titled to a limited partnership, they would be subject to a 'discounted valuation.' Possibly the full partnership interests would be valued at $2 million for estate tax purposes, thus eliminating estate taxes on $1 million.

Generally, assets titled to a limited partnership result in a discounted value of 20 to 40 percent compared to their estate tax value when owned outright. This results in a correspondingly lower estate tax. Several factors determine the amount of the allowed discount. The IRS primarily considers: (1) *Control* the decedent had over the partnership, (2) *Marketability* of the partnership assets and the ability to quickly liquidate its assets, and (3) *Accessibility* of the partnership interests by the decedent's estate.

On the issue of control, the family may, for instance, decide to have the children become the general partners as their parents age. Divesting control from the parents allows for a greater discount on the value of their partnership interest upon their deaths. Cash and marketable securities support a smaller discount compared to a limited partnership consisting of real estate or stock in closely held corporations.

The question of the limited partnership valuation discount is one that has the rapt attention of - and opposition from - the IRS, who routinely contest a decedent's discount valuation and who systematically petition Congress to disallow the discount. Because tax policies and regulations on the subject are likely to change, get guidance from your tax advisor when using the limited partnership for estate or gift tax planning.

The Limited Liability Partnership (LLP)

Most doctors, lawyers, and other professionals carry insurance against malpractice and other types of litigation because claims against these professionals are now a daily occurrence. No professional today, however, can rely solely upon insurance for protection. There are now many other opportunities for professionals to incur liability arising from their practice. The need for sound organizational protection for professionals clearly matches that of the commercial business owner or family with wealth preservation concerns.

Enter the limited liability partnership, a special type partnership created for those engaged in professional occupations such as doctors, lawyers, dentists, architects and accountants. It is called a limited liability partnership (LLP) because it closely resembles the limited partnership, although there are important differences between the two.

While the limited liability partnership protects the professional partner from both debts incurred by the practice and claims resulting from the malpractice of any other partner, it does not protect the professional partner from personal claims resulting from his own malpractice. Moreover, limited liability partnership assets cannot be directly seized by the professional partner's personal creditors, except when the negligent partner was acting on behalf of the limited liability partnership as his principal. Nor can the professional partner's personal creditors easily liquidate his interest in the limited liability partnership, because ownership interest in this type of partnership must usually be owned by professionals from within that profession. This makes the limited liability partnership an excellent option when professionals want to participate in the management of the practice, while still insulating their personal assets from the partnership liabilities.

A limited liability partnership shares common features with other types of partnerships. Like a general partnership, all partners in a limited liability partnership are liable for commercial debts and other partnership actions. However, when a partner is held responsible for malpractice, only that partner is liable. The remainder of the partners are personally shielded from any liability incurred by the professional misconduct of that one partner. Most states that have adopted the Revised Uniform Partnership Act have extended that shield to cover not only tort claims, but contract claims as well.

Despite the continued liability of partners for partnership debts, and personal liability if sued for malpractice, the limited liability partnership is a wise choice for professionals since no partner is liable for another partner's inappropriate or negligent practice. This allows high-risk professions to reap the benefits of forming a partnership without sacrificing personal wealth because of another partner's mistakes.

The professional's asset protection improves when they conduct their practice through a limited liability partnership. Conversely, the general partnership is the most dangerous business structure because each partner then has unlimited liability for all partnership debts. Should you still prefer the general partnership structure, each professional operating as a partner in the general partnership should, at the very least, organize his own professional corporation or limited liability company. These respective entities could then become partners in the partnership.

While this creates a somewhat more cumbersome arrangement than a simple limited liability partnership, the structure provides certain tax, regulatory and organizational advantages. In a general partnership, the partners are all equally liable for partnership debts. In exchange, the partners enjoy the pass-through tax benefits not found in a corporation. In a limited partnership, all partners except one have limited liability: The general partner remains personally liable for any and all partnership debts.

Remember, a limited liability partnership can help to minimize the risk of its partners, but nothing can completely eliminate that risk. Don't mistakenly think that you no longer need malpractice insurance if you form a limited liability partnership. Also, carefully consider taxes, state regulations for your profession, and malpractice insurance when creating your limited liability partnership agreement.

9

The ABC's of LLC's

The limited liability company (LLC) is the first new legal entity to emerge since the 1950s, and it promises to be an increasingly valuable tool in the asset protection arsenal. The limited liability company, first recognized in Wyoming in 1977, helped mining developers attract foreign investors. However, it was 1988 when limited liability company legislation began to spread throughout the nation. The incentive was that the IRS allowed the limited liability company to be treated as a partnership for tax purposes. As with partnerships, the limited liability company allowed *single taxation*. Limited liability company members would be taxed on the limited liability company profits; the limited liability company would itself pay no taxes. On the other hand, the C corporation (not the S corporation) is subject to *double taxation*. The C corporation is taxed on its income, and its shareholders are taxed on whatever distributions are made from the corporation.

There are other advantages that make the limited

liability company a superior business organization in many situations. As a hybrid entity, it features both the limited liability advantage of the corporation with the favorable single income taxation of the partnership. More importantly, a member's interest in the limited liability company gives his creditors only the charging order remedy as seen with the limited partnership (LP). Because the limited liability company offers comparable protective capabilities to the limited partnership, it is an equally attractive vehicle to title and protect personal assets. Moreover, since neither limited liability company managers nor members have personal liability for the debts or liabilities of the limited liability company, it is oftentimes ideal to hold liability-producing assets or to conduct business. Overall, the limited liability company offers several significant benefits over the corporation and other traditional forms of business organizations.

Since much of what I say about the limited liability company also applies to the limited partnership, and considering their several similarities, it is not surprising that one lawyer may recommend that a client use a limited partnership while another recommends a limited liability company. This does not necessarily make either recommendation wrong or right since their distinction is so narrow.

The limited liability company's organizational or structural options also closely follow the limited partnership; but there are differences in terminology. Managers of the limited liability company are called 'managers,' compared to general partners in a limited partnership. Its owners, or members, compare to limited partners.

Limited Liability Company
Advantages and Disadvantages

Although a limited liability company combines advantages

of a corporation with those of a limited partnership, there are several reasons why a limited liability company may be preferable to either type of organization:

- You can avoid double taxation with a limited liability company. Since the limited liability company is not a corporation, you can avoid corporate income tax if you so choose. Income from the limited liability company can be taxed personally to its members, as with a partnership.

- There is a ceiling on personal liability with a limited liability company. The managers and members are both personally protected from limited liability company creditors even when the members participate in managing the company. Remember, general partners of a limited partnership *are* personally liable for the debts of the partnership, and the limited partners of a limited partnership cannot manage the limited partnership without incurring personal liability.

- The limited liability company may require less paperwork and recordkeeping. You only need a simple operating agreement, and you can easily form your own limited liability company. The necessary organization forms are available from the Secretary of State for the location where you want to organize your limited liability company.

Although an excellent organizational choice for many purposes, the limited liability company is not always your best entity choice. There are reasons you might instead choose a corporation or limited partnership:

- The limited liability company is still more narrowly accepted by business owners and professionals than is a corporation or limited partnership because the limited liability company is a newer entity. We have relatively few court cases involving the protection afforded by limited liability companies, and they are less battle-tested than either the limited partnership or corporation.
- Multi-state businesses frequently incur state tax problems should they conduct business in a state in which the limited liability company fails to qualify to conduct business.
- Limited liability companies do not enjoy the corporate advantages of prior IRS rulings concerning the sale of worthless stock or stock sold at a loss.
- LLC membership interests do not enjoy the same 'discounted valuations' for estate tax purposes as limited partnership interests.
- Selling 50 percent or more of the ownership of the limited liability company in any twelve-month period ends any tax advantages the limited liability company may have had with the IRS.
- Limited liability companies cannot engage in tax-free reorganizations.
- Owners of limited liability companies pay higher unemployment taxes on their own earnings than do corporate officers.

As you can see, there is no one perfect entity. You must consider a wide range of factors when deciding upon your best organizational choice. This decision should involve your accountant as well as your attorney.

How the Limited Liability Company Operates

The state limited liability company statutes vary. However, most states conform to the model Uniform Limited Liability Company Act (ULLCA) of 1995. The more important provisions of the ULLCA are:

- A limited liability company is a legal entity separate from its members.
- Limited liability companies may be organized as for-profit or non-profit organizations.
- About half the states allow one-member limited liability companies; the others require two or more members.
- Limited liability company membership interests are non-transferable without the unanimous consent of the other members.
- Interest in future distributions and returns of capital are transferable by a member.
- As the name implies, managers and members of a limited liability company have limited liability. They only stand to lose their investment if the limited liability company is sued or goes bankrupt.
- Limited liability companies can exist for a fixed or perpetual duration.
- A limited liability company is dissolved upon: (1) the consent of its members; (2) dissociation of a member; (3) occurrence of a specific event stated in the operating agreement; or (4) a fixed dissolution date.
- Limited liability company operating agreements may not: (1) unreasonably restrict a member's right to inspect company records; (2) eliminate or reduce a member's duty, loyalty, care or good faith when dealing with or on behalf of the company; (3) restrict

the rights of third parties; or (4) override the legal right of the company to expel any member convicted of wrongdoing, breaching the operating agreement or making it impractical for the limited liability company to carry on business with such a member.

Where to Form Your Limited Liability Company

As with the corporation, you must also consider where to organize your limited liability company. Here, too, there are financial, organizational and legal issues to consider.

Start by researching the financial factors applicable in the state in which you want to do business.

- As with the corporation, you should consider where you will operate your primary business. For example, you may register in a state with low organizational fees - such as New Mexico - but if you plan to do most of your business in another state, you will nevertheless be required to register in all other states where you will do business, which can significantly increase your filing, registration and administrative costs.
- What will it cost to register in the state?
- What are the ongoing annual fees?
- Will your limited liability company be required to pay state or local income taxes?

Also important are the state laws concerning the possible organizational formats of limited liability companies. Evaluate state laws on five key points:

- Can the company members manage or must the limited liability company have an appointed manager?

- Can the limited liability company merge with other types of business organizations?
- Can company members be easily admitted or terminated?
- What standards are imposed on managers for negligence, malfeasance, misfeasance, misconduct, confidence, trust and confidentiality?
- What rights do creditors of a member have to claim a member's limited liability company interests? For asset protection, this last question is most important.

Next consider taxes. What are the organizational requirements to qualify for partnership taxation at the state level? Some states have rigid organizational requirements. These states allow only multi-member limited liability companies to be taxed as a partnership. Other states allow single-member limited liability companies to elect 'pass-through' taxation.

Advantages of a Delaware Series LLC

Frequently a client's asset protection plan will necessitate using a number of limited liability companies for purposes of segregating assets into different entities. For example, you may own five rental properties which should be titled separately so that the liability exposure of one would not jeopardize the other properties. Or the client may have several businesses that operate through different entities with the same objective of liability insulation. I have clients with as many as one hundred separate LLCs. The multiple LLCs may be owned personally by the client or we may establish one or more limited partnerships to be the LLC member (this adds another layer of protection as well as greater opportunity to claim an estate tax discounted valuation), or the LLCs may be owned by one or more trusts.

The obvious problem with the multi-LLC plan is that one must set up and separately administer separate LLCs. To greatly simplify matters, Delaware has recently established the Delaware Series LLC.

With a Delaware Series LLC you can establish a series of cells within one Delaware LLC. Each cell within the series effectively operates as a distinct LLC. Each cell can own different assets or conduct different businesses and have different managers and members as well as operating agreements with varying provisions. They can also file separate tax returns and otherwise operate autonomously from the other cells within the series. The liabilities of one cell remain segregated to the asset of that cell.

The Delaware Series LLC should be considered by anyone anticipating the need for multiple LLCs.

Limiting Personal Liability with a Limited Liability Company

Because both the limited liability company managers and members have limited liability, in this one respect the limited liability company compares to a corporation.

However, in a few states a one-member limited liability company will expose the single member personally for the debts and obligations of the limited liability company, as a general partner incurs liability for the debts of a limited partnership. Moreover, this one member must have sufficient personal assets (set by state law) to meet the foreseeable obligations of the limited liability company. The IRS sets this at 10 percent of the limited liability company's total capital. Neither can this manager be a mere figurehead. Although the single-member's personal liability can be indemnified by others, the manager still has the underlying liability. If you elect to accept personal liability to qualify for partnership tax status in those few states that mandate it, then any indemnity provision must expressly be within the operating agreement.

Of course, every business presents serious lawsuit risks. Your business may not pay its debts, employees have car accidents, customers may be injured, disgruntled ex-employees may sue for discrimination or sexual harassment. It is essential to protect your personal wealth from these and the many other business risks, so it is necessary to organize in a state that insulates the manager from personal liability.

Fortunately, most states allow the limited liability company to accomplish this goal of limiting the manager's personal liability. The *outside* protection for managers and members of the limited liability company is as strong as the corporation's, provided all limited liability company formalities are followed. Only the limited liability company assets are then exposed to limited liability company creditors and lawsuits. The limited liability company manager's and member's personal wealth would be untouchable.

Before you form a corporation, think about the limited liability company. You have the limited liability of the corporation, pay less federal tax on profits and obtain considerably more protection for your ownership interest in the limited liability company than you would as a corporate stockholder.

Because members, managers, agents and employees of a limited liability company are not ordinarily personally liable for the debts, contracts or liabilities of the limited liability company (and have basically the same liability protection as corporate officers, directors and stockholders or limited partnership limited partners - or outside protection), they can only lose what they invest in the limited liability company. However, as with the corporation or family limited partnership, this limited liability does not shield limited liability company members or managers from personal liability for torts they commit personally, contracts they guarantee or in those instances where managers have statutory liability.

How Limited Liability Companies Protect Personal Assets

Then consider inside protection. Generally, a limited liability company member's personal creditor cannot seize or force a sale of the member's interest or claim limited liability company assets, nor can the member's creditor vote the interest of the debtor-member. The member's creditors can only apply to the court for a charging order that instructs the limited liability company to pay income or distributions to the creditor that would normally flow to the debtor-member. This is precisely the same 'charging order' remedy that a creditor has against a limited partner's interest in a family limited partnership. Essentially the creditor gains only the *financial* rights of the debtor-member, not *control* rights.

You should note that the charging order will not (1) give the creditor voting rights or (2) force the limited liability company manager to pay distributions to members or creditors of the member. The charging order only requires that whatever distributions *are* payable be paid to the creditor and not to the debtor-member.

The charging order, then, is as futile a creditor remedy in context to limited liability companies as it is with family limited partnerships. As the manager of your limited liability company, it is you who will decide if and when distributions are paid. Your judgment creditor cannot vote you out as the manager because a member's creditor cannot vote. As long as your creditor has a charging order against you as the manager, you can refuse to pay distributions to members. Nevertheless, you can compensate yourself (and other members) by paying salaries for services, since salaries cannot be seized through the charging order, nor can loans or other compensation paid to managers or members.

You also have the same 'poison pill' option with the charging order against a limited liability company interest. It backfires on charging order creditors for income tax purposes. Since a limited liability company is ordinarily taxed as a partnership, its tax liability passes to its members. A charging order creditor then also gets the tax bill for the debtor-member's share of the profits. A member's creditor would thus be forced to pay taxes on earnings he never received. That's usually a losing proposition.

The problems and limitations of the charging order usually encourage creditors to settle rather than fight. Why sue someone for a remedy that gives you no money, no control and a large tax bill? It would not make sense. If a plaintiff's lawyer knows at the outset of any lawsuit that your assets are safely titled to a limited liability company, then you will probably reach a faster settlement and avoid the expense, time and hassle of defending the lawsuit.

The limited liability company's weaknesses also compare to those of the family limited partnership. Transfers made to the limited liability company *after* you have a creditor may allow the creditor to recover the asset as a fraudulent transfer.

Should a member file bankruptcy, the bankruptcy trustee may also have considerably greater rights to claim the member's limited liability company ownership interest than could be obtained by a judgment creditor holding a charging order. You also have the potential problem of greater profit distributions that may be declared when the debtor-member does not control the manager. Clearly, we would not rely on the limited liability company in these situations.

We can normally improve our protection for a limited liability company member with the same strategies we would use to increase the lawsuit protection for corporate shares or limited partnership interests. For example, we can assess the membership interest, issue proxies and options to redeem the membership interest, encumber or lien the membership interest, or dilute the members' control by selling additional ownership interests.

There are also comparable ways to protectively title a membership interest. For instance, the limited liability company interest owned by married couples may be titled as tenants-by-the-entirety in those states that protect this form of marital ownership. Offshore trusts can own the membership interests in the same manner as we use offshore trusts to be the limited partner in a limited partnership. Limited partnerships may become the member of a limited liability company. This arrangement is a particularly good choice in those states that give more creditor protection to limited partnership interests than they do limited liability company membership interests. The other reason to use the limited partnership to own the limited liability company is for estate planning, which I explain later in this chapter.

It is almost always safer from an asset protection viewpoint to have members in addition to the member who is a lawsuit defendant. Courts are more reluctant to expand upon a creditor's remedy when other members would be affected. Conversely, courts are more likely to authorize the liquidation of the LLC when the debtor is the sole member.

Advantages of the Limited Liability Company

Here is a simple comparison of the limited liability company to the C corporation, S corporation, limited partnership and general partnership:

Advantages of the Limited Liability Company over the C Corporation

1. There is no double taxation for federal or state income tax.
2. There is no double taxation on liquidation.
3. The LLC has the ability to allocate income and losses.
4. There are other tax advantages associated with contributing appreciated property to the limited liability company (which you do not have with C corporations).
5. Membership interest is protected against lawsuits.

Advantages of the Limited Liability Company over the S Corporation

1. Limited liability companies can have more than seventy-five members; S corporations are restricted to seventy-five stockholders.
2. Limited liability companies can make special allocations of income and losses; S corporations must pro-rate profits and losses based on percentage ownership.
3. Limited liability company membership interest is creditor-protected.

Advantages of the Limited Liability Company over the Limited Partnership

1. A limited partnership must have at least one general partner and a natural person who has personal liability for partnership debts and liabilities. The

limited liability company need not have any member or manager who is personally liable for limited liability company debts and liabilities. (Remember, a general partner's liability can be shielded by forming a corporation or a limited liability company.)

2. In most states, a limited partner loses their limited liability by participating in the management of the partnership. Members of the limited liability company, on the other hand, can actively manage the limited liability company while retaining limited liability.

Advantages of the Limited Liability Company over the General Partnership

1. A general partnership offers no limited liability. Each partner is jointly and severally liable for partnership liabilities. Limited liability company members completely avoid this trap; they are neither jointly nor severally liable for the limited liability company debts nor debts created by the other members (except for professional limited liability companies, in some states).

Disadvantages of the Limited Liability Company

While the limited liability company is the entity of choice in many circumstances, it is not perfect. Disadvantages may exclude it from consideration in certain situations. Rather than compare these disadvantages to any particular organizational alternative, simply understand these drawbacks.

1. Not Always Available to the Sole Proprietor

Many states require two or more members to form a limited liability company. Even in those states that allow one-member limited liability companies, the IRS will tax a single-member limited liability company as a C corporation. Any 'pass-through' income tax advantage, therefore, is lost to the sole owner of the limited liability company. Nor can you overcome the disfavored tax treatment of single-member limited liability companies by using a corporation as your second member. The IRS taxes such structures as a corporation, even when a state allows it.

2. **Not Always Available for the Professional Practice**
Many states prohibit the use of LLCs for physicians, attorneys and other professionals. California, for example, prohibits limited liability companies for their professionals. Before setting up a limited liability company to operate a professional practice, check with your state licensing agency or an attorney familiar with your state's limited liability company or professional practice laws.

3. **Risk of Planning Error**
A limited liability company planning error can easily destroy the limited liability company tax advantage. This risk is reduced with corporations and partnerships.

4. **No Estate Tax Benefits**
The limited liability company is not as effective as the family limited partnership for saving estate taxes. Estate planning strategies with family limited partnerships are unavailable with limited liability companies. In fact, recent tax court decisions that disallowed the 'discounted valuation' of a limited partnership interest do not apply to limited liability companies. If you have a taxable estate, use the family limited partnership if you want a 'discounted

valuation' for estate tax savings.

5. **Dissolution Dilemma**

   You may also require the unanimous vote by all members to continue the company after the death, bankruptcy, retirement, etc. of a member. Any one member can then become a holdout and make unreasonable demands on the remaining members to vote for continuation of the company. Fortunately, the IRS requires only a majority vote in these situations to continue the company. To avoid this holdout problem, your LLC articles of organization/operating agreement should require only a majority vote to continue the company.

Assets to Title Your Limited Liability Company

Your limited liability company can own any asset that can be titled to a limited partnership. In practice, I usually prefer that the limited liability company title more dangerous (liability-producing) assets only because the limited liability company managers are fully immunized personally from any debts of the limited liability company. Conversely, the limited partnership's general partner has personal liability. I recommend the limited partnership for 'safe' assets - passive investments, etc. - if only because the limited partnership has been battle-tested for nearly 100 years, whereas the limited liability company, as a new entity, is relatively untested as an asset protection entity. Moreover, the degree of protection can vary between states. I particularly recommend the limited liability company to own:

- Second homes and vacation homes
- Commercial real estate
- Cars, boats, planes, etc.

- Dangerous equipment
- Any operating business.

In rare instances I arranged for a single-member limited liability company to own a primary residence, particularly if the transfer to the limited liability company was necessary to avoid an attachment on the property by a judgment creditor. You may then ask that if both the limited liability company and the family limited partnership can protect such a wide range of assets, why not also title your home to a family limited partnership or limited liability company for the same charging order protection? In fact, some asset protection planners do recommend titling the family residence to a limited partnership; however, the downside is that you then lose your tax benefits. You might preserve your tax benefits by titling the home to a limited liability company.

As a single person, you have a $250,000 capital gains tax exclusion on profits when you sell your home. A married couple has a $500,000 exclusion. Assuming a 15 percent capital gains tax rate, this represents a tax savings of $50,000 to $100,000. For this exclusion to apply, however, you must meet a two-part test: (1) One or both spouses must have owned the home for at least two out of the five years preceding the sale and (2) the house must be the primary residence during those years. If a family limited partnership owns the house for more than three of those five years, you lose your tax benefit. Of course, one solution would be to transfer your home to a family limited partnership for no more than three years and then retransfer the home to your own name for at least two years; however, this is usually impractical.

An alternative solution is to have a single-member limited liability company own the home. If you are married, one spouse (usually the less liability-prone spouse) can be that single-member. Since the IRS disregards single-member limited liability companies for tax purposes, the home should, at least for capital gains purposes, be treated as if it were owned in the name of the individual member. It is impossible to achieve this tax strategy with a limited partnership, which by definition requires at least two owners and therefore cannot be a disregarded entity. Review this strategy carefully with your tax advisor as there is no tax ruling on this point.

The 'due on sale,' clause which is standard in most mortgages, requires the consent of the mortgage lender to transfer property to a limited liability company. Without their written consent, the lender can foreclose. However, lenders routinely consent to such transfers, unless your lender sold your mortgage to Fannie Mae, you are in default on your mortgage, or you are paying a lower than prevailing interest rate. I have had cases when a lender refused consent to the transfer, but it was nevertheless necessary to transfer the property to a limited liability company to sidestep a real estate attachment. I have not had a case where the lender actually foreclosed because of the transfer. Further, there are cases that uphold the right of an owner to transfer property to an LLC or FLP owned by the same party, even absent the consent of the mortgage holder.

The overriding strategy is to segregate your assets into separate limited liability companies. For instance, if you own ten apartment houses, title each in a separate limited liability company. Your ten limited liability companies may in turn be owned by one family limited partnership, with this family limited partnership the common member to all limited liability companies.

10

How Trusts Protect Your Wealth

America's wealthiest families have historically relied upon a wide variety of trusts to protect their wealth from taxes, but now people at every income level use trusts for an even wider variety of purposes. Asset protection is certainly not the least important of these reasons.

Trusts play an important role in your asset protection planning. However, while there are a great array of trusts, only a handful are useful for asset protection. The offshore trust is particularly important for asset protection and, this is discussed in greater depth in Chapter 11 (together with many other offshore strategies and solutions). This chapter covers domestic or US-based trusts.

Understanding Basic Trusts

Trusts are created by a *settlor* or *grantor* (the terms are interchangeable) who provides the funds or other property to be held in trust. As the trust creator, the grantor also sets the terms under which the donated assets shall be managed and distributed.

The grantor names one or more *trustees*. In some cases, this is the grantor. The grantor further designates the beneficiaries who are to benefit from the trust and eventually receive its income and principal. With certain trusts the grantor can be the trustee and beneficiary, as commonly seen with the living trust.

When you think about using trusts for asset protection, you must consider them from several perspectives:

1) Which trusts can protect the assets from the grantor's creditors?

2) Which trusts can protect the assets from the beneficiaries' creditors?

3) How can you improve upon the protection afforded by a particular trust?

4) What asset protection can you expect from the more commonly used trusts?

Trusts That Can Lawsuit-Proof Your Assets

Only an *irrevocable intervivos trust* can shelter your assets from *your* creditors. A *testamentary trust,* with the right provisions, can lawsuit-proof the trust assets from your beneficiaries' creditors.

Every trust can be classified as either *intervivos* or *testamentary*. A living trust, as suggested by its name, is created and funded during the grantor's lifetime. It is an *intervivos trust*.

Trusts that become funded upon the grantor's death are *testamentary trusts*. Since a testamentary trust takes effect by funding upon your death, it is usually created in your last will or living trust and is operative upon your death.

We can also classify trusts as either *revocable* or *irrevocable*. A revocable trust can be changed or revoked by the grantor. Conversely, irrevocable trusts, once established, cannot be revoked or modified. Every testamentary trust is, of course, irrevocable. You obviously cannot spring back to life to cancel or unwind your trust.

What is important about the distinction between a revocable and irrevocable trust is that a revocable trust provides no asset protection. Only an *irrevocable* trust that is presently funded (an *intervivos* trust) can help you if you want asset protection.

There is a downside with creating an irrevocable *intervivos* trust for asset protection. Once you establish and fund your irrevocable trust, you forever lose the ability to cancel or revoke the trust and reclaim whatever property you transferred to the trust. The irrevocable trust effectively causes you to lose both ownership and control over the trust assets. Because of this disadvantage of losing control, irrevocable intervivos trusts are seldom used for asset protection.

In sum, the irrevocable trust protects your assets for the same reason that a revocable trust cannot. A revocable trust cannot provide asset protection because your creditors can step into your shoes and revoke the trust. For example, assets titled to your revocable living trust, are still vulnerable to both present and future lawsuits and creditors. This does not suggest that the living trust is not useful for its intended purpose – to avoid probate, however, you cannot count on your living trust to lawsuit-proof your wealth. For that, you need an irrevocable trust or another protective entity.

An irrevocable trust brings the opposite asset protection results. Because you cannot alter or unwind the irrevocable trust, your creditors have no greater powers than you do to unwind the trust and reclaim its assets.

Also bear in mind that an irrevocable trust must also be a *funded intervivos* trust; that is, you must fund the trust with your assets. Until you do transfer your assets to the trust, they remain *your* assets and subject to the claims of your personal creditors.

There are other limitations to a grantor using a trust to shield his own assets from creditors. One is that the trust cannot ordinarily be settled for the sole benefit of the grantor. As a general rule, a grantor seeking lawsuit protection should retain no beneficial interest, although some retention of income rights based on some ascertainable standard (health needs, etc.) may still allow for a trust to be effective for asset protection. Many states, however, expressly disallow self-settled trusts for asset protection when the grantor can either exercise control over the trust or enjoy its beneficial rights.

Another problem with using trusts as a protective entity is that assets transferred to the trust may be subject to fraudulent transfer claims by the grantor's creditors. Even transfers to an irrevocable trust can protect assets transferred to the trust only from *future* creditors. Present creditors – whether known or unknown - can recover transfers to the trust that would be deemed fraudulent under the Fraudulent Conveyances Act. You should transfer assets to a domestic irrevocable trust only when you are confident that you have no *present* creditors. Of course, you can never determine this beforehand with absolute certainty.

The rule, then, is that you cannot safely transfer assets to an irrevocable trust once you have creditors because such transfers can usually be set aside as fraudulent conveyances. To the extent such transfers impoverish you; your present creditor can recover whatever assets have been transferred to the trust since the transfer to the trust was without consideration (a fair value exchange paid to you from the trust).

As you can see, there are a number of potential pitfalls in the use of trusts to shelter assets from the grantor's creditors. The grantor must use an irrevocable trust, relinquish all control and beneficial interest, and even then the trust remains subject to a fraudulent transfer challenge. Such trusts may be set aside if the court concludes that the trust is only a sham or the grantor retained *de facto* control.

While titling assets in an irrevocable trust may immunize these assets from *future* creditors, lawsuits, and other financial threats, you can see the irrevocable trust's heavy price. You must surrender control, ownership, and any incidental benefits of the asset in exchange for protection. Most people, of course, find this too heavy a price; they want less draconian ways to become lawsuit-proof.

The disadvantages of an irrevocable trust make sense when (1) you would soon gift the assets to your beneficiaries anyway, and (2) you do not foresee needing the assets for financial security during your lifetime. Your 'price,' then, is not particularly heavy. If you do not personally need the assets and the trust accomplishes what you would eventually do anyway - distribute the assets to your beneficiaries (usually your children) at some future time - then you may consider an irrevocable *intervivos* trust.

Avoid Common Pitfalls

You must avoid three common pitfalls if you do create an irrevocable *intervivos* trust. First, don't reserve the power to revoke, rescind or amend the trust, or retain any rights, directly or indirectly, to reclaim the property transferred to the trust. Simply stated, attach no strings to the assets you transfer to the trust. Second, assert no authority on how the trust or its property is to be managed or invested. You can reserve no significant powers over the trust. As the trust's grantor, you cannot be its trustee. You cannot safely use your spouse, a close relative, or even a personal friend as the trustee. Courts closely examine relationships between the grantor and the trustee to determine whether the trustee is serving only as the grantor's 'alter ego.' Unless the trustee is truly independent, the courts will ignore the trust and allow the grantor's creditors to claim the trust assets. A corporate trustee, such as a bank or a trust company, are much less likely to be considered an alter ego and their trusteeship gives your trust that much more credibility.

You can see the obvious difficulties with using irrevocable trusts for asset protection: Since you must permanently relinquish complete control over the trust assets (which few people, of course, are willing to do), most people seek other ways to protect their assets. That's one reason, for instance, why the limited partnership has become so popular. It gives you excellent asset protection, it's revocable and, as the general partner, you enjoy continued control over the partnership assets.

Revocable trusts, such as the living trust, are obviously far more common than irrevocable trusts, if only because they are revocable. While revocable trusts can be extremely helpful for estate planning, they have little or no asset protection value. Your creditors can claim any assets that you transfer to a revocable trust as easily as assets titled in your own name.

Generally, if you can revoke or modify the trust or have the power to reclaim property from the trust, your creditors through the courts can compel you to re-transfer the trust assets for *their* benefit. However, the precise rights of a grantor's creditors to recover property titled to a revocable trust may differ somewhat by state. A few courts have ruled that the grantor's creditors cannot claim the trust assets, notwithstanding that the grantor can revoke the trust or claim its income. However, this is far from the prevailing rule.

Smart Parents, Spendthrift Kids

It is amazing how many parents spend their lifetime scrimping, saving, and sheltering their wealth, only to leave their fortune to their kids who then promptly spend it or lose it in their own financial debacles.

How can you effectively use trusts to safeguard your assets from your beneficiaries' lawsuits, creditors, divorces, etc.?

Perhaps you plan to bequeath significant wealth to your children or other beneficiaries. If you gift your money to them outright, then their inheritance is unprotected from their financial and legal problems.

While we generally do not use irrevocable trusts to protect our clients' assets from *their* creditors, we frequently recommend trusts to protect significant trust assets from their beneficiaries' lawsuits, creditors, and ex-spouses. Usually the beneficiaries are the grantor's children or grandchildren.

Irrevocable trusts may be either *intervivos* or *testamentary*. With an *intervivos* trust, you would transfer some or all of your assets to the trust during your lifetime. Conversely, with a testamentary trust, your assets would go into trust upon your death. Obviously, then, your assets remain vulnerable to *your* creditors until you die, when title to the assets passes to the trust.

However, even a revocable trust can protect the trust assets from its beneficiaries' creditors. Whether you transfer assets to the trust within your lifetime (an intervivos trust) or upon your death (a testamentary trust), the only difference between a revocable and irrevocable trust funded *within* your lifetime is that the revocable trust gives *you,* the grantor, no asset protection. Moreover, the assets in the revocable trust will be included in your taxable estate. On the other hand, assets transferred to your irrevocable trust during your lifetime are excluded from your taxable estate, provided you live at least three years from the date of transfer to the trust.

More Americans with significant wealth now rely upon trusts to protect their children's inheritance. After all, why spend a lifetime accumulating wealth only to lose it to your children's creditors or ex-spouses? Think carefully about *how* you should bequeath your wealth to your kids. Ask not only how *much* to bequeath, but also *when* and *under what conditions* your children should inherit your money.

It is not usually a good idea to part with control of your money during your lifetime by bequeathing it to your kids. For example, you may be inclined to make lifetime gifts to your children by transferring assets outright with the objective of reducing your taxable estate, yet you know the danger when you leave substantial sums outright. Using a trust alone, however, may not be your answer either. A smarter solution would be to hold your assets in a limited partnership, with you as its general partner. You can then transfer a percentage of the limited partnership interests annually to your kids. You reduce your taxable estate each year as you continuously shift your wealth to your children's trusts. Meanwhile, your assets remain safe from *your* creditors because they are titled to a limited partnership. You stay in control of your assets because you are the general partner, and your children's interest is twice protected from any legal and financial problems – once by the limited partnership and again by their trust. Finally, when you die, your remaining partnership interest has a discounted value for estate tax purposes, and your remaining limited partnership interest is easily bequeathed to your children's trust.

Of course, there are literally hundreds of possible ways to combine trusts, FLPs, LLCs, corporations, and other trusts to achieve any amount of lawsuit protection, tax and estate planning objectives, as well as retaining lifetime control over your assets, always an important goal.

Safeguarding Inheritances

To create a creditor-proof trust to fully safeguard the beneficiaries' interest in the trust assets, trust language is incorporated that prevents a beneficiary's judgment creditor from seizing the beneficiary's share of either the trust principal or income. The right provisions also preclude the creditor from exercising any rights that the beneficiary may have to anticipate income, or any other powers of appointment that would weaken the beneficiary's protection.

The first important clause for your trust is the *anti-alienation* or *spendthrift clause,* which directly protects the trust assets from the beneficiaries' creditors. Specifically, the anti-alienation clause prohibits the trustee from transferring trust assets to anyone other than the beneficiary, which, of course, includes creditors of the trust beneficiary(ies). The spendthrift or anti-alienation clause expressly precludes any party with an interest adverse to the beneficiary (a creditor, ex-spouse, IRS, etc.) from making a claim against either the beneficiaries' share of the trust principal or any income distributions. This provision is vital in *every* trust.

The spendthrift clause will not in itself always provide a beneficiary absolute protection. As with most things, there are limitations. For example, several states do not fully enforce spendthrift provisions, and a spendthrift clause may not fully protect a beneficiary from bankruptcy, divorce, or tax claims. Also, it does not protect income distributions that have already been received by the beneficiaries. Then again, spendthrift provisions are often poorly drafted or not comprehensively interpreted. The level of protection, in large measure, is based on the skill of the drafter.

Another important protective measure is to grant the trustee maximum discretionary powers. For example, if your trust specifies that a beneficiary is to receive a trust distribution at age 25, you must also consider whether those distributions are safe if the beneficiary has a judgment creditor or a spouse planning divorce when the beneficiary reaches age 25.

With the discretionary clause the trustee has the right to withhold income and principal distributions that would otherwise be payable to the beneficiary, whenever the trustee believes the funds would be wasted or claimed by the beneficiary's creditors. The discretionary clause also prevents a wasteful beneficiary from depleting or wasting trust assets; which is especially important for grantors whose children are beneficiaries. If you also worry whether money that you entrust for your children will be wasted, then you need discretionary provisions in your trusts so your trustee can better regulate distributions to your children.

You may not think that your child is a spendthrift or someone unable to responsibly handle his or her inheritance; but you may worry about your child's spouse. These same important provisions can also help to keep the trust principal intact if your child dies or divorces. These same protective provisions apply to gifts of any remaining trust principal to your grandchildren or another beneficiary.

The spendthrift and discretionary clauses help to protect the trust assets from your beneficiaries' creditors by allowing the trustee the authority to withhold payments to a beneficiary who has creditors. The beneficiary's creditor cannot force a trustee to distribute assets to the beneficiary. The creditor's remedy is to claim whatever payments are actually paid by the trustee and received by the beneficiary; however, a trustee can always directly pay third parties on behalf of a beneficiary.

While the *spendthrift* clause allows the trustee to withhold payments to a beneficiary with creditors, the *anti-alienation* clause goes further. It prohibits the trustee from distributing trust income or principal to anyone other than the named beneficiaries.

In addition to a trust's discretionary powers, *sprinkling* provisions may be added. Sprinkling provisions are gaining popularity for trusts that are expected to be in force for ten or more years, where the future income or tax situation for each beneficiary is uncertain. The trustee can then modify distributions from the trust through a 'sprinkling' provision that grants the trustee the authority to either disburse or retain principal and income for the duration of the trust, thus determining what each beneficiary receives and when.

As the grantor, you must specify what criteria the trustee will follow when determining distributions, and you may set minimum income distributions when the beneficiary is a spouse or dependent child.

As with a discretionary clause, the sprinkling trust gives you greater asset protection provided you, as the grantor, retain no rights to modify or revoke the sprinkling trust. As with other asset protection trusts, a sprinkling trust must be both irrevocable and free of grantor control. Moreover, a beneficiary cannot be a trustee. Although legally permissible, the trust assets in such an instance would then become vulnerable to creditors of the trustee-beneficiary. A trustee who can distribute trust assets to himself as the beneficiary allows his creditors to stand in his place for purposes of forcing distributions of trust funds, which the creditor can then seize.

A simple example of how a trust that included the many protective provisions works is through the example of a New York accountant client. Jerry owned $600,000 in mutual funds that he wanted to leave to his two adult children, Steve and Stephanie. Jerry and his wife could live quite comfortably without these mutual funds, and he also wanted to save estate taxes as well as provide some security to his children. Jerry, however, had concerns that his kids would unwisely spend their inheritance.

Jerry's concerns were resolved by establishing an irrevocable trust for Jerry, naming his local bank as the trustee. Jerry expressed to the trust officer his distribution preferences, which were incorporated within the trust documents.

Jerry and his wife funded the trust with an additional $20,000 in mutual funds annually so that their gifts to the trust would be tax-free. Since the trust was irrevocable, neither Jerry's nor his wife's future creditors could seize these funds. The trust's anti-alienation, spendthrift, and discretionary provisions also protected the trust funds from his children's poor spending habits, as well as from their own possible divorce or lawsuits.

Jerry correctly foresaw that the trusts would have substantial value. He also could foresee the possibility of its vulnerability due to his children's own lifestyles. With the irrevocable trust, Jerry fully protected his mutual funds from his own creditors, gifted them tax-free to his children, reduced his estate taxes, provided for his children's future (which he intended to do through his will or living trust), and simultaneously protected the trust funds from his children's creditors.

Living Trusts

Having covered trust basics, let's more closely review several common trusts and how they can help you achieve a wide variety of legal and financial goals. Let's specifically focus on whether they can give you (the grantor) and your beneficiaries good lawsuit protection.

The living trust is America's most popular trust because it is an excellent tool to avoid the cost and delay of probate. It also helps you sidestep the general dangers of jointly owning assets. However, as you now know, a *revocable living trust* gives you as the grantor *absolutely no asset protection!*

The reason a living trust cannot furnish asset protection is because it is usually revocable. While it gives you the comfort of knowing that you can change your living trust as readily as you can revise your will; you must also remember that *revocable trusts are vulnerable to lawsuits!*

Even then you must be careful when using living trusts. Living trusts can actually cause you to *lose* lawsuit protection. For example, several states provide that a homesteaded home transferred to a living trust loses its homestead protection. Similarly, assets owned with a spouse as tenants-by-the-entirety may lose their creditor protection afforded by this type of co-ownership when those same assets are titled to a living trust.

Understandably, you must expect trade-offs between the different options to title assets. Without a revocable living trust, however, the court will distribute your assets under a will. This can be expensive, time-consuming and cumbersome. (Probate costs average about 4 percent of a gross estate and the process can delay distributions under your estate for years.) If you bequeath $1 million through your will, your loved ones may pay a $40,000 probate bill and still wait years to receive their inheritances. One way to avoid this is with a living trust, since living trust assets automatically avoid probate.

Of course, your goal is to have the best of all worlds. For example, you would be far smarter to title your assets to a limited partnership (which lawsuit-proofs these assets), and your living trust (which avoids probate) would then own your limited partnership. When you die, your ownership in the limited partnership would transfer through the living trust to your heirs without probate. However, during your lifetime your assets would remain creditor-protected.

Irrevocable Life Insurance Trusts

Life insurance is an important investment and it frequently accumulates a substantial cash value. However, even a term policy can be a valuable asset in that it provides income and support to your family when you die. Life insurance can also pay estate taxes and make funds immediately available to your survivors without the delay or expense of liquidating other assets.

If you do own significant life insurance, then you want to protect it by titling it to an irrevocable life insurance trust (ILIT). An *irrevocable life insurance trust (ILIT)* is an irrevocable trust specifically designed to own life insurance. As with any other trust, the ILIT has a trustee, beneficiaries, and terms for trust distributions.

Your ILIT would own the insurance policy that insures your life. The policy itself would name the trust as the beneficiary. When you die, the insurance company pays the ILIT trustee, who then follows your trust instructions and distributes the proceeds to the ILIT beneficiaries that you named within the trust. Your estate, however, should not be the beneficiary.

An ILIT can either be funded or unfunded. With an unfunded ILIT, your life insurance premiums are not fully paid. You must provide for the future funding of premiums (you would make premium payments to the trust, which directly pay the premiums). With a funded ILIT, the grantor transfers to the trust either a fully paid insurance policy or adequate income-producing assets to pay future premiums.

With both unfunded or funded ILITs, policy premiums must be made directly from the trust funds; the grantor of the trust cannot directly pay the premiums. Unless the trustee pays the premiums, the tax benefits and creditor protection afforded by the trust is lost.

The ILIT is an irrevocable trust, and therefore protects both the policy's cash value and the proceeds on distribution from both the grantor's creditors as well as the beneficiaries' creditors. If life insurance is important for your family's financial security, and your life insurance is not fully protected by your state's laws, then an ILIT is essential for asset protection.

While the ILIT is important for asset protection, it is also important to save estate taxes. Since the ILIT - not you - owns the life insurance policy, the policy proceeds are *not* included in your taxable estate and are therefore not subject to estate taxes.

Why is this so important? Assume that you are single when you die and that your estate is worth $3 million, $1 million of which is life insurance. Let's further assume that when you die you have a $1.5 million death tax exemption. Your estate pays the tax on the remaining $1.5 million, and your estate tax bill is about $750,000. Your ILIT removes the $1 million life insurance from your taxable estate, so you save about $500,000 in estate taxes.

The ILIT also gives you greater control over the policy proceeds than when you own the insurance outright in your name. With insurance owned in your name, your insurance company simply pays your beneficiaries when you die. An ILIT not only lets you control *who* gets the proceeds but, more importantly, *how* and *when* the policy proceeds are distributed. For instance, your ILIT can have your trustee pay estate taxes and other costs (taxes due on IRAs or other retirement plans probate costs, legal fees, other debts, etc.) before making distributions to trust beneficiaries. You could have your trustee pay the beneficiaries directly, or over a period of months or years. Spendthrift, anti-alienation, and other protective provisions can also protect the insurance proceeds from your beneficiaries' financial problems. Finally, the ILIT avoids court interference should a beneficiary become incompetent. Did you know that many insurance companies will not pay life insurance proceeds to an incapacitated person? They require court instructions. Your ILIT avoids this unnecessary complication.

Children's Trusts

If you have children to whom you wish to gift assets, then an irrevocable children's trust (ICT) can possibly reduce your taxes and give you asset protection at the same time. Property transferred to a children's trust is not seizable by your creditors, and it is not part of your estate for estate tax purposes. At least some income from the trust assets can be taxed at the children's lower income tax rates. For these reasons, the children's trust is increasing in popularity.

The ICT or Section 2503 Minor's Trust controls the taxation and asset protection benefits of this trust. The ICT must include a trust document and a trustee with legal title to the trust assets. While the trust is in effect, and while the child beneficiary is under 21, neither the grantor's nor the child's creditors can claim the trust assets.

One disadvantage with the children's trust is that when your child reaches 21, he or she can demand the trust assets. Since it is an irrevocable trust, you, as the grantor, retain no right to withhold distributions from the trust and therefore you cannot prevent your child from receiving whatever assets are owned by the trust. You can only extend the trust until a later age if your child at age 21 consents in writing.

You must carefully consider whether your child(ren) at that young age will have the ability to properly handle the trust property. You no more want to lose the trust assets to an irresponsible 21-year-old than you do to your creditors.

Charitable Remainder Trusts

Gifting assets is, of course, an extreme way to creditor-protect them. However, our tax laws allow you to give away much of your property to charity, achieve asset protection, and still enjoy these same assets during your lifetime. For those who want asset protection and tax advantages from gifting these assets during their lifetime, a *Charitable Remainder Trust (CRT)* can be their answer. The CRT, in sum, allows you to gift your property to a charity, protect it from your creditors, save taxes, retain an income stream throughout your lifetime, and still leave the equivalent value of the gifted assets to your heirs.

As the trust grantor, you select a tax-exempt charitable organization as the beneficiary of the irrevocable trust principal. When you create and fund this trust you effectively make a charitable donation, and you can then claim a tax deduction for the fair market value of whatever assets you contribute to the trust. Although you have gifted the assets' 'principal,' you would be the income beneficiary; during your lifetime the trust pays you a fixed annual income. The net effect is that you get an immediate tax deduction and perpetually enjoy the income generated from your assets.

Assume that you have $200,000 in stocks purchased 15 years ago for only $60,000. If you sold that stock to invest in treasury bonds (for a more stable retirement income) you would pay $21,000 in capital against tax on the profit (15% x $140,000 gain). If your stocks are still worth $200,000 when you die, your estate may then pay another $88,000 in estate taxes (although estate taxes now vary annually). Your heirs would then inherit only $91,000 from the original $200,000 value after estate taxes.

Suppose instead that you don't sell your stocks, but instead transfer it to a CRT. You receive the same annual income that you would get from treasury bonds for the remainder of your life since you could name yourself the CRT's income beneficiary. You could also deduct the $200,000 donation as an immediate charitable contribution. The taxes saved from the charitable deduction would allow you to buy enough life insurance to at least cover the $91,000 that your beneficiaries would have received had you not donated your assets to a CRT. The net result is that you get a large tax deduction this year and the same perpetual fixed retirement income as you would with treasury bonds; you help your favorite charity with your donation, and your trust assets are now lawsuit-proof.

If you have appreciated assets, need a fixed income, and if the CRT's fixed income can adequately cover your retirement needs after inflation, then a CRT may be a sensible choice for asset protection. Since the beneficiary is a charity, a creditor cannot seize the trust principal unless the creditor can argue that your gift was a fraudulent transfer, that you retained excessive grantor control or that there was some other administrative irregularity. The income stream or the grantor's 'payout' is subject to the claims of the grantor's creditors.

One solution to protect an income stream is to instead set up a charitable remainder annuity trust (CRAT) in those states that exempt annuities from creditor seizure.

Qualified Personal Residence Trusts

A Qualified Personal Residence Trust (QPRT) is a special trust to which the grantor transfers his primary residence while retaining a tenancy in the residence for a term of years. At the end of the term, the residence passes to the beneficiaries. The objective is to transfer the residence while it has a lower value rather than when the grantor dies and it has a greater value. Thus the QPRT is basically a trust to reduce estate taxes.

However, QPRTs provide incidental asset protection. The grantor's creditors can claim the grantor's rights to *use* the property for the remaining term of years (or the rental value for those years). The beneficial remainder interest can also be claimed by the beneficiaries' creditors unless the trust includes appropriate spendthrift provisions. Another potential problem is that at the end of the term, the trustee must either distribute the assets (the residence or cash proceeds from its sale) or convert the QPRT assets into an annuity. This is the preferable alternative in states that creditor-protect annuities.

Q-TIP Trusts

Also popular is the Q-TIP (Qualified Terminable Interest Property) trust, which ensures that your spouse receives a lifetime income from the trust assets. The trust principal then passes to your children or an alternative beneficiary upon your spouse's death or remarriage.

Q-TIPs are most commonly used in second marriages since they essentially preserve the estate for the ultimate benefit of the grantor's children rather than the spouse's children or family, who would normally become the beneficiaries if the deceased spouse's estate were bequeathed outright to the surviving spouse. Of course, Q-TIPs are sometimes set up for first spouses when the grantor is concerned that the spouse may waste assets during their lifetime. The Q-TIP essentially serves as a spendthrift trust to shelter the assets from the spouse's creditors or subsequent mates.

One restriction is that income from the Q-TIP trust

must be used solely for the benefit of the surviving spouse during the spouse's lifetime; this condition is necessary to qualify for the unlimited marital deduction. Estate taxes are deferred until your surviving spouse's death.

Unfortunately, a Q-TIP trust won't protect the grantor's assets against creditors because the Q-TIP is a *testamentary* trust, which takes effect only upon the grantor's death. However, the Q-TIP trust is an excellent vehicle to shelter your wealth from a spendthrift spouse, or one who may otherwise encounter future financial or legal difficulties.

While the trust principal remains safe from a spouse's creditors, the income stream flowing to the spouse is unprotected. Moreover, the income must be currently distributed as earned. The trustee has no discretion to withhold distributions.

Some planners use irrevocable *intervivos* marital deduction trusts for asset protection. The objective is to shift assets from the higher risk spouse to the less-at-risk spouse; of course, this is nothing more than another form of lifetime gifting. Such transfers are subject to fraudulent transfer claims. Moreover, the spouse making the gift must also be mindful that the transferred assets may be more easily lost in a later divorce.

Land Trusts

Land trusts are chiefly used in Illinois, Florida, Georgia, California, Colorado, and several other states.

The land trust can own any real estate, including the family home; usually a bank is the trustee. The key question is whether the land trust protects the beneficiaries' interest in the real estate. To some small extent it will if the trust contains the right spendthrift and anti-alienation provisions. You always need good drafting with a land trust.

As the trust beneficiary, you do not directly own the real estate, which is instead titled with the trustee. You own a beneficial interest in the trust; this is personal, not real property.

Owning a beneficial interest in a land trust is not, in itself, sufficient protection from creditors who can seize your beneficial interest. You need a more protective arrangement. One option is to title your beneficial interest in the trust to a limited partnership, LLC, or irrevocable trust.

Land trusts have two disadvantages. One is that it is frequently difficult to refinance property in a land trust. The trust property must then be temporarily reconveyed out of trust to its grantors or beneficiaries to complete the financing. Also, for a beneficiary who wants a Section 1031 tax-free, like-kind exchange, the property must again be transferred from the trust, since a land trust is not considered an interest in real property, but only an interest in personal property.

Privacy, not asset protection, is the major advantage of the land trust. The beneficial owner names do not appear on the public records because the property is directly titled to the trustee. To the extent secrecy aids asset protection, consider the land trust.

Medicaid Trusts

The Medicaid trust is another special purpose trust exclusively used to shelter assets so the grantor can qualify for Medicaid to pay nursing home costs. Medicaid trusts, of course, chiefly interest older Americans who wish to leave their money to their children rather than spend it on long-term care.

A Medicaid trust compares to other irrevocable trusts. The grantor (as an individual or couple) transfers their assets to an irrevocable trust. However, unlike other irrevocable trusts, the grantor can become the income beneficiary while their children or spouse would become the final beneficiaries of the trust. The grantor may continue to receive income from the trust (to the maximum allowed by Medicaid); however, the grantor would now be asset-free so he or she can qualify for Medicaid nursing home assistance.

The Medicaid trust offers about the same asset protection as do other irrevocable trusts. Medicaid trusts prohibit using trust assets for other health care purposes and also limit the beneficiary's income to the limits set by Medicaid. You must create and fund the Medicaid trust at least 60 months before applying for Medicaid. That's one big disadvantage with this trust. Few people can or will anticipate their long-term care needs that far into the future.

Alaska and Delaware Trusts

Both Alaska and Delaware have recently enacted legislation to encourage the formation of 'special' trusts in their jurisdictions that promise added estate planning and asset protection benefits. Their estate tax advantages are worth exploring, particularly if you live in a state with an inheritance tax. Alaska and Delaware trusts are primarily promoting their trusts as alternatives to the offshore trust. Undoubtedly, many Americans are more comfortable with a US-based trust rather than a foreign trust, and this is their selling point.

While the Alaska and Delaware trusts are the most publicized, several other states have comparable trust laws; Rhode Island, Colorado, and Nevada are three. From my analysis, the Nevada trust is probably the most protective domestic trust based on a point-by-point comparison of the trust laws from these competing trust jurisdictions. For example, Nevada trusts impose the shortest statute of limitations for a creditor to file a claim. The settlor can also be a beneficiary and retain some level of control without impairing the trust's asset protection. Delaware, Rhode Island, and Alaska otherwise have comparable trust legislation.

The key question to answer before you establish an asset protection trust in any of these jurisdictions is whether their trusts give you significantly more protection than a comparable trust in your own state. Domestic trusts are compared to offshore trusts in Chapter 11.

In my view, no US asset protection trust jurisdiction offers a sufficiently protective trust, even when they are somewhat more protective than what you could achieve with an irrevocable trust in your own state when there is potential for a fraudulent transfer claim. While the trust laws in these states give you some estate planning advantages, they do not give significant asset protection advantages. However, you should not ignore them for estate planning, and for that purpose you should investigate the trust laws of these few states with your estate planning attorney.

When I want to *totally* lawsuit-proof a client, I seldom use domestic trusts *from any state;* an offshore trust is the answer.

The main flaw with a trust from a more protective state is that it cannot protect you against the claims of *present* creditors. Certainly these domestic trusts are less effective than offshore trusts since a foreign trustee will not recognize US judgments or comply with US court orders. Conversely, the courts of Alaska, Delaware, Nevada or other states *must* constitutionally recognize and enforce judgments and court orders from other states. For example, if a transfer of assets into a trust is deemed a fraudulent transfer in your state, they would be eventually recoverable by your creditor if the transfer to your trust in another state were challenged.

Undoubtedly more states will promote favorable trust legislation in the future; however, the number of trusts established for asset protection in these jurisdictions has not grown dramatically. On the other hand, offshore trusts continue to rise in popularity because they create such formidable barriers to creditors.

Avoid Trust Shams

Promoters of 'pure trusts,' 'common law trusts,' or 'constitutional trusts' ensnare a gullible public. It is usually claimed that since these abusive trusts predate our tax laws, they are immune from taxation, that they protect your assets from creditors, and help you to avoid probate. For starters, the tax claims are nearly always bogus.

'Pure' trusts are usually shams that provide neither tax benefits nor benefits above what you could gain using any other trust. The IRS has cracked down on abusive trusts and their promoters - along with the taxpayers who unlawfully use these trusts to avoid taxes. Remember, any grantor trust requires the grantor to pay taxes on the trust income. On irrevocable trusts, the trust pays the taxes on the income. In either case *someone* pays tax on the trust earnings. A trust is generally *not* a device to avoid income taxes.

Can pure trusts protect your assets? Possibly. The answer chiefly depends on whether the trust is irrevocable and whether you have divested yourself of control over the trust assets. As you can see, the asset protection and tax benefits of any trust will, in every instance, be based entirely on the terms or characteristics of the trust, not on the name of the trust.

From my experience, pure trusts are only simple revocable grantor or nominee trusts. As such, they compare to living trusts, which provide neither asset protection nor any special tax benefits. My advice is to stay away from any organization or promoter that claims their trust enjoys special powers or immunities. Have your attorney prepare - or at least review, any trust that you are considering. You want a trust that will give you every benefit you expect, and not huge tax troubles.

Gifting For Asset Protection

Lifetime gifting can, in some circumstances, be a sensible way to reduce estate taxes and also protect your assets, especially when you shift title to your assets to a less liability-prone recipient.

For example, you can save income taxes by transferring income-producing assets to a recipient in a lower tax bracket. Gifting is also useful to reduce a taxable estate (and estate taxes) while reducing the assets exposed to your creditors.

The annual gift tax exclusion presently allows you to transfer $11,000 annually per recipient, tax-free, provided the gift is immediately available to the recipient. If you and your spouse jointly own and gift property, the exclusion doubles to $22,000 per recipient. A couple with three children can gift $66,000 annually tax-free.

There are ways to accelerate your gifting:

- You can transfer property in exchange for an installment sale note that would be payable annually. In each subsequent year you can forgive $11,000 per recipient, without tax consequences. The note then becomes self-liquidating. This transfer is a 'fair consideration' exchange (the note), and therefore is not a fraudulent conveyance. Of course, your note receivable needs to be correctly titled so that it is protected from your creditors.
- Bypass-generation gifts can also accelerate gifting, although these gifts may impose a generation-skipping transfer tax of 50 percent (plus the gift tax that applies

to larger gifts). You can avoid this with a generation-skipping trust.

- You want to gift those assets that are most vulnerable to creditors and retain those assets that are either exempt from creditors or are otherwise well protected.

- Another option is to transfer property to a minor child through a children's or minor's trust, or gift assets under the Uniform Transfers to Minors Act. A minor's trust is only safe from the grantor's creditors if the trust is irrevocable and the transfer to the trust is not fraudulent. The beneficiary's creditors cannot seize the funds until they are actually distributed to the beneficiary.

Lawsuit-Proof Your Estate

Every indebted testator wants to bequeath his estate free of his creditors' claims. While most people fully pay their debts from their estates, some people do have many more debts than assets when they die. They may even have lawsuits pending against them. Yes, a great number of people get sued *after* they die. You want to arrange your affairs so that your assets pass on to your heirs free of lawsuits or other creditor claims. Here are some ways to do this:

- Title property jointly (or as tenancy-by-the-entirety). Nearly every state passes jointly owned property to the surviving joint owner free of creditor claims against the deceased owner.

- Bequeath your property through an irrevocable trust that was funded during your lifetime (and before you have creditors).

- Make lifetime gifts to deplete your estate, provided these gifts are not fraudulent transfers.

- Invest in fixed annuities or other financial investments. This essentially transforms your wealth into an income stream for yourself, and its value passes debt-free to your survivors.

As you know, your living trust *will not* insulate your estate from your creditors, but even then the living trust offers some asset protection value. For instance, every state sets a time limit within which a creditor must file their claim against an estate. However, when your assets are titled to a living trust you avoid probate. Your creditors, including potential litigants, may remain unaware of your death and their need to file a timely claim.

Disclaiming Inheritances

You may anticipate a large inheritance and anticipate or now have a judgment creditor. Can you judgment-proof your future inheritance? One solution is to disclaim your inheritance. Any beneficiary can disclaim their inheritance. A disclaimer essentially passes the inheritance on to the next generation. The disclaimer is a good strategy when you want your children to get your inheritance rather than risk losing it to your own creditors.

A disclaimer is a complete and unqualified refusal to accept certain rights or property. You can disclaim both gifts and inheritances. Your alternate beneficiaries may be your children, spouse, or any other party you designate to receive the gift. For the disclaimer to be effective, you must observe several requirements: (1) Your disclaimer must be in writing (2) You must not have previously accepted any part of the property or any benefits of ownership (3) Your disclaimer must be received by the transferor within nine months from the date the transfer or document creating the interest (the bequeath or gift) is made.

A testator who plans to bequeath wealth to you, can, of course, during their lifetime change their will to instead direct the inheritance to an entity that would insulate the inheritance from the beneficiaries' creditors. For example, the gift may be bequeathed to:

- A domestic testamentary trust with spendthrift, anti-alienation, and discretionary provisions.
- An offshore asset protection trust.
- A limited partnership or LLC.

In each instance, the full benefits of the gift or bequest can be enjoyed by the beneficiary, partner or member of one of these entities. For asset protection, these inheritors must look ahead to protect their *future* wealth.

Six Tips to Build Trust Protection

How can you increase your trust protection? Here are six simple strategies:

- Use multiple trusts and different trustees for different assets. Creditors find it much more difficult to attack several trusts as opposed to one. Multiple trusts also give you the flexibility to accommodate multiple objectives.
- Consider foreign trusts because they greatly discourage litigation and solidify your protection.
- Incrementally transfer assets to your trusts. Smaller, incremental transfers allow you to better argue that your transfers were not intended to defraud creditors.
- Add 'innocent' preambles to your trust. For example, a stated purpose (such as estate planning) would help

show that your trust was not designed only to creditor-
protect your assets.
- Include in your trust beneficiaries other than yourself.
  Transfers to trusts that are only for the benefit of the
  grantor are not protected against present creditors or
  future creditors.
- Avoid control. The more control you assert over the
  trust, the greater the odds that your creditor can claim
  the trust assets. Use irrevocable trusts, not revocable
  trusts when asset protection is your objective.
  Appoint third party trustees and do not reserve the
  right to modify the trust or dictate how its assets or
  income will be used. These mistakes are fatal to asset
  protection.

Keep Your Estate Plan Current

We also cannot leave the important subject of protecting your
estate without reminding you how important it is to keep your
own estate plan current. People who die without a basic estate
plan only invite legal problems:

- Minimally, you need an up-to-date will (and/or living
  trust) so your estate does not pass by intestacy to
  unintended heirs. Unfortunately, only one in five
  American adults has an up-to-date will.
- Review your will and/or living trust annually. Your
  estate planning circumstances change as rapidly
  as your asset protection needs. An outdated will
  can cause serious legal problems; sometimes more
  problems than no will.
- Besides your will or living trust, you also need a durable
  power of attorney (one for healthcare and one for your
  financial/legal affairs) so someone can immediately

represent you if you become incapacitated. You also need a living will to set forth the circumstances under which you do and do not want your life artificially prolonged.

- Finally, hire a good estate planner, particularly if you have a taxable or complex estate. A good estate planner can save you a fortune in estate taxes (never forget that when you die, Uncle Sam may be your #1 creditor) and show you many ways to achieve your estate planning objectives.

11

The Offshore Advantage

Your simplest and safest asset protection strategy may be to move all your money to a foreign jurisdiction. Why not? This estate and family wealth planning strategy has been popular since the days when Roman emperors relocated their fortunes to foreign lands to preserve their riches for their descendants. Offshore wealth protection is even more popular today because of the lawsuit explosion.

About $5 trillion is now protected in offshore financial centers (OFCs). OFCs feature favorable tax, banking, privacy, estate planning, and asset protection laws. This explains why so many wealthy individuals and families internationally send their money offshore. Only within the last decade or two have so many Americans recognized the many advantages of offshore asset protection and investing. The number of Americans with offshore wealth continues to grow rapidly.

Untouchable Offshore Wealth

I learned from my many years as an asset protection and wealth preservation lawyer that the safest wealth is *offshore* wealth.

I created offshore asset protection programs for hundreds of clients, and I have yet to have one lose offshore assets to *any* litigant. These now financially secure people also enjoy far greater privacy, and as international investors they also oftentimes discover more profitable investments.

Is protecting money offshore *safe?* Rest assured, your money is far safer offshore than it is here in lawsuit-crazy America.

Is going offshore with your money legal? Follow a few simple tax reporting rules and it is 100 percent legitimate.

You may have been programmed to believe that offshore finance is only for crooks, frauds, and the super-rich. Your own financial planner, lawyer, or accountant may advise you to forget about it as being 'too risky, too expensive, too bothersome.' But they would be wrong.

Offshore wealth protection is a popular wealth protection tool and it continues to be because many financial and legal professionals constantly look for better ways to protect their clients' wealth. It is unfortunate that so many American lawyers still rely entirely on domestic asset protection tools and strategies when their clients' money could be considerably safer offshore. When I design asset protection for my wealthier clients I usually blend domestic and offshore strategies. The domestic component shelters their US-based assets such as real estate and business. The offshore structures protect their nest egg or liquid investments. By blending the two, I can usually create the most effective overall protection. Beware of using a lawyer for asset protection planning who is unfamiliar or uncomfortable with offshore strategies. Such a lawyer inevitably shortchanges the client who needs the *strongest* protection.

Why Offshore Havens Provide Powerful Protection

I can give you a long list of reasons why you get the best protection offshore.

First, asset protection jurisdictions won't recognize or enforce US judgments, judicial, or administrative orders (such as from the IRS), so you enjoy jurisdictional immunity. No foreign country can completely ignore every legal order from another country, but certain countries won't enforce US *civil* decrees. These are the countries we use for lawsuit protection.

Because these countries won't recognize an American judgment or civil decree, the creditor must re-litigate its case within that foreign jurisdiction. This may be impractical or impossible for many reasons. One is that the statute of limitations for commencing suit may have expired or the country may not recognize the plaintiff's underlying theory of liability. These countries may impose other procedural obstacles to effectively block creditors and litigation. Asset protection jurisdictions are debtor-oriented. They strive hard to protect their customers' wealth because protection is what they sell.

Asset protection jurisdictions have special laws that allow one to create particularly protective asset protection structures within their country. These entities include offshore asset protection trusts, limited liability companies, limited partnerships, foundations, captive insurance companies, international business companies, hybrid companies, and other comparable entities. Each in its own way can give you considerably more protection than comparable US entities.

Finally, while asset protection jurisdictions are good privacy havens, a good privacy jurisdiction is not necessarily a good asset protection jurisdiction.

The ultimate advantage of offshore protection over domestic asset protection is that fraudulently transferred assets within the US are easily recoverable through the US courts since they have continued jurisdiction over these assets. However, American courts have no jurisdiction over offshore assets. For that one reason alone, offshore assets are far better protected than are US-based assets that remain susceptible to fraudulent transfer claims and other attack mechanisms through our US courts.

This point is important. You never know when someone will raise a claim from the past. Your asset protection plan must withstand these fraudulent transfer claims. There are too few instances where a creditor cannot persuasively argue that there was a fraudulent conveyance. To avoid this vulnerability and uncertainty, you need your money offshore.

OFCs provide enormous debtor protection and impose many legal and procedural obstacles that few creditors can or will overcome. One earlier cited example is their short statute of limitations. For example, claims against your offshore assets must usually be filed within one or two years from the date you transferred your assets to that country. Few creditors can timely challenge offshore transfers. Another obstacle is that the creditor must also *prove beyond a reasonable doubt* that the transfer offshore was fraudulent. This is a very difficult standard to overcome. Nevis (a particularly good asset protection jurisdiction), for example, also requires the creditor to post a $25,000 cash bond before the creditor can commence litigation. Another roadblock is that the creditor must hire local counsel on a fee-only basis. Contingent fee arrangements are not allowed.

The most important procedural obstacle is that an American creditor with a US judgment must nevertheless re-litigate the case within that country and win a judgment from *their* courts before the creditor can attempt to set aside any fraudulently transferred assets. Nor can the creditor even re-litigate the case unless the claim follows rules of liability recognized in that country. For example, discrimination, anti-trust, and many other lawsuits based on American laws give the creditor no opportunity to re-litigate.

These and many other requirements effectively filter most prospective claims against offshore assets. While no respectable asset protection country can completely disregard fraudulent transfer claims, these financial centers can and do make it difficult - *exceptionally* difficult - to pursue such claims.

A final obstacle for a determined creditor attempting to recover offshore assets is that your trustee can relocate your offshore assets to another trust or some other protective entity in another asset protection country. This forces the creditor to begin new legal proceedings in that new OFC. This 'flee' provision - found in most offshore trusts - would cause any creditor to tire from the chase. The trust assets, of course, can continuously be moved to still other countries and structures. This flee provision, or 'Cuba clause,' exemplifies only one of many powerful asset protection provisions found in any well drafted offshore trust. Other provisions can as effectively deprive the creditor any practical opportunity to seize the offshore assets.

This explains why fewer than three out of 100 judgment creditors even attempt to recover offshore wealth. These few cases are typically settled for pennies on the dollar. Without offshore protection, these same creditors would undoubtedly have recovered significantly more. The fact that

97 out of 100 creditors *won't* challenge an offshore transfer strongly endorses its asset protection power.

Understand that in many of these cases the creditor had the legal right to recover the assets as a fraudulent transfer, yet the creditor did not attempt recovery because it was impractical. A creditor can spend enormous legal fees and still never recover a dime in offshore assets, even when the creditor has, at his disposal, the legal remedy. Offshore asset protection makes it impractical for creditors to pursue their claim and your creditor's legal recourse becomes academic when your creditor *won't* assert his remedy.

Select The Right Offshore Financial Center

Which is the best OFC? There is no one best choice. Many offshore jurisdictions offer excellent protection. Focus on five criteria when you select your wealth protection jurisdiction:

- Strong asset protection legislation and a pro-debtor enforcement orientation
- A predictable, sound legal system
- No taxes on foreign capital
- Financial privacy and confidentiality
- No exchange controls.

You may look for other criteria if your objectives for keeping your wealth offshore change. Match your reasons for going offshore to the OFC that best satisfies those needs. For asset protection, unquestionably the most important criteria is the OFC's ability and willingness to protect your assets; everything else is secondary.

About twenty OFCs provide some level of asset protection, but you must closely evaluate these points:

- **Statute of Limitations:** You want the shortest possible period for a creditor to challenge a fraudulent transfer. Only when you reach this date are your prior transfers safe. Statutes of limitations range from an unlimited duration to one-year (Nevis).

- **Non-recognition of foreign judgments:** The country must neither recognize nor enforce foreign judgments. The creditor *must* be forced to re-litigate the case in that country.

- **Burden of proof on fraudulent intent:** Will the country require a creditor who pursues an alleged fraudulent transfer to prove that the transfer was made with fraudulent intent? The debtor should not be required to prove the opposite.

- **Standard of proof:** The standard of proof on fraudulent intent should also be rigid. Some countries require the creditor to establish fraud by a mere preponderance of the evidence. Others demand that fraud be proven beyond a reasonable doubt - a far more difficult standard.

- **Ability to freeze assets:** Your OFC must not allow your creditor to attach or restrain your assets before judgment. Few do.

- **Invalidity of fraudulent transfers or subsequent creditors:** Your OFC must fully protect assets transferred before the liability was incurred, notwithstanding later fraudulent transfers.

- **Clear differentiation of creditors:** Their laws should clearly distinguish between your present creditors who can pursue fraudulent conveyances and *future* creditors who cannot.

You can find OFCs of every size, variety, and political persuasion throughout the world. Bermuda, the British Virgin Islands, and the Bahamas hug America's southeast coast. The Cayman Islands, Turks and Caicos, Nevis, and Antigua dot the Caribbean. The Isle of Man, Channel Islands, Jersey, and Guernsey shadow England. Switzerland, Liechtenstein, Luxembourg, Hungary, and Austria are key European havens. The Philippines, Singapore, and Hong Kong serve the Pacific Rim. Cyprus, Malta, and Gibraltar are Mediterranean OFCs. The Cook Islands, near New Zealand, are another favorite.

Protective OFCs cluster near the industrialized countries whose arcane laws force their wealthier citizens to find friendlier places for their money. The world is shrinking rapidly, however, and your choice of OFC no longer depends upon geography. You can now easily move your money to and invest from whatever country best satisfies your financial objectives. Electronic banking makes it as fast and easy to bank from another hemisphere as from next door.

Offshore stars rise and fall quickly. Newer more competitive OFCs constantly emerge. Gibraltar, the Cook Islands, Nevis, the Marianas, Belize, the Turks and Caicos, and Montserrat are newer offshore contenders. Other bright stars are on the horizon. I currently consider Nevis and the Cook Islands as the most protective foreign assets protection jurisdictions. These are the financial centers I usually use. Every asset protection lawyer has his own favorite jurisdictions and affiliations (trustees, protectors, banks, etc.). Do not expect unanimity when you ask about a best haven.

It is important to understand that you will probably have a multi-national offshore asset protection plan. For example, your Nevis trust may serve as the primary shield, but the trust funds may be banked or invested in Switzerland, Panama, Hong Kong, or elsewhere.

The Asset Protection Trust And
Alternative Entities

The traditional offshore protective entity is the offshore asset protection trust (OAPT). You may know it by other names: The Creditor Protection Trust, Offshore Trust, International Trust, Asset Conservation Trust, Foreign Trust, or Foreign Grantor Trust.

The offshore trust is a relatively new twist to the trust's long heritage. Only since the 1980s have certain foreign countries enacted laws to allow for the formation of asset protection trusts. Most offshore trusts have been established within the past decade, but it is now one of the most popular trusts. Its popularity directly relates to the increased need and demand for asset protection.

You can, however, use offshore trusts for other purposes. Avoiding forced heirship laws, premarital planning, estate planning, Medicaid planning, international business planning, and regulatory avoidance are a few examples. The OAPT is quite versatile.

The offshore trust compares closely to the domestic irrevocable trust, although for many reasons it provides considerably greater protection. One reason is that the offshore trust is a *foreign* trust. That's a critical difference. While your irrevocable US trust always remains vulnerable to your existing creditors and the creditor-friendly US courts, your OAPT is immune. The offshore trust has many unique and interesting protective features:

- **Foreign law governs**: The debtor-friendly laws of the OFC governs its enforcement.
- **Anti-duress provisions:** If a US court should order you as the trust grantor to repatriate the trust assets, the offshore trustee must refuse this demand. Your

trust funds will *not* be returned for the benefit of your creditor.

- **Flight provisions:** The trustee can relocate the trust assets to another OFC if the trust becomes endangered.
- **Discretionary powers:** The trustee can, if necessary, withhold distributions to beneficiaries with creditors.

The OAPT otherwise compares closely to a US irrevocable trust used for estate planning. For example, the offshore trust has a *grantor* (or settlor, donor, or trustor) who creates and funds the trust, appoints the initial trustees and protector and names the beneficiaries. Its *trustee* manages the trust for the benefit of the beneficiaries. (This is almost always a foreign trustee firm.) The *beneficiaries* receive the trust's income and/ or assets.

Unlike the US trust, the OAPT may have a *protector* to oversee the trustee. The protector can replace the trustee and must approve major actions by the trustee. The grantor appoints the initial protector, who should obviously be someone not subject to US court directives.

Any adult or legal entity can be the grantor and create and fund the trust. Parents or grandparents frequently create OAPTs to protect their wealth for their families. Husbands and wives may be co-grantors and combine their wealth into one trust, or they may establish separate trusts. Who becomes the grantor frequently depends upon complex tax, asset protection, estate planning, business, and personal considerations.

For greater confidentiality, you can use an offshore corporation or foreign lawyer to establish the trust as the nominee grantor. Some offshore trusts do not require you to specifically name the grantor, and certain jurisdictions do not require you to record the trust. This also helps to protect the grantor's identity.

Worried About Losing
Control Over Your Wealth?

The most common concern with going offshore is the idea of relinquishing control of your money to some foreign trustee. After all, how do you know that the trustee will not steal or squander your money?

First, it's true that the trust gives the trustee broad powers to do whatever is needed to protect or enhance the trust assets. These powers - found in any irrevocable trust - include the right to sell, buy, lease, encumber, or invest trust assets, defend or prosecute claims, pay debts and taxes, hire other professionals, make loans, and/or distribute income or principal to beneficiaries, and so forth.

The trust purposely grants the trustee broad powers and the grantor no authority or negligible authority. A grantor with more control loses asset protection. However, delegating control over your wealth to a foreign trustee becomes far less frightening once you realize that foreign trustees readily comply with the grantor's appropriate and *voluntary* wishes.

To allay concerns about losing control, you can, through a number of strategies, balance your asset protection goals against retaining some level of control. However, your attorney must ultimately decide how much control you can safely retain without jeopardizing asset protection.

You have other options. You can appoint a protector who will follow your directions. The protector can always block trustee action or replace the trustee. Thus, through your protector you gain *alter ego* control. You can make the offshore trust *revocable* until a specified event – such as a lawsuit – when the trust will automatically become irrevocable. You can also form a limited partnership to be owned by the offshore trust as its limited partner. As the general partner, you would stay in control of the partnership assets within the US until you are sued. You can *then* transfer the partnership assets to the trust. Another option is to become the managing director of an IBC (foreign company), which would be owned by the trust. The funds in the IBC would be under your control. Another alternative is to control the trusteeship until threatened by creditors. For instance, you, your spouse, or another US designee can be the co-trustees with your foreign trustee. Moreover, you or your protector can co-sign the trust bank accounts. Finally, you can keep your trust unfunded and fund it for asset protection only when a lawsuit is likely. We have many other control-retention techniques.

While these and other safeguards can insure that your assets will be handled as you wish, your worries are understandable. Fortunately, you have little cause for concern. Foreign trustees have an impeccable record for honesty and prudence. These professionals are usually fully bonded, licensed, and backed by the reputation of their own countries.

You can find excellent trustee firms in every OFC. Most are lawyers or chartered accountants. Your trustee should also be well established and administer many other trusts and other offshore entities. Active trustee firms also can provide you a wide range of services and deliver those services most efficiently. Expect the attorney who sets up your trust to recommend a trustee firm that has provided his other clients with good service.

Of course, check your trustee's references. How many clients do they serve? How satisfied are they? How has their firm grown? Who within the firm will handle your account? Will they provide client references? Bank references? Bonding? Can they deliver the services you need, such as portfolio management? Are they accessible? Responsive? Are their fees reasonable?

Avoid Three Fatal Errors

Your offshore trust won't be effective for asset protection unless your trust is structured and administered properly. There have been a few celebrated cases of offshore trusts that have failed. Those few cases highlight one or more fatal mistakes that you must avoid.

- **The grantor retained too much control,** allowing the court to determine that the trust was nothing more than a sham. For asset protection, you must give your trustee control over your trust - not only in form, but also in practice.
- **The trust assets were within the United States** where they could then be seized by a US court if the transfer to the trust is deemed fraudulent. Keep your assets offshore.
- **The trust lacked necessary protective safeguards** or the trust was technically defective. Have your trust prepared by an experienced professional.

In some cases, the grantor was ordered by the court to repatriate the trust assets for the benefit of the creditor. When the grantor failed or refused, he was jailed for contempt. I think these rulings were proper in at least those cases where the grantor had *defacto* control over their trust. In other instances, the trust was set up only days before the court proceeding. Ordinarily a court cannot find you in contempt for your failure to repatriate your money if you truly lack the power to comply with the court order, which a properly structured and administered trust should accomplish, and your trust doesn't appear to be a last-minute effort to put your assets beyond the court's reach.

Timing and relinquishing control are both vital to your offshore success. Don't wait until the last moment to protect yourself. Set up your offshore entities well before you have a liability, or at least before you are sued, and don't exercise control over your trust so the court cannot reasonably conclude that you actually have the power to repatriate the trust funds. You are less likely to make these mistakes if your trust is overseen by an attorney experienced with offshore trusts and the rulings in these recent cases.

The Nevis LLC May Give You Superior Protection

The offshore trust is only one of several protective entities that you can use. For example, I now frequently use the Nevis LLC for my offshore clients. However, I still use the offshore trust if my client needs offshore estate planning or to avoid tax problems from transferring appreciated assets to other offshore entities.

I consider the Nevis LLC one of the most powerful wealth protectors. It can give you equal or even more protection - at less cost - than the OAPT.

Nevis, a small Caribbean, British Commonwealth nation in the Leeward Islands, has gained an international reputation for financial privacy and asset protection. The Nevis LLC demonstrates their innovation for wealth protection.

While the United States and several foreign jurisdictions have limited liability companies, the Nevis LLC is particularly effective for asset protection because it has several advantageous features not found in other LLCs. In concept, the Nevis LLC combines the protective features of the offshore trust, American limited partnership, and Nevada corporation into one entity.

The Nevis LLC can be either member-directed or managed by a foreign director. Of course, for asset protection, the LLC should be controlled by a foreign (Nevis) managing director. Contributors of assets to the LLC become the LLC members, whose rights are similar to stockholders in a corporation or limited partners in a limited partnership. The members own the LLC but do not directly manage it. Managerial control rests with the managing director. Through this transfer of control, the contributed assets are protected from US court orders; OAPTs are protected because they are controlled by a foreign trustee.

As the LLC member, you no longer own the contributed assets, which are now owned by the LLC. As the LLC member, you cannot be ordered by a US court to repatriate the LLC assets, because control over the LLC assets is with the managing director, who is beyond US court jurisdiction. A creditor of a debtor-member is limited to a charging order against the member's LLC interest, which entitles the creditor to claim the debtor-member's share of any profit or liquidation distributions from the LLC. However, the membership interest cannot itself be seized by the creditor, nor can the creditor vote or exercise other member rights, such as the right to inspect books and records. In this respect the Nevis LLC compares to a US limited partnership or LLC.

A US court order to transfer or seize the debtor-member's LLC interest would be ignored by the managing director who, under Nevis law, would only be required to recognize a creditor's charging order obtained through the Nevis courts.

Obviously, where a debtor-member owns a major interest in the LLC, the managing director would withhold the distribution of profits that could be seized by his charging order creditor. If the debtor-member has a minority interest, and withholding distributions would conflict with the interests of the other debtor-members, the minority debtor-member may then title his LLC interest with another self-owned Nevis LLC that would serve as a safe recipient for the debtor-member's distributed profits. As with an American LLC or LP, a debtor-member can easily access LLC funds without classifying it a 'distribution of profits.' Payments received as salaries (e.g. as investment advisor), loans, etc. from the Nevis LLC are not subject to the charging order.

Moreover, Nevis law and the IRS impose US income tax liability on the charging order creditor for any LLC profits attributable to the debtor-member. The charging order creditor incurs the tax liability even if the creditor received no distribution. This 'poison pill' feature - also found with US limited partnerships and LLCs, but not with other offshore entities – is another protective feature of the Nevis LLC.

A properly drafted Nevis LLC delegates all important powers to the managing director, who would ignore US court orders to repatriate the LLC assets. If the LLC has two or more members, the operating agreement should require unanimous member vote to change the managing director. This overcomes any court order that would compel a single debtor-member to replace the director with one appointed by the court for purposes of repatriating the LLC assets. The Nevis LLC therefore has similar protective 'duress' characteristics as the offshore trust, except that the debtor-member retains an interest in the LLC and, derivatively, its assets.

A properly structured Nevis LLC, is even more protective than the trust, particularly if you have existing creditors, and a transfer to the trust a fraudulent conveyance, contestable in the trust's jurisdiction.

If a Nevis LLC member has an *existing* creditor, the Nevis LLC ordinance allows the member to transfer his assets to the LLC *without it constituting a fraudulent conveyance,* provided the debtor-member's interest is proportionate to his share of the contributed capital. This transfer is then considered a fair value exchange and one exempt from the Nevis fraudulent transfer statutes. Interestingly, a mere promise of a future contribution by an existing or incoming LLC member can be used to measure this proportionality. It is then possible for the debtor-member to own a minority interest subject to the charging order, although he contributed all or most of the LLC's present assets. This dilution strategy effectively discourages a creditor from applying for a charging order, and it is a feature unique to the Nevis LLC.

It is also important to remember that US limited partnership and LLC law are unsettled on whether a present creditor can successfully recover a transfer to a limited partnership or American LLC as a fraudulent conveyance, even when the debtor received, in exchange for his contributed assets, a proportionate interest in the limited partnership or LLC. (Some courts say that creditor impairment alone is sufficient for the transfer to be fraudulent.) There is no such ambiguity under Nevis law. Investing your money in a properly structured Nevis LLC is not a fraudulent transfer, nor one challengeable by an *existing* creditor.

This is why I consider the Nevis LLC more protective than a foreign trust, a domestic limited partnership, or a domestic LLC. It is legally and ethically defensible to use the Nevis LLC regardless of the financial situation of the contributing member. This point cannot be overlooked at a time when offshore trusts used to shield fraudulently transferred assets are increasingly challenged or subject to stern court sanctions against their grantors.

The Nevis LLC is certainly a more attractive option for attorneys whose clients have existing creditors and where the attorney or professional advisor has professional responsibility and liability concerns arising from a fraudulent transfer to an offshore trust or another protective structure.

In my more serious cases, I want to maximize protection. I use a Nevis LLC as a subsidiary entity of an offshore trust. This 'layered' protection gives my client the best of both worlds.

The Nevis LLC boasts several other significant benefits:

- The Nevis LLC has minimal reporting requirements, and it is not subject to US foreign trust reporting requirements. A US member with 10 percent or greater LLC interest still has foreign corporation ownership reporting requirements to the IRS.
- Although it is tax neutral, the Nevis LLC can elect to be taxed either as a partnership or C corporation. Nevis imposes no taxes on the LLC.
- The LLC can be structured for its profits to flow to the members in any proportion specified in the operating agreement, which may differ from their ownership interest.
- For anonymity, ownership in the LLC can be in registered or bearer form.
- You can appoint a protector over the managing director, as with an OAPT.
- The LLC agreement can include the anti-creditor 'poison pills,' that can be adopted by domestic LLCs. For example, a member's interests may be assessable by the managing director against a charging order creditor.
- The LLC operating agreement may also include a 'flight' or 'Cuba clause' to allow the manager to

expatriate threatened LLC assets to a successor protective structure in another asset protection jurisdiction.

- Managing directors and members of the Nevis LLC are immune from company liability, and creditors cannot pierce the corporate veil.
- Nevis does not require minute books, annual director or member meetings, or other customary corporate formalities.
- The Nevis LLC can be owned by an offshore trust in place of an IBC, or you can use it in combination with domestic entities such as FLPs and irrevocable trusts to strengthen and coordinate your domestic and offshore estate planning and asset protection.
- A Nevis LLC is usually far less costly to organize and maintain than are offshore asset protection trusts.

While the Nevis LLC can replace many offshore asset protection trusts, the offshore trust is still useful for offshore wealth protection, estate planning, forced heirship avoidance, or other purposes achievable only through a trust.

Unquestionably, the Nevis LLC is a worthy upgrade from foreign IBCs, which give you considerably less protection and no advantages.

Other countries are developing their own protective structures. For example, the Bahamas limited partnership is closely modeled after the Nevis LLC. Liechtenstein and Panama private foundations and St. Vincent and Isle of Man hybrid companies are substitutes for a trust or alternatives to the Nevis LLC. The search for 'the better mousetrap' continues; however, only an exceptionally innovative 'mousetrap' can beat the Nevis LLC.

Should You Own Your Own
Offshore Insurance Company?

As a speaker to groups of business owners and professionals on asset protection and tax-favored wealth planning, I am often asked about offshore captive insurance companies.

'Captives' or tax-exempt closely held insurance companies (CICs) are worthwhile both for asset protection and tax deferral if you establish and maintain them properly, if they are suited to your economic needs, and if you qualify for their considerable tax benefits.

The CIC is a legitimate insurance company, licensed to write insurance in the US and registered with the IRS. They are based in an offshore jurisdiction, usually Bermuda or the British Virgin Islands, as these two jurisdictions require a small capitalization and feature favorable insurance and tax laws. Offshore CICs have exploded to over 4,000 companies that write an estimated $60 billion in premiums per year, or more than a third of the total commercial insurance sold in the United States. Fortune 500 companies have long used CICs to protect their excess cash and also to gain tax advantages, but only within the last decade have individuals, smaller business owners, and professionals taken advantage of them.

With your own CIC you can insure all or a portion of your business or professional practices from significant risks such as malpractice or other liabilities or losses for which you would typically carry insurance.

By insuring yourself through your own CIC for 'uninsurable' risks, you get a present year tax deduction and you can pay any claims with *pre*-tax dollars out of the CIC's loss reserves. Your CIC may insure low liability risks or your CIC can transfer some risk to another reinsurer, so you would have little economic risk while enjoying significant tax benefits.

Premiums paid to your insurance company are deductible as an ordinary business expense. Deductions for premiums can, in some instances, exceed $1 million per year.

Beyond annual income tax savings, there are other tax benefits with the CIC:

1) You can postpone capital gains on appreciated assets
2) You enjoy tax-free growth
3) You can reduce or eliminate estate taxes on property transferred to your children.

While specific tax benefits are beyond the scope of this book, these benefits, supported by Congress, encourage substantial tax incentives to small insurance companies.

When you own a CIC as an individual professional, business owner, or member of a group, you can take a significant deduction each year and grow your funds in the CIC completely tax-free, or you can reclaim the funds and pay only long-term capital gains tax. This three-tier tax advantage is unavailable through pensions, IRAs, or other common retirement plans.

In addition to its tax benefits, the CIC offers superb asset protection. Your CIC can supplement your existing liability policy, and such 'excess' malpractice protection gives you the security that you will not be wiped out by a lawsuit above your existing coverage.

Also, pre-tax premiums paid to your own CIC are protected from your creditors and the liabilities of your business or professional practice. This is accomplished without losing control of your offshore funds.

Do you own a business or professional practice that generates $300,000 or more in annual profits? Then owning your own captive insurance company may be just your answer.

Visit my website for more information.

Foreign Corporations Won't Protect You

Most offshore promoters suggest that you set up an International Business Corporation (IBC) to safeguard your wealth from lawsuits. That's bad advice.

An IBC can *privatize* your offshore wealth; however, as you know, privacy is not asset protection. A creditor who discovers that your money is titled to an offshore company can obtain a court order to compel you to transfer your IBC ownership to the creditor, or alternatively, order you to liquidate its assets for the benefit of your creditor. Courts won't believe stories that you simply 'gifted' the money to the IBC or that your money somehow 'disappeared.' Asset protection needs entities specifically designed for this purpose. This is not an IBC. Promoters of IBCs should not sell asset protection as one of its benefits.

It is also a mistake to believe that you can hide your money in a privacy haven bank account. Of course, more than a few people do, but it's still poor protection since your judgment creditor (or the IRS) can force you to disclose your offshore assets. If you lie, you commit perjury. If you disclose these assets, a US court can order you to repatriate the unprotected money for your creditor. A foreign bank account - whether in your own name or in the name of an IBC - is never creditor-protected, because in either instance the account remains under your control, and you *can* comply with a court's repatriation and turnover order or be held in contempt.

Protect As Much of Your Wealth Offshore As Possible

You can protect almost any asset offshore, although you can

most easily protect your liquid assets. Cash, securities, and collectibles (gold and jewelry) are assets that can be physically relocated offshore. Real estate, cars, boats, US securities and other US-based assets must necessarily remain within the jurisdiction of the US courts and are recoverable through our courts if they are fraudulently conveyed to an offshore entity.

You are fully protected only when your trustees, protectors, and fiduciaries - *and* your assets - are offshore and beyond the control and recovery powers of the American courts.

So to be as lawsuit-proof as possible, your goal should be to effectively shift *all* your wealth from the US to an offshore asset protection entity. For example, you can mortgage or sell your US-based assets and move the cash proceeds offshore. Your creditors' only recourse is through the US courts to seize the equity-stripped assets, which obviously would have little or no value to your creditor.

Transferring assets offshore follows the same procedures as transferring assets to a domestic entity. You wire transfer your funds. Your stockbroker can transfer your securities. You transfer personal property by bill of sale or assignment, and convey real estate by deed.

When your primary goal is asset protection, you should move offshore as much of your wealth as possible. If asset protection is not your immediate concern, you may invest offshore only your nest egg funds or whatever excess wealth you do not foreseeably need for your living expenses.

If you are uncomfortable with this, start small. Set up your offshore entity and fund it with a minimal amount. Once you become more comfortable with your offshore fiduciaries, banks, investments, etc., you can add funds. Should it become necessary to effectively transfer your entire wealth offshore, then you already have your wealth protection system in place and also have sufficient confidence to transfer your remaining wealth.

When you have a judgment creditor and need asset protection, any repatriated funds must continuously remain titled to other entities so they remain safe from your creditors. For example, a Nevada or Wyoming corporation may receive the funds, or you may direct repatriated funds to a family limited partnership. You could wire the funds to your spouse's account or to a domestic spendthrift trust, setting yourself up as a beneficiary. The spendthrift trust prevents your creditors from seizing your beneficial interest or the assets in the trust. It is also important to remember that legal battles are eventually resolved and you may need your wealth protected offshore for only a limited time.

Don't Try To Beat The IRS

Go offshore for asset protection, not to avoid taxes. It's that simple. The offshore trust is usually a *grantor* trust, which is tax neutral. The trust pays no taxes, since the trust income is taxed directly to the grantor in the year earned; you gain no tax deferral or tax avoidance. The grantor trust is taxed like an S corporation, limited partnership, or living trust. As an American, the offshore trust gives you neither a tax advantage nor disadvantage.

Nevis LLCs and International Business Corporations (IBCs) are also tax neutral. Don't use them to avoid US income tax. Some promoter may tell you that you can avoid US income taxes by going offshore with your money. Get another opinion from a qualified international tax planner. Except for certain qualified insurance and annuity programs, any income that you or your entities earn offshore is fully taxable in the year that it is earned, whether or not you repatriate it. For more information on IRS reporting requirements, visit my website.

Privatize Your Finances Offshore

As an American involved in a lawsuit, your US bank and other third parties must provide your opponent with any banking records that are subpoenaed. However, your offshore banking records are fully privacy-protected against US court orders and subpoenas because offshore banks in most offshore financial centers are jurisdictionally immune to service of process. Offshore banks in a privacy haven cannot divulge financial information about you to third parties, except as permitted under narrow treaty provisions.

Since offshore banks are jurisdictionally immune to service of process, they equally ban US writs of execution or attachment orders. Thus, while the secrecy laws of most havens generally protect entrusted funds from creditor seizure originating from a domestic judgment and also protect the confidentiality of all financial transactions that pass through the bank, you still need the right protective entity (i.e. an offshore trust, a Nevis LLC) to protect you from a US turnover order.

For privacy you need an offshore bank without American-based branches or affiliates. This keeps the bank outside the jurisdiction of the American courts. Demands for financial information are barred by both the foreign and American courts if disclosure violates the secrecy laws of the offshore haven.

This jurisdictional immunity for offshore banks can guard you against unwanted intrusions into your financial privacy. Banking records that are so readily obtainable within the United States are beyond view of prying government and private litigants if your funds are in the right offshore haven.

Privacy is a major benefit of offshore banking that many American investors overlook. Needlessly exposed finances can get you into serous trouble, and the privacy advantage grows in importance daily.

Another offshore privacy strategy is to convert titled assets, such as real estate or stocks and bonds, into bearer investments (i.e. gold, diamonds, art, stamp collections, coins, and similar collectibles). Bearer investments are easily transported offshore and are completely confidential and private. For more privacy, you can buy and sell collectibles through a third party, such as your own offshore corporation, or Nevis LLC, with bearer shares. They can as easily be reconverted to cash with complete confidentiality and privacy. Private vaults are available in a number of countries to provide even greater secrecy.

For financial privacy, create two separate financial worlds. Your public world is your home country where you work, pay taxes, maintain your bank accounts and investments, and expose the finances you expect the world to know about.

Your private world is offshore, where you keep your 'invisible money' that only *you* know about. This private world shelters your major bank accounts, investments, etc. that you want to keep invisible and private.

To maintain tight secrecy, never mix your two worlds. Avoid direct transactions between the two. For maximum privacy, do not directly transfer your funds from your onshore (public world) bank to your offshore (private world) bank. Use intermediary entities in intermediary havens.

Privacy is a basic right of every free citizen. The fact that so many people want privacy does not speak against them, but against their governments, litigants, and others who stripped them of their privacy. Ignore those who argue that privacy encourages illegality. Financial privacy - for legitimate purposes - must be every American's goal in this litigation era.

Is Going Offshore Your Right Solution?

For all its benefits, offshore wealth protection is not everyone's solution. You must be realistic about what offshore asset protection can accomplish, and what it can accomplish may or may not justify its cost or effort. Candidly discuss your situation with the *right* professional. Nothing can replace a professional evaluation.

You are *not* a good offshore candidate if you cannot become comfortable with the idea that your assets will be controlled by others. Many people who would benefit greatly refuse offshore protection for this one reason. Most people eventually overcome their fears. Others have little choice but to go offshore if they want to save their wealth. Cautiously, they take the plunge. For others, nothing can coax them to redeploy their money offshore. If you are uncomfortable with your wealth offshore, decide whether it is only a matter of learning more or chronic insecurity. If you shun offshore protection in exchange for a less protective domestic asset protection plan, it may be costly. You should not compromise on your asset protection.

Others have shared your same questions, experiences, and fears. How safe will my money be? Will the trustee run away with my money or lose it on some crazy investment? Can I *really* get my money back if I need it? If these are a few of your questions, talk to others who once shared these same concerns. You will find that these people are not only satisfied with their offshore experience, but also find that their wealth is safe and secure.

As one client commented, "You never realize how vulnerable your wealth is here in the US until it is safely sheltered offshore." One Los Angeles physician recently told me, "Before, I was nervous about my money offshore; now I get nervous thinking how easily I could have lost it here."

Knowledge builds confidence and confidence prompts action. That is why I educate my clients: It builds confidence. Your offshore program will get under way with more enthusiasm and function more smoothly when your fears are calmed.

Again, accept no substitute for good professional advice. Educate yourself. You can then more *intelligently* select and work with your advisors. Order a *free* copy of my book *How To Protect Your Money Offshore* (Garrett Publishing). This helpful educational tool answers many questions.

While most offshore professionals are honest, trustworthy, and knowledgeable, every business has its incompetents. Start with an attorney well experienced in offshore wealth protection. Avoid boilerplate plans or entities from non-lawyers or offshore companies unless they are well recommended. Many sell worthless documents and false information to an unsuspecting public. Have your attorney coordinate your offshore program with your domestic asset protection and estate-planning program to create a seamless plan and comprehensive protection.

12

Debt-Shields and Friendly Mortgages

In many cases you must do more than shelter your assets in protective entities. You need an additional firewall. That firewall is to 'strip whatever equity' you can from everything you own, both real estate and personal property. The tactic: Convert unencumbered, vulnerable wealth into debt-ridden wealth, which of course is worthless to a plaintiff.

There are different types of mortgages and liens, but generally a lien is a mortgage or security interest filed against a debtor's real estate or personal property. As the property owner, you still retain title or legal ownership of the property, but you effectively transfer the *economic* value of your property to the mortgage holder. In turn, this reduces the equity in your property available for seizure by creditors or litigants.

Suppose your home is worth more than what you owe on mortgages (or liens) against it. You then have *equity* in your property that is available to a litigant. For protection, you reduce (or 'strip') your equity by increasing the mortgages or liens against the asset. While this is a simple strategy, more terminology may make it less confusing.

You are probably familiar with the term 'mortgage' or a voluntary lien on real estate to secure a debt incurred by the property owner. Some western states call it a 'deed of trust' instead of 'mortgage.' Instead of granting the lender a mortgage, the borrower deeds the property to a third party trustee. With the trust deed, the borrower retains the right to occupy the property provided the debt is punctually paid. The only difference between a mortgage and a deed trust, then, is that a trustee has the right to sell the property at public auction if the debtor defaults. Conversely, a mortgage holder must undergo a more complex court foreclosure proceeding before the mortgage holder can auction the property.

Different terminology is used with personal property. You lien property with a security agreement, or a contract, whereby the debtor pledges his or her personal property to secure repayment of the debt. The personal property may stay in the physical possession of the secured party (i.e. pledged jewelry to a pawn shop), but more typically the debtor retains possession of the collateral. The secured party files a notice of the lien (a financing statement) in a public recording office so third parties are put on notice that the property is encumbered.

Specific drafting and recording is required to create any of these liens; we can leave the mechanics to the lawyers. You may also have multiple liens against the same property. Their priority is determined in the order of public recording.

The point is that with valid liens (whether through a mortgage or deed of trust in the case of real estate, or a security agreement in the case of personal property), future claimants can only seize whatever equity remains in the property (the difference between the resale value of the asset and the total liens). Your asset protection objective: Have as little equity as possible exposed.

Equity-Stripping Discourages Lawsuits

Financial privacy has been demolished by the computer age. Those with exposed wealth are easier targets for lawsuits.

Computers are the lawyers' most powerful tool. The computer allows instant electronic asset searches and financial profiles. Dozens of online asset search firms can, in minutes, reveal all real estate, every company, auto, boat, etc. that you now or have ever owned. These same searches also disclose the mortgages against your property. You then want it to at least appear that everything you own is mortgaged 'to the hilt.' In today's debt-ridden America, owing as much or more than you own is hardly unusual.

Nothing discourages prospective litigants more than realizing that you are mortgaged to your eyebrows. You can own millions in assets, but if your mortgages equal or exceed your assets, then you are not a good lawsuit candidate. Prospective litigants want plenty of equity to seize. When you pledge your assets first to *other* creditors, your poverty becomes negotiating power.

Get a Line Of Credit On Your Real Estate

When should you mortgage yourself to the hilt? My answer is that real estate should always be fully encumbered. Your mortgages against the property should remain as long as you own the property, even if you must periodically refinance to cover the equity build-up as your property increases in value.

Now, you may think, "I don't want a big mortgage. I don't want to pay interest on a loan that I don't need and incur an expense to protect myself against a lawsuit that may never happen."

Refinancing your real estate may not make *financial* sense, but it always makes *legal* sense. This is why I recommend a *home equity* loan. Assume your home is worth $200,000 and you have no mortgage. You can probably get a home equity loan or line of credit against your home for about $150,000 (75 percent of its value). You would actually owe your lender nothing until you draw down your credit line, and this you would do only if you anticipated a judgment creditor. Still, any prospective litigant undertaking an asset search would see only a $50,000 equity in your home because the $150,000 mortgage would be publicly recorded. Now you are a far less attractive defendant because you have significantly reduced your net worth or equity. Besides lowering your exposure to *future* lawsuits, you also gain more leverage to negotiate a favorable settlement if you are sued.

Do you own *any* real estate? Then arrange for an equity loan or line of credit to cover whatever equity possible. Once achieved, arrange a standby second or third mortgage to encumber whatever additional equity is exposed. Yes, you pay loan processing fees, but this is a great investment when you need lawsuit protection.

Encumber Everything You Own

Encumbering your real estate is something to do *now* because you want a profile of 'poverty' to discourage lawsuits. However, if you are already sued or threatened with a lawsuit then encumber *everything* that you own. Remember: *Any* asset can be liened or encumbered as security for a loan.

Place third party liens against your second homes and investment properties, stocks, bonds, art, jewelry, collectibles, business ownership, vehicles, retirement accounts, inheritances, money that others owe to you - *all* your assets.

You can lien your assets separately or through a 'blanket' loan that liens everything to one creditor. This is typically our strategy once a judgment appears likely. Similarly equity-strip your business or professional practice. I discuss that later. Remember – leave *no* asset unencumbered and exposed.

Finding Friendly Lenders

Your next question will be, "How do I find lenders who will equity-strip my assets?"

Look for asset-based lender(s) who loan money and lien assets as collateral. For example, a home equity loan (or refinancing your home to a local bank) creates a valid lien and reduces your home equity. Refinance your business, autos, or boats. Borrow and pledge, as collateral, your investments (or even your bank accounts).

If you have reasonable credit you can probably borrow 70 percent or more of the value of your assets from conventional lenders (banks, finance companies, etc.). Even with poor credit or if you can't for some other reason obtain conventional loans, you can usually find 'hard money' lenders. They charge more for their loan, but paying their steeper financing charges is better than losing your assets in a lawsuit.

Most laymen understand equity-stripping for asset protection; the problem is in the implementation. You and your advisors may not know how or where to find the right lenders or you may not know how to 'defensively position' the deal. Those answers should come from your asset protection lawyer.

There are countless ways to structure secured loans to maximize your protection. I have successfully arranged loans and debt shields for even the poorest credit risk. Our financing arrangements may involve third party guarantees, using the loan proceeds as collateral, back-to-back loans, loans from offshore entities, etc. We have encumbered assets and estates worth up to $50 million through rather complex insurance/financing arrangements. Not only did these deals fully encumber our clients' entire asset portfolio; but the deals also greatly benefited our clients financial and tax picture.

A car dealer client involved in heavy litigation fully encumbered his $2 million home, vacation home, and car dealership worth over $6 million. We ended up with a crazy patchwork of loan deals, but once his assets were fully encumbered, we settled his multi-million dollar case for under $100,000. Without the huge mortgages which effectively shielded his equity, his lawsuit undoubtedly would have dragged on and it would have cost him much more to get rid of the case.

Usually, the debt-shielding opportunities are simpler. Start with banks, finance companies, and other conventional asset-based lenders. Family members and affiliated companies may become 'the lender' if the debtor has more modest assets to protect.

While a debtor's family members - parents, siblings and other relatives - may encumber the debtor's property, closely related parties are nevertheless legally distinct, and liens or security interests between the parties is enforceable provided there was consideration for the loan. Of course, loans from family or affiliated parties make a fraudulent transfer claim more likely. 'Insider' loans are closely scrutinized - as they should be - and to the extent a court determines the loan is a sham or one not adequately supported by consideration (having received money, property, or services of value equivalent to the loan), the mortgage will be cancelled by the court.

Even a spouse may be encumbered with separately owned property in those states with 'common law' property rules. In community property states, only property that is owned and held separately may be granted as security to a spouse. Although one spouse may encumber the assets of the other, the fraudulent transfer statutes frequently make this a challengeable loan, particularly when the mortgage was given after the claim arose. Affiliated business entities may also lien your property; however, in the same manner, a security interest is less likely to be recognized by the courts if you own or control the business entity.

Nevertheless, no rule prevents you from forming a corporation, limited partnership or limited liability company and granting a mortgage or security interest to that entity. Although the mortgage may ultimately be overturned by the court, the computerized asset search may not reveal the relationship between you and that entity. Therefore, a lien held by an entity controlled by the transferor may provide some asset protection in that it may nevertheless deter a plaintiff's lawyer seeking unencumbered assets to target.

A more aggressive asset protection specialist may use creative planning techniques to reduce the visibility of their clients' legal ownership of a corporation, partnership, or LLC. Alternatively, their client may own a minority interest of the business entity that holds the mortgage. With the client owning a minority interest, the client would not 'control' the corporation or LLC. The term 'de-controlled' here describes a corporation, partnership, or LLC structured to achieve this one result.

More sophisticated arrangements are possible. For example, a foreign corporation (an International Business Corporation, IBC) or an LLC, which is de-controlled and not owned by you as the borrower, may be used. A foreign IBC or

LLC can encumber assets of a US property owner who also owns an interest in the foreign entity. Be careful in structuring a foreign entity. You want to minimize the federal tax reporting requirements and the special anti-deferral tax rules that apply to foreign corporations, trusts, and partnerships. In more complex cases you may utilize several levels of customized foreign trusts, corporations, LLCs, charitable organizations, private foundations, or other entities to provide additional layers of privacy and anonymity. Do not, however, use these techniques as tax avoidance schemes.

Frequently, the foreign entities are mere 'shells,' or IBCs or LLCs without legal shareholders and no capital. Only through intensive investigation can a creditor distinguish a shell entity from an operating foreign entity. Therefore, even a shell entity may provide reasonably good asset protection when it encumbers property of a US debtor. However, for maximum asset protection, your foreign entity must be valid and have sufficient documentation so that it will not be ignored by a US judge who must determine priorities among competing lien holders or judgment creditors.

The success of the arrangement lies in the absolute privacy that is available in certain offshore financial centers where plaintiffs' attorneys are denied access to records. The complexities of a multiple layer foreign entity strategy can completely sever the relationships between the US property owner and the foreign IBC or LLC holding a lien on their property.

Take several precautions. First, for confidentiality, use an attorney and a foreign management company to provide the substance necessary to avoid characterizing the foreign entity as a mere 'shell,' or *alter ego*. Again, I emphasize the importance of complying with tax reporting requirements.

On the other extreme, you can sometimes create a

'friendly lien' simply by giving a mortgage to a relative, friend, or even a favored creditor to whom you owe money. What is important here is your ability to show that you actually owe the money and that it is an enforceable debt.

Using Friendly Judgments

Not every mortgage against your property has to be a consensual lien. Perhaps a relative, friend or some other 'friendly' adversary has a potential claim against you. If they were to sue you and win a judgment before a more hostile creditor wins his judgment; then, in such instance the friendly creditor would have first claim against your assets.

I have seen all sorts of 'friendly' lawsuits - ranging from defamation to breach of contract that have resulted in massive judgments which effectively blockaded the defendants' assets against later judgment creditors.

Mortgage Your Business

It is equally important to mortgage your business assets. Shielding your business assets is as vital as protecting your personal assets.

A mortgage against your business can be your best friend when it comes time to combat your creditors. Encumbering your business to a friendly lender positions you so that your lender can foreclose on your business and sell you back its assets to start again fresh.

For example, if your business owns assets worth $100,000 and you have a 'friendly' creditor with a $100,000 mortgage against these assets, and your business owes $200,000 to unsecured creditors, then your friend's mortgage has priority, whether in bankruptcy or under any other liquidation. Your unsecured creditors would recover nothing if your business fails. Without this protective mortgage, your unsecured creditors have first claim to your business assets. While your creditors would not fully recover their debts, they would nevertheless control the future of your enterprise because they could seize and forcibly liquidate your business.

Conversely, with a friendly mortgage, you effectively control your business. Regardless of what a litigant or unsecured creditor may do to collect on their judgment, your friendly mortgagee can always foreclose and re-sell your business's assets to your newly formed corporation. No funds need to change hands since your mortgagee can elect to finance the purchase with a new loan. Again, avoid sham mortgages. Your friendly mortgage must withstand close scrutiny.

Where can you find your friendly creditor? Perhaps a relative loaned you money to begin your business. One client started his desktop publishing firm five years ago with a $250,000 loan from his uncle. While the business is quite successful, why not draw up and give a legitimate mortgage on the valuable computer equipment to his uncle? His uncle may not care if he is repaid, but the uncle's mortgage can stand as a barrier against lawsuits and other creditors.

You may have a friendly supplier. Why not give this favored supplier a mortgage on your business if you're confident he won't come after your business in the tough times? The mortgage will keep other wolves at bay if your business is sued.

Consider becoming your own creditor. Nevada corporations are often formed to be 'suppliers' to the clients' operating companies. Of course, the Nevada corporation may indirectly be owned by the same individual, but 'nominee' officers and directors are used so the affiliation is less detectable. The Nevada corporation could also be owned by an offshore company for further privacy.

The key is not merely to file a mortgage on behalf of

your 'friendly' mortgage holder, but to validate your mortgage with the ability to prove that you actually owe the money. If consulting or other services were provided on credit from the Nevada corporation, can you document what services you received to establish what you owe?

Self-Finance Your Business

Money you loan to your own corporation is money easily lost. You can reduce or greatly eliminate the risk of losing what you invest in your business and at the same time create a legitimate mortgage against your business.

The *wrong* way to finance your corporation is to *directly* invest, whether it is for corporate shares (equity) or as a loan. If your business fails, you are only a stockholder or another unsecured creditor. You reclaim none or little of your original investment, and the bankruptcy court may even cancel your claim or put it behind other unsecured creditors' claims. You will receive no dividends.

However, a shrewd owner secures himself with the assets of the business so the owner's claim becomes *superior* to general creditor claims. However, even then your mortgage against your business may be set-aside in bankruptcy unless you take additional steps.

Have your bank directly loan your business the necessary funds and have your business pledge its assets to the bank as collateral. Your bank will lend to the business because you will pledge your personal assets as collateral for the loan. As a fully secured loan, the bank has little or no risk. Should your business fail, your bank as its secured party will be the first creditor to be repaid from the liquidation of the business. Once repaid, your bank returns the personal assets you pledged as security. Safeguard your investment. Use your bank as your helpful intermediary to insure that your investment is recouped if your business is sued or fails.

Take this strategy one step further. Under bankruptcy law, if a lender is secured by the business owner's personal guarantee, then repayments to the lender from the business within the year preceding bankruptcy may be recoverable as an insider preference by other creditors. Bankruptcy courts reason that the burden to repay the lender should fall upon the business owner, not arm's-length creditors. You can, however, have a friend or relative guarantee your bank loan. You pledge your collateral to this intermediary, who then pledges it to the bank. Since you are not the bank's direct guarantor, bankruptcy of the business does not jeopardize the bank's secured claim against the business' assets. With the bank repaid, your collateral reverts back to you through your intermediary.

Before you invest or loan money to your corporation, review this strategy with your attorney. When you structure your investment through this strategy, you have two big advantages: First, whatever you invest in your business is more fully protected than money invested for stock or unsecured loans to your business. Second, you indirectly control the mortgage on your business *and* can indirectly protect your business from lawsuits and other creditors.

Avoid Sham Mortgages

You can discourage lawsuits with mortgages recorded against your assets because your creditor may simply assume that it is a bona-fide mortgage. To that extent a 'paper' mortgage may discourage a would-be litigant. Don't rely on sham mortgages though. If you *really* want protection from a creditor who may challenge the validity of your mortgage, you must then be prepared to satisfy the court that you owe an enforceable debt for the amount of the mortgage. When your mortgage holder is a friend, relative or affiliate, you can expect close scrutiny of the transaction and the underlying debt. You cannot assume that your creditor will accept your recorded mortgage at face value. More inquisitive creditors will test the validity of your mortgage. If you borrowed money, do you have cancelled checks to prove the loan? If you gave the mortgage to secure a debt for services, can you establish that the services were actually rendered and were reasonably priced?

Another limitation of third party liens is that the total value of the secured party's claim to the collateral may leave an exposed equity. For example, a real estate developer with four separate parcels of land may arrange for a mortgage to be held by a third party in order to reduce her equity in the land. The mortgage granted by the developer to the third party and recorded on the county records has no protection value until a cash loan or other value is given to the developer. If a plaintiff wins a lawsuit against the developer, he can have the county sheriff attach and sell the property to satisfy the judgment. While the sheriff's sale does not extinguish the mortgage held by the third party, this would be cold comfort to the developer, who nevertheless lost her property.

Except for the appearance of a lien against the developer's properties, the developer's arrangement will not withstand a plaintiff's attorney who wants to sell the developer's property to satisfy the judgment unless a valid debt is *presently* owed to the third party mortgage holder. The difficulty for the asset protection planner is to show actual cash loans to the developer to create that valid lien.

What will the developer do with the cash from the lender? If the transaction is small enough, this presents less of a problem. However, you may need complex arrangements for asset protection to protect property worth from $500,000 to $10,000,000. The challenge for clients with millions to protect can usually only be met with creative and aggressive planning. Usually this calls for transferring the loan proceeds to one or more offshore entities or investing the proceeds in exempt assets, such as a Florida or Texas homestead or into offshore annuities.

Another challenge when planning complex third parties liens involves federal tax law. Not every asset protection consultant, attorney or CPA has adequate knowledge of the federal income, gift and estate tax laws to safely apply these arrangements. There are common tax traps that apply to third party liens held by decontrolled entities or some other third party. Because of its tax complexities, many asset protection specialists avoid using foreign entities in their plans. On the other hand, the most effective asset protection transactions require a foreign corporation, trust or other foreign entities for tax and privacy purposes and to remove the liquid assets from the grasp of predatory litigants.

Structuring secured liens on your personal assets or the assets of your business can be effectively accomplished only with careful planning, attention to detail and by observing the applicable laws involved over the life of the lien. A number of hurdles must be cleared in order to avoid problems with the lien itself, such as the fraudulent transfer laws and tax concerns. This complexity creates a two-edged sword. It requires a high degree of knowledge and skill in several different legal areas to succeed. The costs involved can be significant when you consider the legal fees, taxes and special business services, such as foreign managers. Yet, done properly, the complexity of the transaction can impose a formidable barrier to the average plaintiff looking for a fast lawsuit recovery. As more Americans enter the ranks of those concerned about lawsuits and as they educate themselves on asset protection, there will be growing demand for sophisticated asset protection strategies. Third party secured lien arrangements will be high on the list.

Protect The Loan Proceeds

Protecting the cash proceeds from your loan is an easier task than structuring the mortgages. Usually we won't equity-strip a client until we are in crisis mode and a judgment looms. Only then will we complete the loan and transfer the proceeds together with the other liquid assets either into offshore protective entities or into exempt assets. We wouldn't normally use FLPs, LLCs or other domestic entities at that point as such transfers would be too susceptible to creditor challenge as fraudulent transfers.

Ultimately, your end game plan once you are in a crisis mode is to transfer all of your domestic (US-based) assets to some protective entity (i.e., FLP, LLC, corporation, etc.) *and* fully secure the assets to one or more mortgage holders so you leave little or no exposed equity. The loan proceeds are then moved to an offshore trust, Nevis LLC, a self-protected investment (such as certain foreign annuities) or some combination of these entities and investments to maximize your protection.

Loan Payments

One obvious drawback to borrowing to create liens is that you pay interest on your loan, but keep two points in mind: (1) Your loan proceeds are earning money as they are invested (albeit through a protective entity). Your true cost is the 'spread' or difference between your interest charges and your yield on the proceeds; between what your money earns and your interest payment. (2) You will probably need your liens (and loan) in place for only a year or two while a judgment creditor attempts collection. As a practical matter, most judgments are resolved through settlement or bankruptcy within this time period, and therefore a long-term loan is probably not required. The spread may be minimal, and you may even make a profit.

13

A Final Word About Liability Insurance

Before we leave the specific tools used to protect your assets from lawsuits, let me make a few final comments about liability insurance.

In a very real sense, insurance is an asset protection tool because it transfers or shifts the risk of loss on a liability claim from the insured to the insurance company. This is no small consideration. In an age of rampant litigation it can be comforting to know that you have coverage for so many liabilities that may befall you.

However, liability insurance won't solve your every lawsuit worry. While my own observations tell me that far fewer lawsuits are covered by insurance than you might expect that doesn't mean I'm not in favor of insurance. Liability insurance is certainly a good starting point to achieve asset protection, if you bear in mind a few caveats:

1) you must have the *right* insurance,

2) you must carry *enough* insurance,

3) you must understand why insurance is *only* a starting point.

The fact is, you can't completely count on liability insurance. You must supplement it with the other lawsuit protection strategies I discuss in this book.

Liability insurance can also be illusive security. As I have previously mentioned, one reason many people don't protect themselves from liability is because they mistakenly believe that their liability insurance adequately safeguards them. However, no matter how extensive your insurance, you can only transfer *some* risks to your insurance company, not *every* risk.

In fairness, it is not the insurance industry that perpetrates the hoax that insurance is a liability cure-all. The hoax is largely self-inflicted. People *want* to assume that insurance is their answer to the lawsuit epidemic because insurance is easy to buy. Sign a form, write a check and your liability problems are solved. You, too, may argue, "But I have homeowners' insurance, malpractice coverage, business premises liability insurance and even an umbrella policy to protect me against lawsuits." It doesn't matter. The simple fact is that no matter how much insurance you own, *your insurance does not adequately protect you.*

Consider the Many Exclusions

The most common liability insurance policies are (1) general business policies, (2) professional liability insurance policies, and (3) personal liability insurance policies.

General business policies cover specified risks or claims that arise on the business' premises. However, there are many exclusions: intentional torts (wrongdoings such as assault and battery, drunk driving, etc.); acts outside the scope of employment, contract claims, discrimination claims and acts outside the premises (such as working from home) are all examples.

While medical or professional liability policies cover most forms of negligent omission or commission, they may not cover gross negligence, acts involving a violation of law, punitive damages, fines and penalties, product liability, contract claims, or services provided to certain institutions (hospital, HMOs, etc.). These exclusions are of increasingly greater concern to professionals.

Personal liability policies include (1) auto liability policies (2) homeowner's insurance and (3) umbrella policies. Each type insurance has its own long list of exclusions. For example, an auto policy may not cover an under-age family driver or an accident while driving under the influence of drugs or alcohol. A homeowner's policy may not insure a 'slip and fall' on a snow-laden walkway if the snow was negligently allowed to accumulate. Umbrella policy exclusions extend to sporting accidents, liability arising from dangerous instruments (guns, etc.), dog bites, intentional wrongdoings, business-related claims, etc.

A young attorney complained to me that he paid $15,000 a year for malpractice insurance and was never sued until this year when he was hit with a $100,000 wrongful termination suit by a disgruntled ex-employee. He was later hammered with a more devastating $500,000 IRS tax claim. Of course, neither liability was insured since the lawyer's malpractice insurance covered him only from professional liability.

Many of my clients are professionals because they have deep pockets and professionals are frequently blamed when things go wrong. Asset protection is rightfully high on their agendas, which is why they spend many thousands of dollars annually on malpractice insurance. Professionals, however, are exposed to more than malpractice claims. They are also businesspeople who face the same hazards of anyone in business - partnership suits, employee claims, lawsuits from contracts, etc. In fact, today's professional has a greater chance of being sued for something he is *not* insured against than for something for which he *is* insured.

This is true of everyone. The reasons to sue are limitless. New theories of liability are advanced daily by creative lawyers and they are readily accepted by judges and juries. Conversely, liability policies are generally narrowly construed and become increasingly limited in what they cover.

To illustrate this point, about one-third of all federal civil suits involve sexual harassment claims. Yet fewer than one defendant in twenty is covered for this type claim. How will insurance protect your assets from divorce? Tax claims? Debts that you can't pay? Breach of contract? How will insurance safeguard the assets that you leave to your children or shelter your assets from an arbitrary government seizure? You know the answer. It won't.

Even when you *think* a claim is insured, the insurance company often points out a 'fine print' exclusion. For example, I recently had a client sued for over $500,000 on his teenage daughter's car accident. He assumed his insurance policy covered his daughter until his insurance agent advised him that the policy no longer covered his daughter because she had recently moved out of his house to attend college. This one lawsuit cost my client $150,000 to settle. The ways to get into trouble are endless, and insurance too seldom comes to the rescue. *Buy it, but don't rely on it.*

Buy as Much Coverage as You Can Afford

You also need enough insurance. Too little coverage still exposes you to a judgment in excess of your coverage. A good plaintiff's lawyer can manipulate a jury to award bizarre verdicts when measured by any rationale standard.

Runaway juries are hardly a rarity. Yes, we joke about the elderly McDonald's customer who won a multi-million dollar verdict against McDonald's because her coffee burned her, but as you have seen from the opening chapter, ridiculous verdicts for minor injuries are no longer an anomaly. They're routine. That's why our American legal system has become a joke - a bad joke.

What this means is that you can no longer accurately predict what a litigant can recover on their claim. Years ago there was far greater predictability on the outcome of a lawsuit. Juries were sane. Judges reduced outlandish awards. 'Punitive' damage awards where a plaintiff recovered millions when they had insignificant actual damages were unheard of. In those good old days, the courts compensated an injured plaintiff only for their actual loss. Today's courtroom functions to redistribute wealth. How can you be confident that your million or even multi-million dollar policy is *enough*? You can't.

No matter how high your insurance coverage, there is always a litigant who will find a way to sue you for an amount that exceeds your coverage. Most cases today involve excess liability claims; a lawsuit that demands more than the insurance coverage.

While it is true that most cases settle within the policy limits, until that settlement happens you suffer the anguish that possibly - just possibly - the judgment against you will exceed your coverage and you may then lose your assets despite your insurance. Moreover, you must then hire a lawyer to defend you against any potential excess liability.

How much liability insurance is enough? That is a common question. If insurance was free, that answer would be 'all you can buy.' Insurance is not free. The more you buy, the more you pay. You must balance the costs of additional coverage against the risks of less coverage, in terms of the odds of an excess judgment against you as well as what you stand to lose should it happen.

Because you will probably never have enough coverage to insulate you against the insatiable demands of greedy litigants you are bound to encounter, your only solution is to protect your assets against the eventuality by means other than insurance.

Buy Only From Well-Rated Companies

Insurance companies also can go bankrupt. When an insurance company fails, they strand tens of thousands of insureds who relied upon the underwriter's financial stability to protect them from claims.

For example, one insurance company covered hundreds of physicians for malpractice. When they went belly up, scores of doctors with claims pending against them were suddenly exposed both on their present lawsuits and on future claims that could arise before they could buy replacement insurance. Their state insurance commission covered a small portion of each claim, still hundreds of doctors lost their fortunes when they thought they were covered. Even the venerable Lloyds of London almost stumbled into oblivion, leaving its policyholders high and dry.

How financially secure is your insurance company? Unless it is highly-rated you have poorer protection than you may think. *Standard and Poors* or *Best* can give you the financial rating of your insurance company, or ask your insurance agent. Never accept an insurer who has less than an A-rating.

Your Insurer Controls Your Case

Another problem with insurance is that you lose control of your case. It is your insurance company, not you, who decides whether to settle and for how much. This may be unimportant with an automobile accident, but exceptionally important when the lawsuit concerns your professional competence or personal reputation.

For example, as a doctor or some other type professional, you may be convinced that you are in the right and you want your day in court. Your insurance company, on the other hand, may consider it cheaper to settle. Or you may want to settle your case to avoid adverse publicity, but your insurer may insist upon a full-blown trial. In either instance, you and your insurer have different agendas. Forcing your insurance company to comply with your wishes could cause you to forfeit the insurance coverage for which you paid.

An additional consequence of relying on insurance to protect you from lawsuits is that once you are sued, your premiums rise. Given the dismal statistics, you may endure many lawsuits over your lifetime. Your insurance premiums rise with every new lawsuit, even if you win.

For example, before he protected his assets, one physician friend relied chiefly on malpractice insurance. After his insurance company defended four unsuccessful lawsuits against him (three of which went through trial), his insurance premiums rose to $250,000 per year. His insurance will cost him more over the next five years than any single lawsuit is likely to reach and this is not unusual. With insurance, a lawsuit costs you even when you win.

Insurance Makes You an
Attractive Lawsuit Target

I am occasionally asked for my solution to the lawsuit epidemic. While I'm tempted to cite Shakespeare's famous admonition to "kill all the lawyers," I realize that a less gruesome solution is to shut down all the liability insurers and instead compel everybody to protect their assets. In short, I would create a country of *untouchable wealth!*

Liability insurance is one of the more obvious reasons that we have so many costly and frivolous lawsuits. Insurance automatically gives you the 'deep pockets' that attract lawsuits. Whether you are rich or poor, prospective litigants know that insurance companies have plenty of money. Their lawyers also know that most insurers would rather settle even a frivolous lawsuit than fight because it is less costly. Insurance has greatly contributed to the transformation of our country into a nation of litigants.

Because insurance attracts lawsuits and because of the excessive cost of insurance, many professionals and businesspeople are now 'going bare'. They go without insurance.

Going without insurance is particularly vogue amongst physicians who are particularly hard-hit with exorbitant malpractice insurance premiums. High-risk specialists such as obstetricians and orthopedic surgeons pay $100,000 or more annually for malpractice insurance; those in the high litigation states of California and Florida pay appreciably more. However, even general practitioners in less litigious states still fork over $20,000 or more for malpractice coverage each year. And this doesn't buy them much coverage.

This very real cost digs deeply into a professional's earnings already trimmed by cutbacks from managed care programs. Nor is it only a doctor's problem. The litigation explosion also impacts most other professions and businesses. 'Going bare' is now gaining traction in such 'low risk' occupations as law, financial services, and architecture as well.

Cost, of course, is only one factor. Doctors, other high-risk professionals, and business owners now understand that they are frequently sued only because they are well insured. Without liability insurance they would no longer be the 'deep pocket' defendants - particularly if their assets are otherwise well protected.

Many of my doctor clients now practice without liability insurance. However, doing without insurance is not always possible. Many states require insurance as a condition to practice and HMOs and hospitals frequently require their affiliated doctors to carry adequate liability insurance. Where it is possible, however, avoiding insurance is an option. Doing without insurance, however, can only make sense provided your assets are *very* well protected through other means.

How effective is the 'going bare' strategy? One cosmetic surgeon client was threatened by five malpractice suits in the last three years (not one case had apparent merit). In each case we pointed out to the patient that the doctor had no insurance and that his assets were fully protected. Not one prospective malpractice litigant sued. If our doctor had ample insurance, he would undoubtedly have had five lawsuits with which to contend.

One practical problem of going without liability insurance is that you must pay the defense costs if you are sued or alternatively face a default judgment - a particularly undesirable outcome when you believe that you are in the right. And defense costs do not come cheap. It can cost $100,000 or more to defend against even a routine liability or malpractice suit.

A good compromise solution is to retain a local law firm to defend you should you be sued. Your annual retainer can cover any litigation costs whether or not you are sued. In addition, some of our professional and business clients retain us to keep them completely judgment-proof, and we continuously monitor their finances to keep them fully protected. Thus, in these cases, the professional has his defense costs covered in advance and can remain confident he will not lose his assets even if he should lose a case. Of course, the professional usually informs his clients or patients that he is without liability insurance, so they are less likely to sue in the first place.

Many more legal defense fund insurers are now springing up. They sell insurance to cover *only* your defense costs. Legal defense coverage, coupled with solid asset protection, can for many professionals, be an excellent alternative to huge malpractice premiums.

Still, this is not everybody's answer. Your insurance premiums may be a bargain, considering the risks; from a statistical viewpoint, however, this is unlikely. Emotionally, you may want to insure yourself against every possible lawsuit danger no matter how remote the odds, provided the insurance is affordable. Others go to the other extreme and refuse to admit risk. This attitude is certainly more understandable for those with few assets and who can't afford insurance, but these are not usually the people who are sued.

Buy Insurance from Your Own Insurance Company

Physicians and other professionals in a group practice have options that fall between buying expensive insurance and 'going bare.' Sole practitioners (or smaller groups) can frequently benefit from these 'insurance alternative' programs by joining or forming purchasing cooperatives or IPAs (Independent Physician Associations).

Another increasingly popular option is to form your own captive insurance company, particularly if you pay significant premiums ($200,000 or more). The Captive Insurance Company(CIC) is a legitimate insurance company licensed to write insurance in the US. It is registered with the IRS, but is based in an offshore jurisdiction, such as Bermuda or the British Virgin Islands. Most CICs are established in these two countries because of their smaller capitalization requirements and their favorable insurance laws and taxes. Funds in the CIC can be maintained and managed in the US. Offshore CICs now number over 4,000 companies that write an estimated $60 billion in premiums per year - more than a third of the total commercial insurance sold in the United Sates. Fortune 500 companies have long used CICs to protect their assets and as tax advantages; however, only in the last decade have individuals, business owners, and professionals started to take advantage of CICs as well.

The CIC can also be a powerful tool to build wealth through tax-deductible contributions from a business or professional practice, since the premiums paid by the practice to the insurance company are deductible as ordinary business expenses. Beyond the annual income tax savings, other tax benefits of the CIC include: (1) capital gain postponements on appreciated assets, (2) tax-free growth, and (3) reduction or elimination of estate tax on property transferred to children.

When you own your own CIC you have the flexibility to customize your insurance coverage in ways that are not possible with commercial third-party insurers. For example, some physicians prefer a malpractice policy that pays only the doctor's legal fees (with a choice of attorneys), but does not pay creditors or claimants (what we call 'shallow pockets' policies). This prevents a prospective defendant from appearing as a 'deep pocket,' which is itself a necessary asset protection strategy today. The CIC also has the flexibility to add coverage for claims unavailable through traditional malpractice policies. Wrongful termination and harassment violations are two examples. Even when you can purchase broad coverage policies from traditional third-party insurers, you would not have the powerful tax advantages. In essence, the question becomes: When you want insurance to protect your assets, why give away the potential profits and tax benefits to a commercial insurance company? Why not form your own company?

In addition to its tax benefits, the CIC also offers you asset protection. Your CIC can supplement your existing liability policy and such 'excess' malpractice protection gives you the security that you will not be wiped out by a lawsuit above your traditional coverage limits. The CIC may even allow you to reduce your present insurance.

Don't Rely on Your Employer's Insurance

Your employer's insurance does not guarantee you adequate protection. For instance, your employer's coverage may not be obligated to defend or pay a judgment against an employee. Employers ordinarily share liability with the negligent employee; therefore, any judgment against the employee usually also creates a judgment against the employer. The employer's liability - paid by the insurer - covers the employee liability. Nevertheless, employees who rely on their employer's coverage run several risks. For example, what is your protection if your employer is *not* liable for your errors or omissions on acts outside your scope of employment? What protection do you have if your employer's policy is terminated without your knowledge? What if your employer's insurance is inadequate? What if multiple employees are named as defendants, as is often the case? The shared liability limits may not adequately protect you. What if your employer's plan is a claims-made policy and covers only claims made during the policy period? If your employer changes liability coverage or you change jobs before a lawsuit is filed, you may not be covered. Finally, what if you lose your job? Since the possibility of job loss or job change is real; a lawsuit after your employment ends, gives you no coverage.

Review your employer's policy. Satisfy yourself that your employer's insurance underwriter must defend and protect both your employer *and* you. Also, evaluate your employer's financial stability. Companies in financial difficulties frequently lose, reduce, or cancel their insurance. Your best option when you are employed is to buy your own supplemental insurance.

Assert Your Rights

When you are sued, your insurer must in good faith defend you or you may have a claim against the insurer for any judgment that arises in excess of your coverage. Your insurance company can also incur liability for any excessive award unless it notifies you of the excess claim and settles or attempts to settle the claim in good faith. Your insurer cannot refuse a reasonable settlement offer when the refusal exposes you to excess liability.

Your insurance company may decline coverage on certain claims, but even on questionable claims, always demand that the insurance company defend and indemnify you. Your insurance company may then defend the lawsuit while reserving their rights not to pay any judgment, or the insurer may then litigate the issue of its liability under the policy. If there is any possible question as to whether a claim should be covered by your insurer, then retain an attorney to represent your interests. Do not rely on the attorney hired by the insurance company. Remember that your interests will not always coincide with your insurance company's. An attorney *on your side* is invaluable to protect your rights as the insured.

Intelligently Buy Insurance

Despite arguments against buying insurance, you may want or need insurance protection for a variety of reasons. For instance, you may question whether you can adequately protect your assets, or liability insurance may be mandated by regulation, customers, or competition.

In my many years of practice I have seen enough mistakes in buying insurance for asset protection to offer a few suggestions on how you can buy insurance more effectively:

- **Rely on one insurance agent:** You need an agent who understands your business or profession, its special risks, the coverage you need, and how best to buy it. Insurance is complex. You need an agent on your side who can handle your insurance needs as effectively as you would expect your asset protection lawyer to handle your asset protection planning. When you buy liability insurance through one agent you can also avoid insurance gaps or coverage overlaps.
- **Buy sufficient coverage:** If you have any significant assets, you probably need a minimum $1 million coverage per claim. Nothing less will give you meaningful protection against high awards. Check the costs of increased coverage. To save money it is always best to increase your deductibles (or the portion of the claim that you pay).

- **Buy an umbrella policy:** Umbrella insurance is your best insurance buy. It covers you from many liability claims that are not covered (or inadequately covered) under general liability policies. For example, it was State Farm's Umbrella Insurance that paid most of President Clinton's defense costs as well as the settlement on the Paula Jones case. Many claims not covered by your underlying policies will be handled by an umbrella policy. Check with your insurance agent.

Transferring risk through insurance is a good first step toward creating *untouchable wealth*; however, it is seldom the most cost-efficient way to achieve it.

One architect client explains it this way: "I paid about $70,000 annually for a comprehensive professional liability policy to protect my $2 million net worth. I have since replaced a big share of my insurance coverage with rational thinking. I have retitled my assets so they can never be seized by creditors - no matter what or how large their claim. To achieve this level of protection cost me less than $10,000 and perhaps another few thousand a year to maintain. Since I now carry considerably less insurance, I save about $50,000 a year; but my protection has greatly improved because I no longer rely only upon insurance."

My architect friend gives good advice. Insurance is important and it has its place, but it's never the entire answer if you want the *safest wealth*. For that you need your own asset protection plan.

14

Your Next...
(and Most Important)
Steps

Reading and learning about asset protection is a wonderful way to begin the process, but without the next step - implementing your plan - you only have a gesture in the right direction. So, here in four simple steps is what I want you to do the moment you finish this book.

Step 1: Commit to Action

As with any goal, you need a commitment to action. Asset protection isn't something you should do in two months…or next year. It may then be too late. Set a deadline for completion; a definite timetable within which you will have competed this important goal.

Step 2: Organize Your Team

Your asset protection plan will necessarily involve those most intimately involved in your finances. Building your team is important. For example, you should not ignore your spouse who will rightfully become alarmed if you suddenly and inexplicably re-title marital assets for unknown and suspicious reasons.

Anticipate and allay those fears and uncertainties. Involve those entitled to know the reasons for changing your financial affairs. With candid explanation comes understanding and cooperation. Which close family members and trusted friends can administer your financial game plan as trustees or executors? Your business partners or key business associates are examples of potential asset protection teammates. But confine individuals involved in your financial affairs only to the financial matters that specifically involve them.

Be careful what disclosures you make to your team. Your spouse may understand asset protection is a key objective, but why needlessly reveal this to friends, relatives or others who should instead believe your goals involve good tax or estate planning? While asset protection is legal, your actual intent may become an important factor if an asset transfer is later challenged by creditors. You then gain no advantage if a friend or associate testifies that asset protection was your only objective.

Your team should include only people you can unquestionably trust to faithfully implement your plan. Cautiously evaluate the extent each can be trusted, and whether they will remain trustworthy under stressful circumstances. And can they professionally handle their responsibilities? Asset protection planning requires you to objectively evaluate others, and this is as critical as selecting the right legal strategies.

Step 3: Recruit the Right Professionals

Asset protection planning also requires the right professionals for your team.

Lawyers and legal considerations will most influence your plan, but other factors are also important. For safe and sound tax planning, your accountant may participate. To achieve your investment objectives – liquidity, yield, safety and growth – requires a good financial planner or investment advisor. Your banker may be needed to refinance your assets or your bank's trust department may become the trustee of your new trust. Your insurance professional also becomes important when annuities or insurance are part of your plan.

Professional coordination is vital when you have a significant net worth, diverse assets or complex investment objectives. Those with more modest wealth may need only their attorney and accountant.

Successful asset protection plans depend less on the number of advisors than on the *right* advisors.

A skilled asset protection attorney is absolutely essential. Unfortunately, few attorneys have the background or training in asset protection. Your family lawyer may be proficient in other legal matters yet knows little about asset protection.

Fortunately, you can find legal talent. Most asset protection lawyers originate from within the legal specialties of bankruptcy, corporate law and probate. Bankruptcy lawyers reconcile disputes between debtors and creditors and either chase or protect assets. Corporate lawyers are familiar with the numerous asset protection entities – corporations, limited partnerships, limited liability companies – and commonly handle asset protection. Estate lawyers are especially expert with the various trusts, gifts and other asset protection structures also used for estate planning. Usually they have a good knowledge of asset protection.

To find a good attorney, call your local bar association. They may know who can best help you. I work closely with asset protection lawyers and consultants nationwide and may possibly refer you to an asset protection specialist.

Interview your prospective attorney carefully:

1) Check references from other asset protection clients.
2) Evaluate the attorney's answers to your questions, as well as the questions posed by the attorney.
3) Discuss fees and costs.
4) Determine whether you are comfortable with the attorney.
5) Determine if the attorney will design and implement your plan and defend it should it be challenged. Whether your plan withstands a creditor attack is its acid test. Your lawyer must be confident that he or she can win that contest.
6) Evaluate your attorney's experience and credentials in asset protection.

Selecting the right attorney is mostly intuitive. You are relying upon this individual to be your 'safety net,' as John Mathews would say. However your interview proceeds, you must have that clear sense that this is a professional who knows the options and has sufficient interest in you to explain each option and how he or she would ultimately create that 'bullet-proof' plan – should it become necessary. Without that sense of confidence you have the wrong professional.

Location should not be a governing factor. For example, my own clients come from throughout the country. A good many I have yet to meet face-to-face. Through the modern world of telecommunications we have nevertheless served as the architect for some of the most complex plans.

Step 4: Stay Proactive in Maintaining Financial Secrurity

Your professionals won't have every answer. You must take your own counsel. Continue to learn the fundamentals of asset protection, just as you would master the basics of sound investing or tax planning.

Why this advice? First, only with personal knowledge can you measure the competency of a prospective asset protection lawyer. Second, when you stay abreast of new asset protection strategies, you maintain the best asset protection. Third, you can then implement many asset protection strategies yourself, while your attorney handles the more complex procedures. A knowledgeable client can immeasurably add to his asset protection plan in so many different ways.

Learn! Read other books on asset protection. Attend a few asset protection seminars. When you are proactive rather than a mere bystander, you best ensure the success of your wealth preservation program.

With that, I wish you and your family lifelong financial security.

Index

ABOUT THE AUTHOR

One of America's leading wealth protection specialists, Arnold S. Goldstein Ph.D. has helped thousands of individuals, families and organizations gain complete lawsuit protection.

You may have seen or heard Dr. Goldstein discuss his powerful financial strategies on radio and TV talk shows (including CNN, CNBC and NBC's *Today Show*), or as a seminar and meeting speaker.

You could have read about his wealth preservation concepts in numerous business and finance magazines: *INC, Fortune, Money, CFO, Entrepreneur, Success, Venture, Business Week, Bottom Line,* to name a few.

Possibly you may have found your path to financial security from his best-selling books, *Offshore Havens or Asset Protection Secrets,* or his more than fifty other books on wealth protection.

A veteran wealth preservation specialist, Dr. Goldstein is founder of the Florida and Massachusetts firm of Arnold S. Goldstein & Associates. He is a member of the Massachusetts and federal Bars and a member of the Bar of the US First Circuit Court and US Supreme Court.

He holds five academic degrees (including graduate law degrees, an MBA and a Ph.D. in economic and business policy from Northeastern University, where he is professor emeritus). He has served on the faculty at several other universities and as a post-doctoral research scholar on offshore trusts at the London School of Economics. Dr. Goldstein resides in Delray Beach, Florida with his wife Marlene and their two labs, Shadow and Coco.

Questions, Free Updates and to
Contact the Author

- with comments about this book ...

- to receive a free asset protection e-mail newsletter...

- to order other books by Dr. Goldstein ...

- for Dr. Goldstein to speak at a seminar or meeting, or to attend one of Dr. Goldstein's seminars ...

- for a free, confidential, preliminary asset protection consultation ...

Call Today 561.953.1322

....It Only Takes a Phone Call to Put My Asset Protection Expertise to Work For You

Are you ready for your very own financial protection plan? Give my office a call and let's arrange a personal consultation to put together a plan that will give you the best protection possible against any financial or legal problem.

Whether you have few assets or enjoy considerable wealth...you'll have the confidence that what you own is more safe and secure once we meet and begin to safeguard your future.

It's easy to arrange. Simply phone our office. There's never an obligation when you call and, of course, upon request, we will send you a brochure describing our firm's services.

**We serve individuals and
businesses nationwide.**

Arnold S. Goldstein & Associates, LLC
Telephone: 561-953-1050
Fax: 561-953-1940
e-mail: asgoldstein@asgoldstein.com
Visit our website: www.asgoldstein.com